Industrial Genius

INDUSTRIAL GENIUS

The Working Life of
Charles Michael Schwab

Kenneth Warren

UNIVERSITY OF PITTSBURGH PRESS

Published by the University of Pittsburgh Press, Pittsburgh, PA 15260

Copyright © 2007, University of Pittsburgh Press

Manufactured in the United States of America

Printed on acid-free paper

10 9 8 7 6 5 4 3 2 1

Library of Congress Cataloging-in-Publication Data
Warren, Kenneth.
    Industrial genius : the working life of Charles Michael Schwab
/ Kenneth Warren.
        p.   cm.
    Includes bibliographical references and index.
    ISBN 0-8229-4326-3 (alk. paper)
    1. Schwab, Charles M., 1862-1939. 2. Industrialists—United
States—Biography. 3. Steel industry and trade—United States—
History. I. Title.
    HD9520.S3W37 2007
    338.7'6691092—dc22
      [B]   2006036183

In affectionate memory of Fred Hetzel

CONTENTS

ILLUSTRATIONS

PREFACE

On a sunny Sunday morning in late July 1879 a youth of seventeen and a half years arrived in Pittsburgh by train from a small village along the Allegheny Front in western Pennsylvania. He had not been far from home before and, being a lively person, probably was keenly interested in the view from the rail car all the way down from the hills. As he recalled years later, however, it was as he neared his journey's end that he was bowled over by what he saw: "As the train rounded the curve, the great smoking stacks of the Edgar Thomson works, the flaming converters belching forth, made such a vivid impression upon my youthful mind that it will never fade. I thought I had seen the very acme of what might be accomplished in an industrial way. It then appalled me as something gigantic, something never to be duplicated."[1]

A few weeks more than six decades later, on Thursday, 31 August 1939, a day of light rain and mild temperatures, the liner *Washington* arrived in New York harbor carrying 984 passengers. It was the last large passenger ship to leave Hamburg for America before the German attack on Poland and the resulting war crisis disrupted shipping schedules. Many eminent Americans had taken the opportunity of its departure to get back to the peace of their own country. As disembarkation got under way, an elderly passenger was carried by stretcher to an ambulance, which was then driven the short distance to an apartment on Park Avenue.[2] There, less than three weeks later, the patient died.

The young train traveler and the sick old man from the liner were the same individual. Between the two events he had been one of the most powerful, successful, charismatic, and for a time one of the wealthiest of the great industrialists of the Gilded Age. He was Charles Michael Schwab, the most renowned of all American steel magnates with the single exception of Andrew Carnegie. Although Schwab is less well known, his career may be claimed to be as fascinating and thought provoking as that of Carnegie, the man he always recognized as his master. Carnegie was actively involved in iron and steel for fewer than forty years; Schwab's career was half again as long. The former was very much a man of the nineteenth century, but Schwab's working life stretched from the full flowering of the age of steel in the 1880s to the time when his industry was struggling to adapt itself to the very different steel requirements of an age of mass consumption. Carnegie created one great, world-leading company. Schwab ran that company for him, moved on to head for a time the biggest industrial enterprise on earth, and after that built up from a modest beginning what became the world's second ranking steel company.

Contemporaries seem to have had no doubt that Schwab was an industrial genius, but he was more limited than some of his peers. He was unquestionably one of the great "captains of industry" at a time when that title was a term of approbation, but it was his misfortune to live on into a time when it began to be used in denigration. Compared with many other tycoons he was a consummate "salesman," not in the narrow sense of that term but in his ability to convey the impression that business was being conducted for the common good and that all would be well. In his last few years the endless repetition of this message, his failing health, and above all external circumstances made it seem a generally inappropriate quality. Andrew Carnegie and Henry Clay Frick knew Schwab well and valued his exceptional business talents. In contrast to them he proved himself at a variety of levels, from departmental and plant management to overall command of vast corporations and even a government-controlled, nationwide business. Like Carnegie he was confident and extraverted, but he lacked the "master's" breadth of interests and the nagging conscience whispering that wealth should be used for the benefit of society. Carnegie spent the last decades of his life organizing a wise system to disburse his wealth; Schwab was less philanthropic but saw his fortune gradually dwindle. At the end of life Carnegie left only a generous competence for his family; Schwab had no close surviving family and died in debt. Although a more congenial character than Frick, he had no passion similar to Frick's love for art or, for that matter, for anything outside business to counterbalance his commitment to material progress and money making. In short Charlie Schwab epitomized some of the favorable aspects of the Gilded Age and was one of its more attractive personalities, but he also personified its limitations and unfavorable impacts on society.

In spite of the inherently fascinating aspects of such a man's life, a word of justification is needed for this account of his career, because in 1975 Robert Hessen produced an excellent biography entitled *Steel Titan: The Life of Charles M. Schwab*. Hessen's study is one on which any subsequent writer on Schwab or the fields of business in which he was engaged is thankful to draw. It was the fruit of scholarly research, including interviews with surviving members of the Schwab family and some old friends, many now no longer alive. The case for a new study of Schwab can only lie in a radical difference of perspective and the availability of archival material not accessible to Hessen.

An essential consideration in the writing of history, including biography, is the perspective of the project: its selection of what is most important and its interpretative framework and value system. Hessen acknowledged an intellectual debt to Ayn Rand, and his account of Schwab bears the signs of her inspiration. This study reflects a different set of values. Like Hessen and Rand, I recognize that impressive achievements resulted from the aggressive, acquisitive drive of industrial capitalism. How could one avoid doing so when it is obvious that this ethos and the business qualities accompanying it laid the foundations for the prosperity that has spread so widely through society in the years since Schwab's death? On the other hand, might there have been other less ruthless and more physically, economically, and socially "efficient" methods of securing such ends? Was confrontation with or even the grinding down of workers the only way of dealing with labor?

This book is not an attempt to write a complete life, for it would be difficult or perhaps impossible to contribute anything new to details of Schwab's family life or to the admittedly small section of Hessen's book dealing with Schwab's affairs. Time and mortality have removed many of the sources on which he was able to draw, and neither my competence nor my inclination lies in those directions. On the other hand I have not wholly neglected Schwab's activities outside industry, for they too were an essential part of the man and were affected by and in turn influenced his business success and wealth. Another guide I followed in these more peripheral aspects was that if I had anything new to contribute, I considered it worthwhile to do so.

In many instances, I have focused on different themes than did Hessen, and throughout I have tried to place the story within and not to isolate it from the broader context of the industrial developments of the time. Some important sources not available when Hessen wrote have been drawn upon, filling out topics that previously were covered in a necessarily scanty fashion. Researching the industrial career of Charlie Schwab depends on examining materials scattered among a number of libraries and record centers. His years in the Carnegie enterprises are richly recorded in the Carnegie papers housed in the Library of Congress; in the Frick papers, which were held in the Helen Clay Frick Foundation in Pittsburgh when I worked on them but are now in the Archives of Industrial Society of the University of Pittsburgh; and in the Carnegie Steel section of the immense record collection of the United States Steel Corporation. Schwab's involvement in Bethlehem Steel was traced in the archives deposited in the Hagley Museum and Library, Wilmington, Delaware, and the National Canal Museum (NCM) in Easton, Pennsylvania. The Pattee Library at the University Park campus of Pennsylvania State University has other relevant papers. I would like to thank the librarians or archivists of each of these centers for their helpfulness. In particular I wish to record my appreciation of the expertise and encouragement of Lance Metz of NCM, who has kindly read and commented on the manuscript. Perhaps I should also add that my forthcoming history of the Bethlehem Steel Corporation, provisionally entitled *The World's Second Steel Maker*, also covers themes relevant to Schwab—hopefully with not too much repetition.

Believing that academic reconsideration of so prominent a figure in the folklore of American capitalism may now be profitable, I have aimed to provide a new and different but complementary interpretation of the life of a leading industrialist. Seeking scholarly detachment I have tried to avoid either doctrinaire denunciation or uncritical deference. Even so I hope this record and interpretation of his life also shows that, though at odds with some of his actions and values, I found it hard to avoid being fascinated by Charlie Schwab's achievements and personality.

Industrial Genius

1 ☙ Early Years to Homestead

A young German named Charles Schwab, who came from Baden-Baden, settled in Bedford County in south-central Pennsylvania in 1830. A few years later, he went northward into Cambria County, making his home in Loretto, a village on the heights of the Alleghenies. In 1857 he moved a few miles eastward to the Appalachian valley town of Williamsburg. There his eldest son, John, joined him as a weaver. When he was twenty-two John Schwab married Pauline Farabaugh, a former neighbor in Loretto. Their first child was born in February 1862 and was baptized Charles Michael. When the boy was twelve, his parents moved back to Loretto, where John went into the livery business and obtained a contract to carry mail. The family's wealth was slight.

Although Charlie seems to have been a bright boy at school, he grew up in an economic backwater, a little community showing few signs of the dynamism already transforming other parts of the state and the national economy. Even so, he gained some intimation of the ferment that lay beyond—though it is important to recognize that much of what he later claimed he could recall seems to have been shaped or at least colored by later experiences. A vivid example of this sort of retrospection, one whose very form seems to owe a good deal to the work of professional myth makers, was his recollection of one childhood view:

> Many a time I would stray from home over the hills and to the top of
> the range, where I could see the tall chimneys of Johnstown send-

ing up their plumes of smoke. Often I lay on a hillside to watch those streamers. Along toward dusk tongues of flame would shoot up in the pall around Johnstown. When some furnace door was opened the evening turned red. A boy watching from the rim of the hills had a vast arena before him, a place of vague forms, great labors and dancing fires. And the murk was always present, the smell of a foundry. It gets into your hair, your clothes, even your blood.[1]

The steel works of the Cambria Iron Company that Schwab claimed to have viewed from his hillside were actually eighteen miles away and separated from Loretto by a jumble of other hills.[2] But other direct connections with the wider spheres of economic growth were beginning to filter through to the neighborhood. As a teenager Charlie helped his father haul goods and carry passengers to and from the small local rail station of Cresson, four miles from home on the crest of the Allegheny Front. There he first set eyes on Andrew Carnegie, whose summer home was nearby. Long afterward and characteristically, he was eloquent about Carnegie's influence on his life but rather vague about its chronology:

> It is nearly forty years since I first knew Mr. Carnegie. As a boy I met him when he sojourned on the Alleghany [sic] Mountains for his summer outings, and I little thought at that time, when I held his horse and did trivial services for him, that fate in later years of life would so intimately throw our lives together, and that I would become the friend and associate of such a great man. . . . [A]s I look back upon those days of boyhood, . . . I feel now the strength of that personality and the influence it had upon me in after life.[3]

After Schwab attended the local Catholic college, sometime during midsummer in 1879 the steady but limited country routines of the young man were broken when he began work. He traveled seventy miles from home to become an assistant in a grocery store. The store was in Braddock, a small community, but one whose fortunes were inextricably linked with the dynamism of what was then a leading growth industry: steel manufacture. The largest interest in the Edgar Thomson works, which had then been in production for only four years, was held by Andrew Carnegie. Here, as in the other burgeoning mill towns of the Monongahela valley, ways of life, social structures, the built environment, and the pace of change were all radically different from those to which Charlie Schwab had been accustomed. It took sixty years for Loretto's population to increase from 100 to 240 in 1900; the census taken a few months after

Schwab's arrival in Braddock showed that the industrial town already housed 3,300 souls. His home area was and remained relatively unspoiled by "progress"; the valley to which he came had once had its own idyllic landscape, but it was now well along the way to man-made desecration. Economically speaking, it was an unqualified success.

In the year of Charlie's arrival new records were being set by the iron and steel industries. National output of pig iron was 19.1 percent higher than in 1878, the tonnage of Bessemer steel was up by 26.8 percent, of rolled iron and steel products, 30.4 percent, and of steel rails, 23.8 percent. In some respects Pittsburgh did even better, the net profits for the Carnegie associates being 70.55 percent higher than in 1878. Given such a setting, the restless energy of locally booming business, and the pervasive atmosphere of the possibilities and prime importance of material achievement, no more propitious occasion could have been envisaged for the arrival of an able, energetic, and ambitious young man. It was indeed a remarkable conjunction of time, place, and individual character. Charlie Schwab, though only in his eighteenth year, was bewitched by the outward signs of industrial achievement and was already given to dreams of his own part in a yet greater future. In such circumstances the dull routine of a job behind a store counter could not provide satisfaction for long. All that was needed was a role model for the new possibilities and value systems and the chance to change direction from retailing to a job more obviously in the stream of the times. Opportunity and inspiration came together in the form of the general superintendent of the Edgar Thomson steel works.

Having proved himself in the iron business, as early as 1868 Andrew Carnegie had ventured on a small scale into Bessemer steel at the works of the Freedom Iron and Steel Company at Lewistown, in central Pennsylvania. This venture was a commercial failure. Four years later, after returning from Britain where he had seen bigger plants operate successfully, Carnegie decided to try again, this time on the outskirts of Pittsburgh. With an eye to sales prospects, he named the new steel plant and rail mill after the president of the Pennsylvania Railroad, Edgar Thomson. Asked to approve the use of his name for the works, Thomson is said to have responded, "I fear they will do me little credit." He died in May 1874 and therefore did not see how quickly and decisively his doubts proved unfounded. The first Bessemer blow occurred on 26 August 1875, and six days later the first rails were rolled. During 1879 the Edgar Thomson (ET) works rolled seventy-six thousand tons of steel rails, almost exactly one-eighth the national output. In early fall that year, as Charlie Schwab was settling into the routine of the grocery store, a major change was made in top management at the ET works. William P. Shinn left after an acrimonious dispute with Carnegie; William R. (Bill) Jones, general superintendent since the plant began production, was now given greater powers. Devoted to the pursuit of high productivity, Jones made the ET works a marvel of the metallurgical world.

The chronology of Schwab's introduction to this dynamic industry is by no means clear. It seems probable it was only about eight weeks after he arrived at the store when he was offered and accepted a job at the steel works. The details are lost in the mixture of fact and what eventually became an industrial myth, uncritically repeated, with the latter more assiduously propagated than the former, particularly by image makers. Bill Jones was a customer at the grocery store, noticed the brightness of the young man who served him, and asked if he would like a better job as a laborer. Charlie seems to have joined the Edgar Thomson engineering corps on 12 September 1879. Some doubt may be thrown on this date as it was a Friday, at first sight a rather unlikely day to start a new job. Whatever the truth, late in life Schwab particularized and overdramatized the event: "If I had not sold that 10 cent cigar to Bill Jones, I might still be selling dried apples over a counter."[4] Another story that may be apocryphal but was all of a piece with the attitudes of his later life was that Schwab's response to Jones asking if he could drive stakes was, "I can drive anything." All in all it was an auspicious beginning, scarcely modified from sheer bravado by the fact that during his schooling in Saint Francis College in Loretto some time was devoted to aspects of both surveying and engineering, or that, as author Robert Hessen suggests, in this new job Schwab got by for some time with a mixture of pretended knowledge and quick learning. To help himself further, he is said to have studied mathematics in the evenings. As compared with the ten dollars or so a month he earned at McDevitt's store, he earned a dollar a day at the Edgar Thomson works.[5]

Six months or so after he began work at the plant, that is, sometime during spring of 1880, the temporary transfer of Peter Brendlinger, head of the engineering corps, to the company's Scotia iron ore mining operations gave the still barely eighteen-year-old Schwab another break—the opportunity to take his place. In fact, reliable dating of his progress is unsure, depending as it does on his recollections more than half a century after the event. Eugene Guifford Grace, later chairman of Bethlehem Steel and a close associate in the last thirty-five years of Schwab's life, suggested he became chief engineer two years after starting work; Hessen, drawing on the notes compiled by S. B. Whipple, indicated six months. Even less credible is biographer Joseph F. Wall's claim that within six months of starting work as a stake driver, Schwab was superintending the construction of new blast furnaces at Braddock. He provides no evidence, and at that time Schwab had absolutely no experience with blast furnaces. On prima facie grounds it seems most unlikely that men with the business sense of the Carnegie brothers or as ever-watchful as Henry Phipps would entrust a project costing many thousands of dollars to an unknown youth with no technical background. In fact, at that time the blast furnaces at Edgar Thomson were under the control of Julian Kennedy, a man ten years older than Schwab and a highly trained engineer.[6]

Shortly after being promoted into the engineering corps, Schwab became a staff member in the drawing office, where his dedication to work once more earned Jones's respect. Again, myth making has been active where detailed information is lacking, it being said that he gained rapid promotion by excelling in an exercise especially framed to see which of the draftsmen would accept an extra burden of work without grumbling. A rare specific date in all the flux of rumor and conjecture seemed to be provided many years later by James Farrell, who, as president of the United States Steel Corporation, must be assumed to have had command of the resources to find the truth. He revealed that Schwab first applied for a job in the Edgar Thomson mills on Sunday, 12 September 1880. On the other hand, it is disturbing to the confidence to note that this date was exactly a year after Schwab is said to have first been employed at the plant—and that 12 September 1880 was a Sunday.[7]

Experience continued to increase Jones's trust in the lively young man, and he began to use Schwab as a means of communicating his daily commercial reports to Andrew Carnegie, whose office was in central Pittsburgh almost ten miles away from the plant. Carnegie too was impressed by the combination of charm and obvious talent in the carrier.[8] Even so, for some years it was Bill Jones who was the most important influence on Schwab. He was a man well suited to inspire a keen, able, ambitious, and still impressionable deputy.

When William R. Jones joined the Edgar Thomson Steel Company in 1873 he was thirty-four years old and, after years of work at the Cambria Iron works, Johnstown, an experienced steel maker. In 1873 construction of the new Edgar Thomson works was still in its early stages. Jones became superintendent in September 1875. Apart from his technical competence, he possessed two other vital qualities: he was both highly competitive and able to instill this commercially valuable attitude in his men. Year after year rail travelers passing through Braddock would see an immense

Captain W. R. "Bill" Jones.
Reprinted from H. N. Casson, *The Romance of Steel*
(New York: A. S. Barnes, 1907).

broom towering above one or another of the Edgar Thomson blast furnaces. Its transfer from one stack to another indicated which of them had
recently made a clean sweep of the world blast furnace production record.
A similar drive for production was pursued in the steel department. In
1874 Alexander Holley reckoned that the plant he had designed would
make 30,000 tons of rails a year; during November 1879 it rolled 11,037
tons.[9] It gained a lead over contemporary European practice not only by
installing new equipment, by superior design, and by the advantages of
the large, standardized mill runs possible under U.S. marketing conditions but also because of the gradual development of a distinctively American production ethos: a focus on high productivity coupled with unceasing striving to be at the head of the field. In short, the achievements at
Edgar Thomson were a special case of a national characteristic. As early
as 1877, 22 converters in the United States, each averaging 5 tons in size,
produced two-thirds as much steel as 114 British converters of larger average capacity.[10] The plant's 1880 output of 138,000 short tons ranked Edgar

Thomson ahead of all the steel plants in the nation. The following May, in a paper on American Bessemer steel and rail manufacture presented at the Iron and Steel Institute in London, Jones attributed the large outputs directly to the keenness shared by managers and workers: "As long as the record made by the works stands the first, so long are they content to labor at a moderate rate, but let it be known that some rival establishment has beaten that record, and then there is no content until the rival's record is eclipsed." Given such conditions of work, it was easy to conclude that progress and expansion had no limits. In 1880, when Schwab joined the work force, the Edgar Thomson plant's daily ingot steel capacity was 450 gross tons; by March 1887 output averaged 968 tons a day.[11]

Charlie Schwab now moved into this frantic but exhilarating industrial atmosphere; given his own aspirations, he responded positively to its challenges and opportunities. Years later he spoke of Jones as "my best friend of early life. . . . How proud to be known in after-life as one of 'Capt Bill's Boys!' . . . a true man among men." In a less euphoric moment he also described him as "an impetuous, hustling man." At the time his response was devotion to the work: "My whole object in life then was to show him my worth and to prove it. I thought and dreamed of nothing else but the steel works." In fact, the situation provided more than a chance to please his immediate superior. Looking back, he reckoned that by the early 1880s Jones, though only in his early forties, was tiring, and the superintendent accordingly began to delegate more and more work to Schwab. The established reputation and production psychology of the works, the inspiring example of Jones, and possibly his wish to pass on more routine work to an assistant in whom he placed increasing trust created a most favorable milieu for an ambitious young man. There is circumstantial if little direct evidence of his early aspirations as he put down roots in the area. In May 1883, aged only twenty-one, he married Emma Eurania (Rana) Dinkey, a local girl whose brothers worked at Edgar Thomson. Their carefully posed honeymoon photographs from Atlantic City were revealing. Arms folded, Charlie seemed solidly self-confident. In contrast with the otherwise identical background in Rana's photograph, he stood with his right foot firmly planted on a "log." When they returned to Braddock, they moved into a very modest home, a small wood-framed cottage. Many years later he recalled the time and place as the happiest period of their lives. Despite the new domesticity the drive for advancement was undiminished. One indication of this drive was that in his early years at Edgar Thomson Schwab would typically be up at 5 a.m. ready for the day's work.[12] The marriage not only failed to moderate his zeal for work but also provided another

Charles M. Schwab, May 1883, at the age of twenty-one.
Courtesy of the National Canal Museum, Easton, PA.

potent industrial "myth," the truth of which is difficult to verify. Charlie began to use the room originally intended as Rana's sewing room as a place in which to teach himself the rudiments of metallurgical analysis. By now he had caught the attention of other Carnegie associates, and a major help in equipping his "laboratory" was a gift of one thousand dollars from Henry Phipps—a generosity Schwab later failed to acknowledge in his rather parsimonious assessment of the owner of the second largest interest in the Carnegie operations. In marked contrast with Schwab's attempt to make good his lack of scientific knowledge, Jones, though continuing to make important innovations in steel works equipment, affected skepticism about scientific research. As he once put it, "Damn it Charlie, chemistry is going to spoil the steel business yet."[13] Despite the difference in their ages, Schwab became Jones's friend as well as a workday colleague; he even gave piano lessons to Jones's daughter.

Meanwhile Schwab's progress in the field of iron and steel works engineering continued. An early triumph was his design for the construction of a bridge in Braddock to be used for transfer of molten iron across the tracks of the Baltimore and Ohio Railroad. He completed this assignment in 1885, in two-thirds of the time allocated to him, and he received recognition from both Jones and Carnegie: a diamond studded pin from the former and a monetary reward from the latter.[14] Above all, such successes suggested he might be suitable for still greater responsibilities. The progress of the Carnegie associates provided him with the necessary opportunity.

In 1881 the Lucy Furnace and the Edgar Thomson steel works were merged and the resulting conglomerate was known as Carnegie Brothers. Five years later a second firm, Carnegie, Phipps and Company, was formed with another big steel operation at its core. On the south bank of the Monongahela River, two miles closer to the center of Pittsburgh than Braddock, the borough of Homestead was incorporated in 1880. Its population was then 596, but industrial development was already under way. A glass plant was the pioneer in 1879, and then in October that year a group of special steel producers, incorporated as the Pittsburgh Bessemer Steel Company, went looking for a site on which to build a new bulk steel works and chose Homestead. Their first steel was poured in mid-March 1881, but not until August was the rail mill at work. For a time this new mill threatened to be a major competitor for established producers, including Edgar Thomson. Then labor unrest, partly the result of insensitive handling by management, hamstrung its operations. On 16 October 1883 the Carnegie interests bought the troubled Pittsburgh Bessemer works for a reported $1.2 million. It was not in good condition. During the first five months of 1884 its net earnings were $44,353, equal to an annual profit of $106,000; that year net profits at Carnegie Brothers amounted to $1.3 million. The newly acquired works needed to be revamped.[15]

In the mid-1880s it seemed for a time that steel rail production had reached a plateau. National output decreased each year from 1883 to 1885, and the average production for all three years was 79.7 percent of the 1883 figure. In light of these circumstances the decision was made to equip Homestead to roll other products. By summer 1885 its rail mill had been modified to produce steel beams. In spring 1886 work began on a plate mill, and in 1887 a new cogging mill was installed to serve the structural steel operations. Even more important, Carnegie Brothers decided to branch out in steel making technology; to its existing Bessemer capacity the company added an open hearth shop of four thirty-ton furnaces. In 1887 the company invited bids for construction of a universal plate mill, which was expected to have the largest capacity of any mill of this type worldwide.[16] The plan for this new mill provided Schwab with the opportunity to make his next major step forward, for he was given his own managerial post at Homestead, as assistant superintendent under Julian Kennedy. There seems to have been some tension between the two men, with Schwab reckoning that Kennedy, who in formal training was much more highly qualified, was jealous of his success. Kennedy soon resigned, and Charlie Schwab became general superintendent of the works. He was not yet twenty-five.[17] The next few years proved his senior colleagues had been right in seeing Schwab as a man of quite exceptional qualities and promise.

It is said that it was on Jones's recommendation that Carnegie chose Schwab as Homestead superintendent, though he was now familiar enough with the young man to make his own judgment. Apart from his increasing skill, experience, and enthusiasm, another reason for Schwab's promotion seems to have been that he had proved he could get on well with working men. Given the part that labor troubles had played in the failure of the Pittsburgh Bessemer Steel Company, such ability was particularly valuable. His annual salary, which had been $120 when he sold groceries and $300 when he drove stakes, was increased to $10,000.

Before taking over at Homestead Schwab was sent to Europe to look over the practices of some of its leading steel works. Later he recalled his first European visit as being in 1883. He may well have taken the trip that year, but by the time of the recollection he was not wholly reliable as to dates.[18] He contemplated using open hearth steel in rail manufacture, and it seems likely that his transatlantic trip was as much to see good melting shop practices as to become familiar with particular finished products. By 1885 the United States outproduced Britain in Bessemer steel by more than 16 percent, but in open hearth steel Britain made 583,000 tons as compared with Germany's 276,000 and 133,000 tons for the United States. The leading British district for open hearth steel was Scotland, whose works made 81 percent more than those of the United States. Naturally, works there received Schwab's special attention, and he recalled that he brought back with him a man called Purvis, who was then involved in the first open hearth steel made at Homestead. By 1888, having used the acid open hearth process, Homestead pioneered basic open hearth steel making in the United States.[19]

Although the Bessemer process was used for years at Homestead, major expansion depended on the new open hearth shops. As late as 1890 converters accounted for well over half the tonnage at Homestead, but it already made ninety-two thousand tons of open hearth steel, one-sixth of the national total.[20] In other respects too the works grew rapidly in im-

portance. By the mid-1880s the federal government was considering expanding the navy, and the ability of the steel industry to supply armor
and ordnance became an important issue. By now the government had
made several inquiries into the state of the armaments industry, examining manufacturing works both domestically and in Europe. The Bethlehem Iron Company made the most positive impression, but in spite of his
initial doubts about entering the new trade Andrew Carnegie was soon
eager that his own companies should also be at the forefront in this field.
Accordingly, during 1886 Schwab and Carnegie's cousin, George Lauder,
made visits to the leading armor plate works of Europe. In December the
secretary of the navy, William C. Whitney, invited bids for five thousand
tons of armor. Julian Kennedy drew up plans for an armor plate mill, and
because armor required steel of a quality best produced in open hearth
furnaces, the firm decided that the new mill should be at Homestead.

All in all it is clear that Schwab, as general superintendent, gave full
satisfaction to the controllers of Carnegie, Phipps and Company, of which
Homestead was the central operation. Unfortunately, little evidence has
come to light of the ways these successes were achieved. One factor was
undoubtedly beyond his control; consumption of the products made there
was growing more rapidly than was the case with rails. In fact, for a time
Edgar Thomson, operating as Carnegie Brothers, found it increasingly
difficult to hold on to the share of the nation's rail business it had supplied in the early1880s. Between 1883 and 1890, both good years, national
output of rails increased 61.7 percent; that of all other categories of rolled
steel, 807.8 percent. Homestead's high level of production reflected the
major capital outlays made by its new owners. Basic open hearth production was an important departure, and Schwab later claimed he had gained
a reputation for always trying to adjust to their customers' needs.[21] Yet,
however great the success, Carnegie always pressed for greater output and
lower costs. Believing that they were paying too much for labor, in December 1888 he urged William Abbott, chairman of Carnegie, Phipps and
Company, to go over things carefully with Schwab to see if Homestead's
work force could be reduced at the beginning of the new year: "The force
might perhaps be reduced in number 10 percent so that each man getting
more wages would be required to do more work."[22] Naturally, such action was unwelcome to workers. Next summer a major strike was mounted
against a Carnegie plan to replace flat-rate per ton wages with a system
based on a sliding scale. Schwab's part in the dispute was a secondary
but essential one, that of keeping the works as calm as possible. Abbott
handled the negotiations, but, despite having prepared his company to

fight the men, he compromised when there were signs that physical confrontation might become violent. He recognized the union and made a three-year wage arrangement in return for the workers' acceptance of the sliding scale principle. The letter in which Carnegie criticized Abbott for giving way was not unkind, but by implication it compared him unfavorably with the general superintendent: "So glad Schwab proved so able. If we have a real manager of men there Homestead will come out right now. Everything is in the man." A few months before, in a letter to Carnegie Brothers about outlying works at Beaver Falls being a continuing drag on their success, Carnegie had given further indication of his regard for Schwab, albeit as a member of a promising group: "A man like Borntraeger or Schwab, or one of Schwab's promising young men, should be selected and given full charge."[23]

Edgar Thomson

In September 1889 circumstances beyond his control or that of any of his colleagues suddenly changed the course of Schwab's career. Jones was severely injured while helping his men clear a blockage of material in one of the Edgar Thomson blast furnaces, and he died two days later. Immediately there was speculation as to his successor. Many names were brought up for discussion, and it apparently came as a surprise to many local individuals when on 1 October, at Schwab's own request but apparently against Carnegie's initial inclinations, he was transferred from Homestead to take the "Captain's" place. His own replacement at Homestead was John A. Potter, three years his senior and a man who, like him, had begun humbly, having started at age fourteen as a greaser in the Lower Union Mills. On Thursday, 10 October 1889, Henry Clay Frick, chairman from the previous January of Carnegie Brothers and Company, introduced Schwab to his new colleagues at Edgar Thomson. The general superintendent was well received on his return to the works in which he had first revealed his promise. Edgar Thomson was as yet the bigger of the two main Carnegie steel works, and Schwab set out to improve its standing. He later recalled how deeply committed he had been, but he was to claim this level of commitment for every stage of his career. If the noise from the mills ceased for any reason, the change would awaken him in the middle of the night. On Sundays he spent the morning at the mill, and, after an afternoon with friends, returned there by 6 p.m. His dedication achieved a good deal in terms of improved equipment and in relation to labor.

Within a few months it was recognized that Jones's successor was in

The Edgar Thomson Steel Works in 1890.

many respects at least his equal. A new converter and new mill were at work, and, as Frick reported, "The men are extremely well-pleased with the new order of things there and it is considered by everyone that the Works certainly are in better shape than ever." Carnegie welcomed this sort of assessment: "So glad Schwab grows in your estimation—thought he would. Potter is to be proved, Schwab has been."[24] The flow of letters from the new general superintendent to the chairman recommending plant improvements seemed to be unceasing. Most of Schwab's requests were approved and were justified by the operating results. Over the first two-thirds of the year monthly rail output averaged 27,500 tons. Schwab was unsatisfied. In September 1890 he asked for $5,000 to $6,000 for a new pressure pump: "I expect to increase our product very materially and feel sure that, unless our pressure system is somewhat increased, we will be greatly delayed on this account." Frick gave approval next day.[25] Almost immediately after this exchange, Schwab visited the South Chicago works of their great rival, Illinois Steel. There he saw a new blooming mill, which he believed could deal with 30 percent more steel than any mill in the United States. He was challenged as well as impressed: "Since returning from Chicago my only thought has been how to remodel our mill to make it as nearly like Chicago's mill as possible without a large outlay of money." He estimated the cost of necessary changes would be $21,368: "I know of course our calls for many improvements and repairs have been very heavy this past year, but I know of no improvement that will give us any better return." Again he was promptly and fully backed by Frick, though this time the letter of approval sounded a note of caution: "I have your favor of the 27th and note carefully the changes you desire to make. I trust you are correct in your estimate of what they will cost;

and hereby approve of their being made."[26] Next year, Schwab kept up the pressure. The results vindicated him. In the last four complete years under Jones, 1885–1888, Edgar Thomson averaged 11.02 percent of national steel rail production. He was in command for almost three-quarters of 1889, when its share was 18.37 percent. In 1890 and 1891, under Schwab, its share of the nation's rail output reached 19.13 percent.

In his concern for the performance of the works under his direct control, Schwab had an inclination to invest in plant improvements in an endless pursuit of more operational efficiency, whatever the capital cost. Although Frick remained supportive, as chairman and a partner in the firm he had to adopt a wider perspective, and he therefore had to urge that his irrepressible general superintendent exercise some restraint. An interesting example of this relationship came in late September 1891 when Schwab submitted suggestions for changes in the Bessemer shop. As usual, Frick replied promptly. His brief letter avoided a tone of harsh refusal but was a masterpiece of quiet caution:

> This is somewhat of a new departure, and I trust you have given the matter sufficient thought so as to be quite clear that after the change is made it will be of the benefit you say, and that the cost will not exceed $25,000. The next time you are in I should like you to call on Mr. Lovejoy [the Carnegie Brothers secretary] and let him show you the amount of money you have already spent at Edgar Thomson this year for improvements. I think it will make you open your eyes. However, I will talk this matter over with you the next time you are in, or I am out, and if, on further investigation, you still think you are correct, it is likely I can prevail on the Board to agree to the expenditure.[27]

At Braddock as at Homestead, Schwab's success in increasing production was partly achieved by pitting one gang of workers against another. This technique for raising productivity Jones had already used with great success—and, notwithstanding his popularity, with scant regard for the long-term well-being of his men. During this period Schwab also proved his abilities in handling recalcitrant workers. Fuller consideration of this issue is important, for one of the most persistent and important myths about Schwab is that he had some magical way with workers and, in an era of hardness, was a more understanding and sympathetic employer than most. Except in the case of his skills in managing the media of his day, this myth was by no means true, as he was to show time and again throughout his career. On the labor front, his record at Braddock was a mixture of giving the men their due, squeezing down pay scales, and dealing very firmly with disputes. An example of the first came in October 1890 when he suggested that the increases in output, with no significant rise in worker numbers, meant that men in the furnace department were undertaking 27 percent more work than a year before. He wanted to increase their wages, but the changes he proposed in converting department rates would add only 1.6 cents to a ton of ingots (the average price of Bessemer pig in Pittsburgh that year was $18.85 per gross ton) and in the rolling mill, an additional 2.1 cents per ton for the cost of rails.[28] Moreover, while recognizing that the men had a grievance about wages and being willing to put this situation right, he was still careful to keep a close watch on them. On Saturday evening, 13 September 1890, a body of workers, mostly from the rolling mills, held a meeting in Braddock attended by William Weihe, president of the Amalgamated Association of Iron and Steel Workers. Schwab, knowing that the meeting had been called, "placed myself in position to get all the information possible" and delivered to Frick a sixteen-page typed report on what had happened and on the general labor situation at ET.[29]

A few months later, as the agreement with their blast furnace workers expired, he was faced by an outbreak of violence. The action is vividly brought out in letters written at the time. Men in the stockyard left work at 6 p.m., breaking their contract six hours before it expired. A gang of about 50 continued to fill coke. Unfortunately, a group of workers identified by the popular term "Hungarians" reportedly spent the evening of New Year's Eve 1890 in Wolfe's Saloon. Before midnight they gathered at the corner of Thirteenth Street and set off toward the works "to clean out" the men still there. Called in, Schwab arrived at the same time as a mob of about 60 men. Largely drunk, the "Huns" drove away some of the men still working their shift and caused material damage, but by 3 a.m., when Schwab wrote a short report on the incident, the yard was clear. Having the names and addresses of a large number of those involved, he intended to inform the authorities and have them jailed at once. He sent for the sheriff and hoped to swear in 20 to 30 special police officers. Wolfe promised he would not open his saloon next day. However, despite these moves, the struggle was not over. In the middle of New Year's Day about 250 reportedly drunken Hungarians attacked the furnace department, and all those working there were forced to quit work. Schwab wanted to call in Pinkerton agents, but within a few hours he had decided that would not be the best course of action. He told Frick he was willing to allow the furnaces to stand idle for two or three weeks until the men saw sense.

Frick favored using the sheriff to protect the property.[30] After the sheriff arrived Schwab called together those men who had remained on the job and pointed out to them that "it was simply ridiculous" that 500 Hungarians could deprive 3,000 men—"honest workmen," as he characterized them—of their employment. By ensuring that the sheriff swore in some of the loyal employees as deputies, he expected that by evening he would have at least 100 men defending the furnaces. To arm them he had twelve Winchester repeating rifles, small arms, and clubs. He assured Frick that if the "Huns" attacked again, "I am determined to drive them out, no matter at what cost, or sacrifices . . . should the opportunity come to-night we will make it mighty hot for these people."[31] The whole episode had made clear that he was not a man to capitulate in the face of labor militancy.

In October 1891 Schwab completed a new settlement of wage scales with the Edgar Thomson workers. There seemed reason for requiring reductions: it was a direct consequence of the huge capital outlay on new plant. Increasing productivity resulted in higher wages for employees who were paid according to the tonnage they produced. In making adjustments at this time Schwab also managed to remove all bonuses and to ensure that laborers who had previously been on fixed rates were placed like others on a sliding scale related to the price for rails. Sending his new schedules to Frick, he added a handwritten note in which he triumphantly stated,

> I hope you will be satisfied with the results. . . . The total percentage of reduction is much higher than I had at first anticipated as being able to secure, but as I said before one is never able to tell just what can be done in a settlement of this kind until he actually meets the men he has to deal with. . . . [I]t gives me pleasure to report that I not only secured much below the maximum figures which you gave me as being what you were willing to accept, but as a general thing I have secured figures slightly below those which I first recommended to you as being the extreme reduction we should ask for, and which I did not believe we could get without considerable trouble. I am glad to have been mistaken in this.

He also claimed in his note to Frick that the men had accepted the new schedules without complaint or "any bad feelings on account of this heavy reduction. With one little exception the best of feeling and humor was maintained throughout all the conferences." Overall, he estimated the savings achieved in the converting, blooming, and rail mill operations amounted to $8,771 a month. To this savings he expected to add a further

$5,353 because of the redundancy of thirty-eight men resulting from new equipment to be installed beginning 1 January 1892. His pride in what he had achieved was emphasized by repetition: "I take this opportunity of saying that the reductions secured this time are by long odds the heaviest reductions we have ever secured at Edgar Thomson. . . . I have done the best I could everything considered and I trust you are satisfied with the results."[32]

As chairman of Carnegie Brothers, and by general agreement the outstanding resident partner, Frick was generally greatly impressed but occasionally outraged by his immensely talented but temperamentally very different deputy. Events in the first half of 1891 illustrated these varied aspects of his relation with Schwab. During mid-January Frick rebuked him for slowness in stockpiling coke at a time when labor disputes were looming in the Connellsville district. In April he sent Schwab a short, stern note: "If you have not already done so I should like a written report giving full particulars of the accident at Bessemer yesterday. Hereafter in all cases let me have such reports promptly. I prefer to get my information direct rather than through newspapers." A few weeks later nepotism was the problem, but the means whereby he had learned of it were again also in question: "Newspaper item says that A. C. Dinkey is to be appointed Superintendent of Rail Mill. I hope this is not correct. You cannot afford to appoint a brother in law to such a position." In this case Frick's opinion was decisive, and Dinkey remained for the time being secretary to the Homestead general manager.[33] A third contact between the chairman and general superintendent was on a happier note though there was a less positive minor theme. Frick sent on a letter that George Lauder had written to John Leishman, the vice president of Carnegie Brothers: "I was much pleased to see the excellent position of E.T [Edgar Thomson] today and have read Schwab's report to Frick with interest. I cannot quite see the force of his logic as well as I can of his results but this is all right. You know it was said of a celebrated judge that his decisions were always right and his reasons for such always wrong." In September at the end of a long letter to Jay Morse of Illinois Steel, Frick reported a recent insight by Schwab regarding a possible up-and-coming rival: "I might add that our General Superintendent, Mr. Schwab, has returned from a visit to Sparrows Point, and I will have, to take with me to New York, a complete report on that works, together with Schwab's idea of its output, based on what he saw and what the President of the Maryland Steel Company, Mr. Wood, told him." Frick sometimes found Schwab's methods of conducting business annoying. In mid-October this annoyance was made clear when

Charles M. Schwab in the early 1890s.
Courtesy of the Carnegie Library, Pittsburgh, PA.

the latter was working on the labor agreement of which he was to be so proud. Frick wrote, "Mr. Lovejoy has shown me your message wherein you want the comparative wages and comparative earnings of Homestead, Braddock and Duquesne. I told you very plainly, the other evening, that I did not wish you to bring in the question of what wages were paid at Duquesne and Homestead, and I do not think you would gain anything through it if you did. Make no mistake about this."[34] His appreciation of Schwab's abilities was shown early next year when the company decided to start iron making at the Duquesne works they had bought fifteen months earlier. Frick informed Carnegie that he was going over there to select a site for the new blast furnaces and that James Gayley and Schwab were going with him.

From the company's point of view Schwab's management practices were fully justified by reduced costs and its increased share of the nation's rail business—20.45 percent in 1891. As the new year began Carnegie wrote in jubilant tone from New York to the chairman, "Schwab's success is splendid. He is really a 'Number One' superintendent."[35]

Sometime in the early 1890s Schwab was offered a large salary by British entrepreneur Arthur Keen, who had major interests in the iron and steel industry of South Wales and the Black Country of England, to transfer his genius as a steel mill manager to the United Kingdom. It was fortunate that Schwab turned down the blandishment. In 1892 Edgar Thomson pushed its share of the nation's rail business up to 21.49 percent, but before that operating year was complete, Schwab had again been switched to new duties. This time the cause was not a catastrophic accident, as with the death of Jones, but a reaction to a long-fought and unusually bitter labor dispute.

The Homestead Strike and After

The worst episode in the history of the Carnegie associates, and possibly the most notorious episode in American labor history, was the Homestead strike. By the time he wrote his autobiography twenty years later, Andrew Carnegie had managed to persuade himself that if Schwab rather than Frick had been in charge this bitter conflict might have been avoided. As it drew to its close Schwab was moved back to Homestead, "and 'Charlie' as he was affectionately called, soon restored order, peace and harmony. Had he remained at the Homestead works, in all probability no serious trouble would have arisen."[36] It was a thought-provoking idea, but it glossed over and sanitized much of the reality.

The Homestead strike began on 1 July 1892 as the labor agreement Abbott had negotiated three years before expired. Its course over nearly five months has been studied, written about, and discussed by innumerable writers for more than a century.[37] For present purposes the details are unimportant, but the financial and still greater human costs give some indication of the harm and anger that simmered on after its formal end. Losses in wages were about $2 million, the cost to the state in maintaining troops in the area was approximately half a million, and there were other losses from the effects of rioting. The violence had been vividly reported by watchful newspaper reporters. The number of casualties was a matter of dispute, but there had been much bloodshed, injury, and loss of life. One assessment of the toll conveyed something of the horror: "At least 35 deaths were directly or indirectly caused by the strike. Besides those killed in the battle of July 6th [when an attempt by Pinkerton agents to land at the works was met by gunfire], many soldiers contracted fever, which resulted fatally; one soldier was shot accidentally by a comrade, another was killed by the cars, one striker committed suicide, one was drowned, one was killed by the cars, several non-union men died from fever and several were killed in the mill, and one was murdered by another non-unionist." The Carnegie Steel Company paid a high price both in material terms and in reputation. In 1892 the industry had a record year, with crude steel output rising 26.2 percent from 1891; at Carnegie Steel the increase was only 10.2 percent. Net profits fell by $300,000 or almost 7 percent.[38] All told, it was an appalling record.

Company resistance had been led by Frick, chairman of the Carnegie Steel Company, the new firm that from 1 July 1892 combined the previously separate Carnegie enterprises. There seems no reason to question the general assumption that it was above all his unyielding determination that caused the dispute to drag on for so long and to cause so much hurt before the workers gave in. However, to appreciate the atmosphere in which reconstruction at Homestead began it is important to recognize that the power and essential spirit of the company, as focused in Andrew Carnegie, was fully behind Frick's inflexible stand, although in retrospect the situation was often represented otherwise. Carnegie seems not to have anticipated a long fight, but he undoubtedly endorsed one if it should prove necessary, writing from England early in May, "I really do not believe it will be much of a struggle. We all approve of anything you do, not stopping short of approval of a contest. We are all with you to the end." Five weeks later, and three before the strike began, he remained supportive: "Of course you will win, and win easier than you suppose, owing to the present condition of the market." Much later, and looking back to the violent clash between the strikers and the Pinkertons on 6 July 1892, which shocked the nation and reverberated far beyond it, Carnegie presented himself as cut off from an active role in these horrible events by distance. He summarized the situation long afterward in words well chosen to convey shocked innocence: "I was coaching through the Scottish Highlands on my holidays and did not hear of the lamentable riot at Homestead until days after it occurred. I wired at once that I would take the first steamer home, but was requested not to come."[39] The latter part of that statement seems to have been true, but he had heard the news and had reacted to it far more promptly than he pretended. The day after the violence he wired Frick, "Cable received. All anxiety gone since you stand firm. Never employ one of these rioters. Let grass grow over works. Must not fail now. You will win easily next trial." Ten days later, when he wrote to his cousin, George Lauder, it seemed to be the mechanics rather than the morality of the bloody confrontation that he criticized: "Matters at home *bad*—such a fiasco trying to send guards by boat and then leaving space between River and fences for the men to get opposite landing and fire." He continued to represent himself as much more acceptable to the workers than the implacable Frick. Wall summed up admirably, "In time Carnegie even became convinced that the workers had sent him a telegram that read, 'Kind master, tell us what you wish us to do and we will do it for you.' Unfortunately, nowhere in his personal papers could he find such a telegram. . . . [W]ithout any corroboration [he] told of the telegram in his autobiography anyway." On 18 November Frick sent a single-word message to inform him the strike was over: "Victory!"[40]

Some weeks before Frick sent that cable, Schwab had been moved to Homestead to sort out the situation that the so-called "victory" would leave. He went back with the prospect of unceasing pressure from Frick to assert the primacy of management's wishes, the less explicit but equally firm commitment of Carnegie to the same values, and confidence in his own powers to put things right. On Tuesday, 18 October 1892, he took over as general superintendent. His appointment brought about a number of moves by other leading figures in the management team. James Gayley replaced Schwab at Edgar Thomson. On the same day, the Edgar Thomson chemist resigned.[41] More directly Schwab's transfer meant the effective end of John Potter's prospects in the company.

In contrast to his transfer to Edgar Thomson after the death of Jones, there was on this occasion some initial reluctance to move on Schwab's part. He later and publicly confirmed this reluctance: "I was asked, much against my wishes[,] to reorganize and take charge of the Homestead works. I finally consented to do so."[42] From a letter Schwab wrote to Frick on Sunday, 16 October, it seems that neither Potter nor Gayley would know until Frick saw them of the moves his own transfer would require of them. That weekend he was unwell, but his handwritten letter provides fascinating insights into his mind at a crossroads in his life. Notwithstanding his indisposition, he thought and expressed himself well:

> The Doctor has advised me to stay in today, but I will be all right in the morning. I have been thinking about your visit to Homestead tomorrow with a good deal of anxiety. Will meet you at City Farm station tomorrow at whatever time you telegraph me. In talking to John [Potter] try to impress him with the fact that my greatest regret was supplanting him and that I was most anxious to see him well provided for which as you know is quite true. In this way I can get better service from him in the future. If he gets an idea that I rejoiced in his failure he might not be of much use to me afterwards. As for Berg [P.T. Berg, a highly talented Swedish engineer, in whom Carnegie in particular seems to have had great confidence], I believe that John

and he will arrange to go together, that is that John will take him for his draughtsman to the city office. I hope this can be prevented, 1st because I should like to retain him at the works and 2nd because it is not conducive to best discipline to provide places for subordinates simply because they do not personally like the superintendent, as was done once before in his case. I would not object to such an arrangement in 6 months or a year, but would not like it now. I believe after arranging matters with Potter tomorrow morning, if it can be arranged to notify Gayley and let me go over matters with him on Monday afternoon and evening so that when I go to Homestead on Tuesday I can stay right there. For the first few weeks I will be obliged to be there almost night and day so I can learn and become acquainted with both turns fully and quickly. I am sorry I cannot go in to-day but think it better to be in good shape for next week. It is hard for you to understand how I dislike leaving old E.T. works—13 year[s] here. [He seems to have discounted the years 1886–1889 already spent at Homestead.] I dare not think of it. But one thing sure. I am determined to make this the greatest work of my life—and am eager to get at it. Only have patience with me and don't expect too much until the strike is broken. Give me the same support you have always given me and I will take care of the rest.[43]

On Tuesday, 18 October, after the regular meeting of the board of managers Frick issued a press notice: "The following appointments were approved by the board of managers this day: Mr. John A. Potter, having resigned the general superintendency of Homestead Steel Works, has been appointed chief mechanical engineer of this association with office at No. 42 Fifth Avenue. Mr. Charles M. Schwab has been appointed general superintendent of the Homestead Steel Works. Mr. James Gayley has been appointed superintendent of Edgar Thomson works. Mr. D. G. Kerr has been appointed general superintendent of furnace department[,] Edgar Thomson works. All taking effect today." The company maintained the changes represented promotion for all those involved, and as a result the local press reported regarding Potter that "as a reward he has been given a position which is not only more responsible but valuable pecuniarily."[44] (A little over a year later, and still puzzled by the way he had been displaced, Potter resigned and left Carnegie Steel for the Cleveland Rolling Mill Company.)

On the day these changes in top management were announced Schwab began work. As Frick told Tom Morrison, general superintendent at the Duquesne works, "Mr. Schwab will carry out the policy we outlined when we went into this strike." He had been at Homestead that morning and "was much pleased to see the way everything is running. A number of old men are coming back today and appear very glad to get back." The returning workers were vetted individually. This process gave the management a chance not only to weed out those regarded as subversive but also to downgrade some of the others because, "not being able to get their positions, all were willing to take anything they could get." Schwab was in charge of the selection. Frick's biographer, George Harvey, was generous in his assessment of the way Schwab carried it out. Large numbers broke away from the strike on 17 and 18 October, "all of whom were cordially greeted personally and few turned back by Mr. Charles M. Schwab."[45]

At this point the strike still dragged on, and Homestead was operating with a work force of about two thousand men, roughly fifteen hundred fewer than the normal complement. No more than about one in ten of those at work had been employed there before the strike; the rest had been transferred from other plants or were strikebreakers brought in from outside.[46] Schwab assessed the situation he had inherited with remarkable speed. On the day after taking charge he reported to Frick how bad things were in both plant and labor force. Indeed, he judged the situation so critical that he sent his report that evening in the hands of his secretary, Reinhardt, direct to Frick's home, "Clayton," in the Homewood district of Pittsburgh: "Have met many discouraging things indeed, since starting at this place that it would be impossible for me to tell you by letter. The converting mill is in terrible condition. . . . Coupled with this fact, it seems impossible to urge the men. . . . All our Foremen and Superintendents here lack energy, vitality, and it seems impossible to get them started up, in fact, the men seem completely worked out, and they will have to be very gently nursed, as their positions are not the most desirable under the circumstances and might leave us in a still worse condition."[47] Frick dictated his reply to Reinhardt. It was typically inflexible in relation to the strikers but strongly supportive of Schwab:

> Do not be in the least discouraged. We all expect that it is going to take some time to settle this matter properly. I am perfectly aware that you will put into it all the energy and good judgment that any one can, but with that I know it is going to be hard work to make things run smoothly, or show any decided improvement. I am perfectly aware of the fact that things generally are in bad order and of course that will operate against you for a while, but let me repeat, do

not allow anything of that kind to worry you; just keep at it, doing the best you can, and, as I said to you before, do not allow the fact that you are not getting along as well as you would like, lead you to put yourself in a compromising position with any of the old employees who are still on strike.

Three days later Frick informed Schwab he was to be given a substantial material incentive for tackling these problems, a two-thirds of 1 percent interest in the Carnegie Steel Company, backdated to 1 July, the day on which the strike began.[48] Welcome though it was, at the time the amount must have seemed scarcely adequate recompense for the struggles Schwab could vaguely see ahead.

An important point that had not been spelled out in the company notice of the managerial changes was that, while Schwab was to give his main attention to Homestead, he would also continue as general superintendent of Edgar Thomson, Gayley being only its superintendent in everyday matters. By his overall command of the two main Carnegie Steel works, Schwab was in some respects already the key man in the organization, with the single exception of Frick.[49] Even though his biggest and most immediate challenges lay at Homestead, Schwab continued to live in Braddock. News of Schwab's financial incentive brought an uncommon note of criticism from Carnegie, then in Milan. It came in a letter to Frick reviewing promotion and shares in the partnership:

> *Schwab* of course deserves increase. Still it would have been [an] appropriate time to give this *after* he had settled in Homestead and became a Homestead man exclusively—and made Homestead a success—He can never have the needful influence until he goes and lives among his men and becomes the first man of the place—I saw a note in a Braddocks paper he was still to live there but of course that's absurd. Homestead men cannot be made a tail to a Braddocks Supt or to Edgar Thomson—am so glad Schwab feels he has a great field at Homestead and trust he will see that the sooner he goes to live among his "own people" the better.[50]

Schwab's great task of rehabilitating Homestead could not get under way until the strike was over. On Tuesday evening, 25 October, he was at home when three representatives of the strikers came to the door: "They said they had been sent over to see if there was no way by which I would meet them, or any of their men, to discuss the situation. I told them plainly, and very bluntly, that it was impossible for me to do so; that we had out-lined our policy and it would not be deviated from, one iota." He felt their presence and attitude was "another indication of their weakness, and enormous pressure which is being brought to bear against them."[51] The resolution of the men was now crumbling, and striking employees were returning daily. Things dragged on into middle of the next month, but on Friday, 18 November, there was a large influx of mechanics and laborers, and three days later the local lodges of the Amalgamated Association of Iron and Steel Workers called off the strike. There are widely varying accounts of the way in which Schwab received men who returned to work; on balance it seems that he conducted the operation with an effective mixture of approachability and cool-headed selectivity. Writing in the early aftermath of the dispute, journalist Arthur Burgoyne, although generally sympathetic to the workers' cause, recognized that Schwab "was known to be a genial and amiable gentleman" and in general presented his actions in a favorable light. Hessen put a very rosy gloss on the proceedings: "Schwab himself greeted the returning strikers, not *en masse*, but individually—calling the many old-timers he remembered by their first names. His approach, so unlike Superintendent Potter's dour formalism, made him all the more popular with the workmen." Some labor historians have not been so sure. Samuel Yellen noted that "the new superintendent, Charles M. Schwab, not bound by the promises of Potter, discharged many inexperienced scabs to make place for the indispensable services of the former workers. . . . Many skilled men, also, were on the blacklist and could get work in no mill throughout the country." A generation later Philip S. Foner wrote that those who returned on 21 November had to line up in front of Schwab, who checked their names off in a book in which the most active strikers were listed. Many were turned away; others got work but at much reduced rates of pay. A few weeks after the return, the *National Labor Tribune* reported that some men who had previously earned four dollars for an eight-hour day were now having to work twelve hours to earn half that amount. It is difficult to be sure which of these interpretations·is nearer the truth, but the fact that Schwab received an endorsement from his chairman is some indication that he was by no means too soft with the recent strikers. On Friday, 18 November, the day the mechanics and some general laborers had flooded back to seek work, Frick wrote, "Over 500 men applied individually for their positions while I was there, many of them valuable men in all departments. Not being able to get their positions, all were willing to take anything they could get."[52]

Almost forty-five years after these events, Schwab recalled his earliest days at Homestead. By this time he was prone to view the past in a favorable light, but if it is anywhere nearly accurate, his account confirms that he managed to combine a direct and understanding attitude toward the workers with a considerable measure of hardheadedness:

> When I went to Homestead . . . I went freely among the workers, without fear. Some others were afraid I would be attacked, and on one occasion, when there was some shooting, they thought the shooting was directed at me. I stood on the top of a box car and watched what appeared to be an incipient riot. Instead it was merely a "celebration." I had the strike leaders, one group at a time, in my office. I told them I proposed to open the plants and to *take the old men back*. I talked to them about their problems and the company's problems, as man to man. I told them I didn't want inexperienced men in our mills, and that any real grievances would be adjusted. But I said firmly that as far as the Amalgamated was concerned, we would have no union whatsoever in our works. "That," I told them, "is a situation that cannot and will not be changed. Otherwise we should have to close down completely and dismantle our plants." When I said that, they knew I was telling them the truth because I had always told them the truth. I took the men back as individuals, not in a group. The record of every man was searched, and he went back to work on his own merits.[53]

In his approach to the selection of his work force from the combined ranks of striking employees and those who had been brought in to work during the strike, Schwab was strongly supported by his two most powerful colleagues, Frick and Carnegie. Carnegie's controlling influence came from his combination of predominant financial interest, close surveillance, and shrewd insight. Frick started from the logical but not very imaginative assumption that, having won the strike, management could dictate terms for the future.[54] Carnegie too looked for high achievement. Writing to Frick from Venice he said, "I got one big religious picture (fine copy) might do for Schwab at Homestead. . . . We must show our men there who have gone into the best of all Unions—a union with their Employers—that they are no longer considered as outcasts. I hear the men have been very jealous of the favorite 'Braddocks'—important give Homestead evidence of our tender regard now."[55]

Forty years after the Homestead strike an account of the remedial actions that followed was published as part of an article entitled, "The Story of Charles M Schwab." Given its source, the *Bethlehem Review*, it can only have come from Schwab's own recollections. Its very positive note had some foundation in the objectively verifiable events of the time, but overall it was another splendid example of the weaving of an industrial myth:

> He determined not only to cure the ills at Homestead, but to do so with maximum speed. During his early months there, he frequently was on the job 72 hours at a stretch, sustained by occasional catnaps, feeling the need to be always on call night or day, getting acquainted with the men individually, visiting their homes, giving ear to their grievances, recognizing the justness of much of their resentment, granting that both sides had made errors, convincing them that the only solution for capital and labor was to work together, and assuring them that every man was welcome to bring any problem direct to him and find sympathetic understanding.

According to the article, Schwab was said to have displayed "patience, tact, and energy."[56] This heroic image was one that time and again Schwab proved able to reproduce. It would be perhaps his greatest strength as an industrial leader.

2 ❦ Manager and Executive

On Monday, 21 November 1892, the day on which the local lodges called off the Homestead strike, Frick wrote to Schwab, who had by then been in his new post for five weeks. His letter was in some ways a manifesto for the new Homestead; it set hard targets but ended with a solid endorsement of the man who would have to reach them. It dealt with labor, referred to Schwab's senior staff, and outlined the company's expectations and the general superintendent's own position. Because of the recent electoral success of the Democrats on a reduced tariff platform, it was necessary to reduce costs. The work force must be subdued: "We have now put the labor matter in a most satisfactory shape at Homestead, and it rests entirely with you as to how long it will be kept that way." But Frick was not happy with Schwab's choice of senior deputies: "[W]e must keep in mind that something may happen to you sometime, and your assistant should be a man capable of succeeding you. I know you will not let sentiment interfere with completing your organization: The stock-holders of this Association will, and do, expect great things from you at Homestead. . . . No man ever had a better opportunity than you now have to make a perfect organization, and I am glad to say I believe no works ever had at their head, as General Superintendent, a better man to make a complete and efficient organization." In view of the foregoing, his letter ended on a rather strange note: "Hew to the line, but treat all men kindly."[1]

Judged by statistics of production over the next few years Schwab's management at Homestead was an outstanding success. Between 1891, the last clear year before the strike, and 1896, national output of raw steel increased 35.3 percent, from all Carnegie plants by 72.5 percent, and at Homestead by 127.7 percent. During the next two years Carnegie Steel production rose 57.9 percent, and Homestead's rose 64.9 percent. In 1891 the Homestead works provided 31.8 percent of the company's steel output, by 1896, 41.9 percent, and two years later, 43.8 percent. As volumes increased unit costs fell sharply. This remarkable record was achieved by sustained effort on the part of management, large-scale investment in new plant, and unremitting attention to cost reduction, particularly in labor. By standards other than tonnages and costs per ton, however, these years were by no means such an unqualified success. (For statistical data, see tables 1 and 2 in appendix B.)

Schwab's emphasis on improving the physical plant was not surprising given his record in the three preceding years at Edgar Thomson. He stressed it from the beginning: "The converting mill is in terrible condition and with their present machinery it is going to be a very difficult matter to increase product materially. . . . We had a big break in the slabbing mill, which has delayed us since yesterday, having no spares on hand."[2] Before long he was moving on from repair to betterment and extension. As he pushed ahead he had to cope with a major crisis in their armor plate department.

In fall 1890 Carnegie, Phipps and Company had signed its first contract with the U.S. government for steel armor plate, to be made at Homestead. The vital importance of meeting obligations in this sector was a source of concern during the strike, and at this time the government found it necessary to deny a report that some plates had been returned as defective. By the end of the year important decisions had to be made about the construction of ancillary plant for the armor department. For instance, on 6 December, fifteen days after the formal end of the strike, Frick wrote to Schwab about the selection of a heavy hydraulic press. His letter provided more evidence that the new general superintendent was being drawn into top management, with its privileges as well as its responsibilities. It also reflected Frick's personal prejudices and perhaps his view of those of Schwab:

> I have arranged for Mr. Matthews, of Whitworths, England, to be here on Friday. Would like you to come in Friday evening next in order to take dinner with me at six p.m. at the Duquesne Club. After dinner we will have a meeting at this office with Mr. Matthews and

some of our people. It would be well for you to arrange to have Potter at this office, say by half-past seven on Friday evening, and anybody else whose views on the Press you would like to have. Do you not think that it would be well to have Julian Kennedy with us that evening. It is a very important matter.

Schwab's level of commitment was revealed in that within two days of this meeting he had sent Frick a request for a new forging press. He made clear both his high ambitions in armor and his expectation that the trade might be very profitable: "We are now in the armor plate business, and like all our other products we want, and must lead our competitors. Lead them not only in our ability to make as heavy, or heavier plates than they, but especially in the quality of our material." Capital outlay would be high but would be well covered by sales: "Even though the press did cost complete $750,000 the profit from one single plate per month would pay 6 percent interest on the investment, and there is no doubt whatever in my mind but that the press would be a good investment." Schwab's responsibilities in their developing armor business extended well beyond plant management. The following summer Lauder sent a telegram from Manchester to Carnegie in Laggan in northern Scotland, asking him to get letters of introduction for Schwab to John Devonshire Ellis at John Brown's of Sheffield, a pioneer in modern armor manufacture. In August Schwab was in Europe examining tools and the ways of finishing forgings in the works of Krupp, Whitworth, and other armor makers. Matthews had written saying he was sorry to have missed Schwab's visit to the Whitworth plant and offering to "run over."[3] Just as things seemed to be progressing well, a crisis occurred. Another rumor casting doubt on the quality of Carnegie plate supplied to the U.S. government proved to be well founded. The resulting controversy dragged on for almost a year, involved two government inquiries, and caused a public scandal that threatened an untimely end to Schwab's advance.

Allegations of fraudulent practices in the armor department were made by four plant employees and sent on by a Mr. Smith, a Pittsburgh attorney, to the secretary of the navy. A naval board of inquiry in secret session decided that Carnegie Steel should be fined for failing to follow approved procedures. As general superintendent, Schwab inevitably came under suspicion, even though Carnegie, writing to President Cleveland, described him as incapable of defrauding his government. However, testimony from William Ellis Corey, superintendent of the armor department, involved Schwab. Of the four matters of complaint against the company two were shown to be either groundless or unimportant. Two serious charges remained: that test results had been falsified and that some plates selected for examination had been re-treated before the tests were carried out, without the government inspectors' knowledge.[4] By spring 1894, at which time Schwab was also involved in sharp altercations with Frick about the dismissal of a man called Buck from the plate mill testing laboratory, it seemed Schwab could be forced to resign. Press reports that he had offered to do so were confirmed by his own recollection that by late April "I felt that the unfortunate circumstances concerning Armor were so strong as would compel me to retire from these works."[5] Despite their disagreement, throughout this difficult period Frick was supportive, on 12 April Schwab telling him that his "talk to me while at Homestead on Tuesday has done me more good than anything that has happened since our unfortunate trouble." Now that Schwab had spent a year in "reconstructing and building" the works, he asked that before being forced to leave he should be given a period in which he could run them in his own way to demonstrate that they could perform satisfactorily: "My only request therefore is that you grant me this opportunity—I don't feel like retiring from Homestead an acknowledged failure." He added a postscript showing both the strain under which he was operating and his dependence on Frick's goodwill: "I do feel that I ought to be ashamed of myself for troubling you further with my talk the day you were here and trust you may overlook it knowing my overstrung feelings on this unfortunate armor affair."[6]

During summer 1894 the Committee on Naval Affairs conducted an inquiry into the alleged armor plate "frauds." Testifying on 6 July, Schwab mounted a vigorous defense. He was fully satisfied that all care, precaution, and science had been used to make good armor, and he criticized each of the three naval officers who in the previous December had fined the company for producing material inferior to that specified in the original contract. He denied the statement of Prof. Philip R. Alger, a naval officer now acting as professor of mathematics at the Navy Department in Washington, that the company demanded a certain output of armor, and he rejected the accusation by Capt. William T. Sampson that he was working for a large output because he would benefit from it financially. He was particularly outspoken about Lt. A. A. Ackerman, who when he came to Homestead "seemed as ignorant as a school boy about the manufacture of armor." The committee concluded that Carnegie Steel had indeed sold the government defective plates. [While recording this conclusion, Schwab's biographer, Robert Hessen, somehow also manages to maintain in both his text and an appendix that Schwab was wrongly associated with this "fraud" ever afterward.] Schwab's fears that he might have to resign proved unfounded, but the episode left a scar. Seven years later, asked by the Industrial Commission to state what Carnegie Steel made, he replied, "[W]e made nearly everything pertaining to the iron and steel business—rails, billets, armor, many lines of that sort. I mention armor because it is well known."[7]

There is little evidence that worry about the armor inquiry hindered Schwab in pushing ahead with plant improvements with his usual zest and naive, almost boyish, enthusiasm. But another early blow to progress came from the sharp depression of 1893. After a period of national economic growth in which gross national product (GNP) had risen year after year for a decade, the economy suffered a sharp downturn, with GNP at constant prices falling 5.2 percent from the 1892 figure. Starting with railroad failures—which by summer had already brought seventy-four companies owning thirty thousand miles of railroad into receivership—and then affecting banks, other financial institutions, and manufacturing, the contraction had a severe impact on the steel industry. In 1893 output of rolled iron and steel was down more than 19 percent from production in 1892. In Pittsburgh an estimated sixteen thousand men were out of work, with estimates for Allegheny City ranging from three thousand to ten thousand while the mayor of McKeesport put the figure there at six thousand. For a time the program for reequipping Homestead and rebuilding its work force and morale was hit hard. In mid-May Schwab recorded that, except for armor, they had not run at full capacity in any department since February: "April was especially bad and I am afraid to look at results for that month. In April the converting mill was shut down for one week on account of no orders. Thirty-five inch mill was shut down all month. Forty inch mill made blooms for three weeks in April. Slabbing mill was shut down for ten days. Plate mill was off for five days, and Twenty-three and Thirty-three inch mills rebuilding, and generally it was the worst possible month." Things quickly improved after that so that by mid-May they were again running full and Schwab was hoping to surprise Frick on cost and production.[8] In fact the harsh conditions that year were less harmful to the interests of Homestead than of the other Carnegie Steel plants. National iron and steel rail production fell by 27 percent but that of structural shapes was down only 15 percent; Bessemer steel tonnage was 23 percent less than in 1892, but open hearth output rose 10 percent. Even so it was a hard year, and by early December it was known that one thousand of Homestead's thirty-eight hundred workers would have to accept wage cuts of up to 40 percent. There were renewed rumors of Schwab's resignation.[9]

Both throughout the nation and at Carnegie Steel, the production of steel rose in 1894, though in the case of the former the level reached was still well below that of 1892. In May Schwab reminded Frick that while the Homestead construction program was under way, he had expressed a wish that when it was completed, Frick would come over with Leishman, Lauder, Henry Curry (treasurer of the company), and other partners and spend enough time there to be shown all around the works: "I now feel that we have reached that point and nothing would give me greater pleasure and satisfaction than to show you fully where all your [*sic*] money has been spent and the conditions the works are now in generally. It would require a full half day."[10] It seems the visit was not made, for almost seven weeks later Schwab wrote again to his chairman, this time spelling out in more than fourteen typed pages what he had done since taking charge. The list of improvements was long, and in every case costs had been cut sharply. His tone was remarkably self-confident, a quality that could have been described as arrogance but for the evidence with which the claims were supported. (He even explained that he had written the account "without wanting to appear egotistical.")

> Starting with the Bessemer works. This mill was built by Julian Kennedy and was very poorly constructed. Vessels were not of the right shape and had to be changed. He cast in the old-fashioned way. I changed all this and cast on cars, necessitating a complete change of track and yards. . . . The Converting Mill is now in excellent condition. . . . The principle [*sic*] improvement in the Open-hearths has been in the better design of furnaces enabling us to turn out big tonnage and consequent reduction of labor. . . . I don't believe any one ever came near such figures as we are now getting . . . [in the] 23 and 33 inch mills. . . . When I assumed charge of these works, the plans of these mills were made and the machinery ordered and had they been built as planned originally, we would never have rolled successfully on these mills. . . . I have every confidence that these two mills will be amongst the most successful mills we have. . . . I now come to the 35 and 40 inch mills. The extent of changes and improvements on these mills has been most marked and nowhere in the world is there a mill so well equipped. . . . . I have never completed a piece of engineering work that I feel better satisfied with, than I do this

beam mill and yard arrangement. It has been the admiration of everybody who has inspected it.

After making reference to the armor department, he summed up on a note of triumph:

In conclusion, I might state that the Homestead plant, taken as a whole, is complete and finished in every department. There is nothing of any consequence to be desired. It is the first time I have ever been connected with any works that I could say, it is finished and complete and to my entire satisfaction. When I think of the short time, less than 20 months ago, when I came to take charge of the Homestead works, it seems almost incredible that all this work could have been crowded in such a short period, especially as the first four months were almost entirely taken up with reorganization and repair, as a result of the strike. It is almost impossible for any one who was not on the ground, to understand the extent of work that was necessary after our strike was over, and this during the severest winter imaginable. Then followed in rapid succession all this planning, improvements starting etc.[11]

In spite of these remarkable achievements, his pleasure with what had been done, and the claims of completeness, predictably Schwab proved to be still unsatisfied and indefatigable in pressing further. He was soon requesting money to install electric cranes, having calculated that in the thirty-two-inch slabbing mill these cranes would cover their cost within a year in savings on oil fuel alone, "to say nothing of the inconvenience or cost of repairing the old machine." On the light beam mill the electric cranes would cut fifty cents off costs and again pay for themselves inside a year.[12] In the two weeks prior to 28 November 1894 he wrote a total of eight letters to Frick about methods of running the mills or installing new machinery to improve productivity and costs. Through eighteen months up to December 1894, the company spent $4 million on upgrades at Homestead. Even then Schwab was not finished. In June 1895 he sent nineteen typed pages to the new president of Carnegie Steel, John G. Leishman, urging greater use of the basic open hearth process at both Homestead and Braddock. Six months later he reported that he had spent two weeks designing a new open hearth plant. If the plans were approved he could have the sixteen furnaces built and operating within six months. With ancillaries they would cost $1.09 million.[13] He eagerly pursued ways of making open hearth operations more efficient; for example, he wrote to David Evans in the Cleveland district in England asking for clarification of a published statement that Evans's company had derived little advantage from the use of hot metal. He explained his interest by mentioning that he was arranging at considerable capital outlay to bring Edgar Thomson hot metal to the Homestead melting shops. In each instance Schwab was pursuing his ideal of a perfect plant. In November 1894 he had provided Frick with a simple statement of his motivation: "I enclose you herewith a number of recommendations for improvements at the Homestead Steel Works, none of them very large as to total cost, and I may say, none of them absolutely necessary, but all would add much to the completeness of the works and cheapness of production. There is none of them that I would not put in if the works belonged to me and had the money to do it with."[14]

At the end of 1896 Schwab set off in another direction, with plans to further process some of the steel they made. He sent Leishman a general outline for a large plant to make axles at Homestead.[15] As this scheme for forward integration showed, not only was he driving for general expansion but he also had a good grasp of the economic principles that should govern large, capital intensive industry. Evidence of this insight was particularly apparent in what he wrote on the effects of utilization rates on overall costs, taking up and giving substance to Carnegie's perennial enthusiasm for "running full." Contacting Frick during the 1893 depression about "much complaint" of their high costs of production, he pointed out that it was up to their sales department to get them the necessary orders:

> Homestead works, taken as a whole, is designed and equipped for large output, and when we are obliged to run slowly as for the last two months, we are badly arranged for cheap production. It is almost impossible to have a big and modern plant like Homestead make a good showing on half production. . . . The mills are so arranged and properly, that it costs nearly as much for day labor to make 100 tons a day as to make 400 tons a day. . . . Give us work to do and let us run our mills and costs will come right all right. . . . Of course I understand that material cannot be sold, but the fault of bad showing in such instances are [sic] not entirely chargeable to the mill.[16]

Taking the matter further, by the end of the following year Schwab was pressing Frick to recognize that they needed to sell any semifinished steel their rolling mills could not use in order to improve their overall performance: "I want to see you this week if possible, about the running of our works during the dull season. I have carefully gone over and figured out this matter in every conceivable way, and there is only one conclusion to be reached. We must run the works, especially Open-hearth, on Sunday nights and Saturdays. Our gas bills which are very high, go on almost the same whether furnaces are producing or standing idle." He reviewed the capacity of their slabbing mill and the new blooming mill and the calls on their output from their own finishing mills. To run the two primary mills at full capacity "therefore means that we would have to sell 5,000 tons of slabs per month to outside customers, and 4,000 tons of large sized blooms. You would be surprised to find how very much difference this will make in all our costs. I know of nothing connected with the works that is of so much importance as this and I hope you will take up this matter as soon as possible so that by January 1st we can run as outlined above, and in my former letters to you." Two weeks after this plea for high operating rates to cut unit costs, he committed himself to a complementary approach, "close shaving," reducing costs in 1895 as compared with 1894: "In other words, expect to make a clean saving by practice, labor, running expenses, etc., of one-half million dollars for this year."[17]

Clearly, a central consideration in Schwab's success at Homestead was his relationship with Frick. When he first went back there, determined to make a success as general superintendent, he was anxious for the chairman's support. Frick was wise enough in the ways of good management not only to give him this support but also to withhold it when he thought that to do so would strengthen Schwab's own grip on the situation. Gradually the relationship changed as, realizing his own powers, Schwab began to assert his independence. In October 1894 he was already taking the initiative when he sent eleven typed pages to Frick: "[S]o much has been recently said about the apparently high cost of making girder rails at Homestead, as well as the irregularity of quality of same . . . that I take the opportunity of submitting a report to you on this subject." A month later he explained the changes he wanted to make in handling their spare machinery and further pressed the sale of semifinished material: "It is quite impossible to make anything like a decent showing running the way we now are, and shall be very happy indeed to learn that you have decided to sell this class of material."[18] In December he sent the chairman a long memorandum on the new wage scales to be published on Christmas Eve. This time Frick broke with his own practice of not communicating with the press. His statement was a more or less direct quotation from Schwab's memorandum, but he was generous enough to add a sentence of his own: "I take pleasure in saying that the ability of the company to maintain a higher average wage than most of its competitors has been largely on account of the success of improved machinery lately introduced by the general superintendent, Mr. C. M. Schwab, whose plans have been uniformly successful."[19]

As well as undertaking this vast program of expansion and overseeing everyday production performance, Schwab exhibited striking mastery in other fields, evidence of his intelligence, rapid command of data, immense capacity for work, and also perhaps an ability to tap the knowledge of subordinate officers. Some of his reports were fairly sophisticated analyses. For instance, in summer 1895 he produced an internal memorandum, "Advantages of Location for Open-hearth plants as compared with Bessemer," and a subsidiary discussion of how competitors would be situated if they too went over to the open hearth process. A year later he sent Carnegie a concise comparison of the cost of making a ton of open hearth structural steel at Homestead as compared with Chicago. There, Indiana coal was used for producing steam and Pittsburgh coal for heating and melting. From melting shop through the blooming and finishing mills Schwab assumed 2,626 pounds of coal would be needed in each place per ton of open hearth beams, and he concluded that the total fuel cost per ton of beams would be $0.89 at Homestead and $2.46 in Chicago.[20]

Amid all the pressures of everyday production routines, the planning and undertaking of major extensions, and his ever watchful oversight of the labor situation, Schwab also showed skill in organizing and pressing his chief assistants and in defending their interests. P. T. Berg, who had been Potter's supporter and then became chief engineer, was now brought effectively under Schwab's own direction. In November 1894, sending Berg a list of schemes, Schwab began with a command: "You are hereby directed to go ahead, with all possible speed, with the drawings for the following improvements which I wish to push along as rapidly as possible." His letter ended with another assertion of authority: "The above list of improvements I wish to make during this winter and wish you would push them forward with the utmost speed."[21] He organized his deputies in order to make maximum use of their experiences. This strategy became clear when, early in 1896, Homestead was visited by a group from the Bethlehem Iron Company. The visitors recorded that every Monday at noon a "school" attended by thirteen superintendents of various departments was held in Schwab's private dining room to consider any questions that had arisen in the week.[22]

Despite all his authority and command of the situation, Schwab seems to have had one blind spot—he had no compunction in supporting the advancement of family members. In summer 1894 he wrote to Frick—who always denounced any semblance of nepotism—in support of a wage increase for his brother-in-law, Alva C. Dinkey, "an exceptionally capable man," whom both Jones and Laughlin and Westinghouse had been trying to poach. Late in 1896 he was in contact with Leishman about his own brother, Joseph E. Schwab, then moving from Homestead to the Union Mills: "To give my unbiassed [*sic*] opinion, I consider this young man one of the very best, brightest and ablest in our employ. I think no doubt he would have advanced much more rapidly had he not been associated with me."[23]

Throughout his years at Homestead, Schwab was under great pressure and was often worn down by it. In his early months he felt he lacked full support from his immediate subordinate. He wrote to Frick, "As you are aware, these past four months have been devoted to all sorts of work as occasion may require; that the assistant superintendent which I have at Homestead, and upon whom the burden of such duties should fall, has not been a man who was most suited in disturbed times such as we have had." A few days later he requested a first, short relief from his duties: "Since the middle of October, as you are aware, I have been working very hard indeed. Often three and four days and nights at a stretch. In this time I have not been absent from the works a single day. As a consequence I am commencing to feel worn out and cannot sleep at nights. Now that I am about to start another big job . . . I respectfully ask for three or four days rest, believing that I can now spare this time without loss to the company, and be in much better shape when required."[24] Eighteen months on, he ended a fourteen-page letter, most of it a triumphant record of his successes, with a final paragraph that made clear how heavy the strain had been:

> One further request. Personally, I feel worn out, disheartened, and thoroughly discouraged. It is necessary for me, under any conditions to have a rest. This I think you can understand better than anybody, knowing what I have had to go through here, this past year. I will arrange the time, etc., as may suit your convenience and decision in the matter, but should like to have a rest this time, entirely unmixed with any business matters. The greater part of my vacation last Summer, was, as you remember, spent studying the best methods and plans for our new Press and Harveyizing shops [for armor plate]. I should like in my vacation this time to be entirely free of any work.[25]

But the pressure, some of it self-imposed, was unabating, and in summer 1896 he was so preoccupied with work that he was planning only a short vacation of one week to ten days for "going up into Canada for a little fishing."[26] Inevitably, despite his youth, enthusiasm, and strong will, this regimen had a bad effect on his health. Photographs taken a few years later show a man who was confident but not particularly fit.

Considering the matter from the point of view of company interests, there can be no doubt of Schwab's remarkable success at Homestead. Naturally, he grew in the esteem of Carnegie. More interesting in some ways, and certainly better documented from this period, are Frick's assessments of him; Frick's own outstanding talents were those of a manager of company strategy rather than plant operations. Schwab's steady progress must have been challenging to his chairman, a man twelve years his senior. Usually Frick was warm in his praises, but sometimes the marked difference in their temperaments can be seen in the ways in which he criticized Schwab. In summer 1893, when business was depressed and Schwab was away—apparently spending much of his time studying armor processes—Frick sent Carnegie a memorandum about reduction of salaries. In it he commented on the ways various sections of their business were run. Their engineering department was not satisfactory, but

> Duquesne under Morrison, and the Upper and Lower Mills and Beaver under Dillon are economically and carefully managed. Edgar Thomson is gradually settling down to a more economical management. . . . [T]he worst case of all is Schwab's management at Homestead. There is no question but what he has great ability, but it is too largely used to make himself popular. He is recklessly extravagant in everything he does for himself or any one else, and I regret to say in many respects unreliable; tells you only that which he thinks will please, without regard for its correctness, and in that way has even mislead [sic] you. I feel that he has outraged the confidence I have reposed in him in many ways. . . . The management at Homestead is the embodiment of all that is reckless and extravagant. . . . There is too much of the fire works order about everything he does. You remark in your letter that "he is really our most important manager." I would amend by saying he occupies the position that should be filled by our most important manager. On his return, he shall have, as he always has had, my warm support, when he gets down to the business, but I do not propose to be deceived by him in the future, nor will I be put off by plausible excuses. Have already started in to institute many economies at Homestead that it is not necessary to give you in detail. Might say, however, that he had my brother-in-law, Marshall Childs, in a position I did not think he was capable of fill-

ing, and I told him so frequently. I dropped Mr. Childs a note several days ago to hand in his notice to the Assistant Superintendent. Want no relatives of mine, or my wife's, in our employment at Homestead or elsewhere. . . . It is really astounding, when I come to look into it, how he has been mismanaging the business at Homestead.[27]

During the middle months of 1894—a time at which, it is important to note, Frick himself was suffering severe mental strain—he was again highly critical. At the end of March he instructed Schwab to dismiss Leo Bullion, who was in charge of one of the Homestead plate mills and against whom certain allegations had been made about irregularities in conducting tests. Schwab acted promptly, but Bullion stayed on at the mill for a few days so as to pass on necessary information to his successor. Unaware of this arrangement, Frick reacted angrily: "It seems to be very difficult to get anything into your head, or to have you follow out instructions as given you." A few days later, to Carnegie, he again expressed extreme opinions:

> My conviction is that Schwab is not, and never will be, an economical Manager. It is not in him. He has some good qualities but is fearfully extravagant; does not follow his business closely and keep at it like Morrison, Dillon, etc. You know I like him personally very much, in many ways, but do not think that you can point to one instance, where he has made the concern any money in operating. Visit his home and you will find the same extravagance prevails there. As I was passing there this morning, on the train, I noticed all the electric lights burning in broad day light. As we are almost now through constructing, a few months will determine whether we can afford to have him in charge of operating at Homestead.[28]

After this outburst Carnegie obviously pressed Frick further on some of these criticisms, for early in June he took up the matter again, this time acknowledging the fascinating qualities of the man they were considering but at the same time touching on what he saw as other weaknesses:

> Mr. Schwab is perfectly familiar with the differences in costs, and in justice to him, I must say that owing to the extraordinary amount of construction and reconstruction on hand he has probably not been able to give the operating department the attention he should. There is no question about the man having a brain, and a fine one, but I doubt whether he will ever be able to get down to work, and give matters the close attention that they must have to bring proper result. You ask what Mr. Lauder thinks of him. He has the highest

opinion in the world of him, but Schwab is such a magnetic fellow that when he particularly lays himself out to capture a man he does not have much trouble in doing it, and making him believe about everything he tells him. You are quite right. We cannot get every quality in one man, but I cannot agree with you in saying that Schwab's men like him. Some particular pets of his do like him. There is but one thing necessary however, to have his men like him, and that is to get them to understand that his word can be relied upon under all circumstances. That is what he lacks. Do not think I should say that he deliberately lies, but he has a careless way of making promises, which are very little to him, but everything to his employees, and I have at all times impressed upon him the utmost importance of never making a promise to his men that he did not live up to; that he could make mistakes of that kind with us, but with his men never, and we would see that every promise he had made was carried out, although we might not approve of his having made it. He certainly does deserve the credit for what success we have had in Harveyizing, and am sure there is no mistake in new 35 and 40 inch beam mills, but am afraid that money spent in re-constructing 23 and 33 inch mills has not been spent to the best advantage, but Schwab is certainly responsible for that. In all these matters write you freely and fully, and when an opinion is put into cold type it looks very much different from what it would be if we could talk it over.[29]

What is to be made of Frick's very sharp criticisms of Schwab? In the first place it must be granted that he was probably becoming somewhat resentful of their manager's success and ability to charm, the latter a quality that, in business at least, he himself conspicuously lacked. In addition, Frick was approaching what in December 1894 seems to have become a nervous breakdown, which caused him to resign the chairmanship—only to regain the title but with reduced functions and powers early in 1895. Both these circumstances would point either to inaccuracy or at least exaggeration in his assessments. On the other hand some of his indictments of Schwab have the ring of truth about them, even if the tone in which he presented them was unduly black. Finally, Frick's highly critical remarks were counterbalanced by his own words of high praise. Indeed, in September 1895, again for Carnegie, he provided a very different assessment of the general superintendent's achievements:

Homestead is in remarkably fine condition. Schwab tells me and shows me costs for last month are lower than ever before, notwithstanding the bonus. If that works could be run smoothly the output would be enormous and cost exceedingly low. Duquesne, it seems to me, lacks the presence of a good organizer; do not think Mr. Morrison has the qualities necessary to get furnaces down to good working basis, even with the help of Mr. Gayley, who, of course, does understand [the] metallurgical part of the business, but has demonstrated in the past that he was not a good manager of men.

He now went so far as to suggest that Schwab's jurisdiction should be extended to include Duquesne.[30] In fact, when some eighteen months later Schwab's regime at Homestead ended, he never again operated as a plant manager. Instead he moved into the leading position in the Carnegie Steel Company. However, thirty-five years later he revealed how seriously he had taken Frick's commission. He spoke of his achievements there in almost biblical terms: "I find my greatest happiness in thinking of those days in Homestead when I labored to bring a thing to perfection entirely by myself. In the evenings I would go into the hills and look down on my work, and I knew that it was good, and my heart was elated."[31]

Although at this time he seemed to be preoccupied with work, Schwab was already developing a taste for the material rewards of success. Coming from humble economic circumstances, Schwab, with his now increasing means, wanted a more comfortable home than the small house in which he and Rana had first lived. In the early 1890s, as superintendent at Edgar Thomson, he built a house in Braddock, near the home of Spiegelmire, who had been his first employer in the town some twelve years earlier. As early as spring 1893 Schwab's new home was described as a "palatial residence"; by the end of the decade it was reckoned the best house in the borough. Of similar style to Frick's "Clayton," with red brick, massive rough stone facings, and slate covered round corner towers, appropriately for the business hierarchy of the time its interior was finished to a standard slightly lower than that in the chairman's home. The woodwork was good, and the house had some excellent friezes. A striking feature was a large painted glass window of a blue-clad female figure. Outside, the fair-sized plot contained stables. Most of the money for purchasing and then decorating the house had been advanced by Carnegie Steel.[32]

There are scant records of Schwab's social life in Braddock. It is known that in May 1893, when he and Rana celebrated the tenth anniversary of their marriage, a great party was held at their home. The Edgar Thomson and Homestead works bands were both there, an event Schwab considered to be a sign of a new harmony following the bitter labor re-

The Schwab home in Braddock, PA, in the 1890s.
Courtesy of the United States Steel Corporation.

lations of the previous year. A press account described the banquet as "in keeping with the other details, the dishes being epicurean and diversified." Most of Schwab's near neighbors were in comfortable circumstances, but his prospects were advancing faster than any of theirs. Once, in a group walking home from the local Roman Catholic church, conversation incongruously turned to wealth, and Schwab promised that if he became a millionaire he would give each of those present $1,000. In a relatively short time he had done so. But he by no means ignored the needs of the local community. In 1903 he and his wife made a joint gift of a new church to the people of Braddock. It cost $125,000. On Sunday, 22 November that year, the Schwabs joined twenty-five hundred others in a dedication service for the new Saint Thomas Catholic Church. Already there were signs of a tendency to spend to the limits of his increasing income. Eight years before, when Father Hickey had asked him to lend his church $600, Schwab inquired of Leishman whether it could be provided by the Homestead pay office: "I would loan this money to him personally but I haven't got it to spare."[33]

Managing Labor

It had been the firm intention of the Carnegie Steel Company and especially of Frick that labor matters should be once and for all "put in good order" at Homestead. As he expressed it to Schwab on the day the strike formally ended, "It is not who you can get to work for you, but who will you have? It is not, 'how much will you take and come and work for me' but it is 'what will you give me if I take this position, or that.'" From a modern perspective it seems an extraordinary attitude to adopt toward a work force, for it implied that, having been beaten in the struggle to unionize, labor was to be molded as the company wished. One aspect of this molding involved a wholesale reallocation of jobs. As Schwab reported six months later, 54 percent of all the skilled employees had worked for them before the strike, but of this group only 18 percent occupied the positions they had then held.[34]

At the time of the strike the works had sometimes been referred to as "Fort Frick"; the fortress mentality continued after the strike ended. A stark outward sign of the new, stricter regime at the works was the requirement that all employees should enter it by passing over the bridge at the main entrance. The local press explained both the rationale and the implications of this new rule: "Using the check system is what makes this order imperative. It is very inconvenient to many of the mill men as they are compelled to walk from one quarter to one half mile out of their way to get to their work." Even more oppressive were the routines that had been established to deal with the workers' bitter resentment. Most ominously, their suppressed anger manifested itself in a disposition to prepare for another round of action against management. Schwab was fully involved in the campaign to root out the ringleaders, but he also gradually tried to do something to improve labor relations.[35] He brought to this long struggle the advantages of a strong and outgoing personality and the respect it seemed to secure for his approach.

In spring 1893 Schwab reported examples of his methods to Frick, whose own way of dealing with problems would have been much less personal and direct, though he would probably have been no more determined than Schwab in getting the result the company wanted. His account indicated that his powers for all practical purposes extended beyond the boundaries of the works into the town and even involved the civic authorities. Through March and April there had been "occasional rumors of trouble, street fights, annoyances to non-union employees, etc., but nothing of any consequence. Commencing in April, I decided to take a very strong hand in such proceedings and thought it time they should end. So I undertook to investigate every squabble whether it occurred in the town, or works, and deal with the guilty parties severely." He gave three examples of his actions against those disturbing the settled order, whether they were old employees or workers the company had brought in during the strike. His actions seemed to have an element of arbitrariness as well as decisiveness:

> One day I heard that an employee of the Plate Mill, a head shearer, and an old hand, had called another man a scab. I immediately went down into the mill, brought the parties together, found that the charge was true and instantly discharged the offender, at the same time taking occasion to state that any employee, no matter how important, would be dealt with in the same manner. I had probably six or eight of such cases all told, within the two months of March and April. I also watched the town closely. As an example, an old German employee who resided in Homestead, and one of our new men, was being constantly annoyed by people yelling in his yard and about his house. I had a policeman secreted in his yard, when two young men came in his back yard and started to annoy him they were then promptly arrested and fined by the magistrate of the town and discharged from our employ.[36]

Whether or not Frick was concerned about the legality of some of these actions, he sent Schwab's letter to and discussed his policy with the company's legal advisor, Philander C. Knox.

Another incident at the same time called forth a rather arbitrary way of problem solving:

> On the first day of May we had a little incident that I was very glad of, and I believe strengthened us very much. We completed the 23 and 33 inch mills about the middle of April, and until the first of May, when the work was entirely experimental, we paid the men fair daily and tonnage rates. On May 1st, I formulated a new scale for these mills in which I paid the principal men by the ton and all unimportant positions by the day. This scale was given to the men on the day before it was to go into effect. The next morning everything started off all right, but about 9 o'clock all the pit furnace hands, except the heater, quit and tried very hard to have the roll crews quit with them. I was sent for, and when I arrived a few minutes later, found an excited crowd. We then had the men who struck, imme-

diately put out of the works, and filled their places with other men
in about twenty minutes, and started off again. The heater himself,
who, by the way, was John Evans, whom you will remember, had
remained a passive spectator, but when he started to work with the
new men, commenced growling and sulking. I did not lose much
time with him, so I told him we did not want any one to work for us
who was dissatisfied and told him to take his bucket and go home
and stay there. He protested a little, but I was firm and sent him off.
I then noticed the roll crew standing together talking earnestly. I
went up to them and said if any of them wanted to quit work, that
now was the time to do it, as I wanted to know at once just who
was going to work and who was not, and that, if we were going to
have any trouble, I wanted it right now. They went to work without
a word. The mill was not stopped twenty minutes and we were entire masters of the situation. About noon, twenty or twenty five men
(old employees) came up from Homestead and said they had heard
that some of our men had quit work and they would like to go down
and get their places. I told them the places had all been filled. I have
since learned that the whole occurrence had a most wonderful effect
on loud talking people. The men in other departments of the works
never noticed or seemed to care what these men did, and I am satisfied it was the opportunity of showing everybody just exactly how
we intended conducting our works. Had we had organized labor, we
should surely have had no end of trouble. To sum up, am happy to
report the labor situation could not be in better shape.[37]

Given his report, that conclusion seemed of questionable validity.

Apart from dealing promptly with disputes, Schwab labored unceas-
ingly to cut wage costs. Sometimes he gained his end by making the employees work harder. In June 1894 he informed Frick of a strike of thirty
laborers in the fitting shop: "They are the men who handle the material
to and from the fitting shops, and struck because they wanted eight men
to a gang instead of six men. We have been working with six men to a
gang for the past four months, and have done the work satisfactorily. We
have not as yet been able to get men to take their place, but expect to do
so within a day or two. It will never do to accede to such demands, or we
would have trouble every day. They are mostly Hungarians." One reason
for reducing wages was the same as he had encountered at Edgar Thomson: huge investments in machinery greatly increased productivity and
had given "tonnage men" inflated payments. Even when the system was

reformed the workers would still be in a good position. As he reminded Frick, in June 1892 the company had taken "great pains" to explain that whatever the reduction in rates, their men would earn as much or more under the new scales at the increased tonnages than before. A year later he confirmed this outcome and concluded, "None of the men have any reason to complain of the results of the strike except those who returned too late to obtain their former positions." He continued to reduce pay scales to counterbalance capital outlays.[38]

Following the policy Carnegie Steel was now committed to, Schwab kept up an inflexible hostility to any attempt at combination among the men: "My own idea is that if the men hold any meetings or attempt to form any organization, we should be prepared to be fully informed of all that goes on and unhesitatingly discharge any men connected with this movement. In this way our peace will be secure for a long time and it will be easily done if taken at the start." On the other hand, he made an effort to win men over by leniency in times of hardship. The recession of 1893 provided an opportunity in relation to the rents for the 331 houses the company then owned in Homestead.[39] Another successful approach was through social and recreational provision for their employees. As they reached the first anniversary of the strike, one of his police-and-oversight staff members told him there were "expressions on all sides favorable towards the Company, and I believe that your action in backing up the Homestead Athletic Club, Base Ball Club and Steel Works Band has had much to do with bringing about this feeling." Three years later, Schwab sent Carnegie a Homestead newspaper containing an account of a musical contest he had arranged for people of Welsh origin: "They as a race are hard to control, but I think you will always find them on my side." He went on to ask for financial support for building an industrial school, first for local boys but later for training girls as well.[40]

In five years Schwab made Homestead a remarkable steel making operation, one that in size and probably also in efficiency was a world leader. Unfortunately, his ceaseless pressure for higher productivity, superimposed on the legacy of the strike, also made it a soulless industrial monster. Men, like machinery, became items to use, write off, and replace. This principle was in accordance with the general industrial practice of the times; Homestead was exceptional only in the degree of its "success." In 1890 in reply to a query about the "recklessly rapid" driving of American blast furnaces, the president of one American steel company had remarked, "We think that a lining is good for so much iron and the sooner it makes it the better." Unfortunately, the same principle was applied to hu-

man beings. Gang foremen were called "pushers"; all too often "pushing"
led to accidents.[41] An example of Schwab's apparently casual attitude to
human welfare came during a spell of extremely hot weather in July 1894.
An explosion in the converting mill allowed metal to fall on the cinder-
men working below. He took the calamity in his stride: "Four men were
burnt; two I think seriously and will likely result in their death. The other
two will surely recover within a couple of weeks. Both men who were fa-
tally injured were married and have families." Next day he reported,

> Are getting along the best possible, handicapped as we are by this
> extremely warm weather and accident of yesterday. Will endeavor
> to worry this week through as well as possible. Think that Sunday
> night will again put us in good shape. . . . Yesterday, as you will
> note, was one of the warmest days for many years and our OH men
> dropped off like flies. . . . You have no doubt heard that the two men
> who were so badly injured yesterday, have since died. Indications
> seem to be that we will have cooler weather tonight, so we will soon
> recover and be on our feet again.

A few days later, and again in a matter-of-fact tone, he turned to the question of compensation for the accident: "Before you go abroad, wish you
would instruct me as to your wishes in regard to the two men who were
recently burned to death at our Converting mill, each having left a family.
The family of Anthony Dimond is entirely destitute. I have been told that
the family of Mr. Nelson, who reside in Braddock, have or will receive,
considerable insurance. I will endeavor to ascertain whether this is actually so, and will advise you, and regulate any contribution that we may
make to them, accordingly." Eighteen months later another fatal accident
was caused by a ladle tipping over in the open hearth shop. Reporting to
Leishman, Schwab seemed to make the company interest his main concern. Since the accident everyone "feels nervous and insecure with the
present arrangement and we would no doubt be liable to some extent in
case of accident." As a result they would have to make similar ladles perfectly secure, and they expected to have them changed in about ten days.
On the human side there was a note of expediency in his report: "In view
of the fact that this accident has occasioned considerable talk, I think it
wise that an early adjustment be had with the widow."[42]

On the other hand, there is evidence that, despite all the pressures
of work and the depressing physical environment of Homestead, Schwab
managed to hold on to and express some warm human qualities. Generally concerned with keeping wages down and squeezing more work out

Charles M. Schwab in the mid-1890s.
Courtesy of the United States Steel Corporation.

of his employees, he could be open and helpful to people who had scant claim on his time or generosity. One instance from this time combined sentimental motivation, a sense of decency, and straightforward goodwill. Somehow he had learned of the needs of Albert F. Malloy, who originated in Loretto but now lived in Bridgeton, a small village twenty miles from Terre Haute in the corn belt country of western Indiana. For some reason spurred into recollection, in July 1895 Schwab wrote aggressively to "Dear Sir":

> Some four or five years ago, at considerable personal inconvenience, I loaned you a certain amount of money with which to finish your education and start in business. While I do not so much mind the fact that you have not paid it back, as you have had some difficulty in getting started, yet I feel sorely grieved that you have never sent me a single line as to how you are getting along, or what your prospects were of paying back this money. I cannot even imagine what

excuse you will have to offer for such conduct. In all my experience I
have never had any person act so ungrateful as you have done. This
was not to be expected, inasmuch as you were a school mate of mine
and from the same town, and I doubt if you would ever have succeeded in earning enough money to have completed your education
if I had not helped you out. You had no claim on me whatever for
this money, and I did it as a mere act of kindness. I wish you would
write me and tell me just what you intend doing. Yours truly.

Notwithstanding his previous silence, Malloy responded promptly, and
two weeks after his first letter Schwab wrote to him again, this time in a
very different tone:

I trust you will excuse the delay in replying to your letter, but I have
been East and since my return have had so much business to attend
to that my time was all taken up. It is with pleasure I write you this
letter and I sincerely wish you every success in your very good resolve. Believe me I have none other than friendly feelings toward
you. It is not a question of the money which I loaned to you, but
the question of you doing what is right and making a good man of
yourself, and as long as you do this, there is no one who would more
willingly help you than myself. The arrangement you propose relative to returning the money is perfectly satisfactory to me. I hope you
will turn over a new leaf and do what is right and you will find my
friendship strong, if not stronger than ever. Write me occasionally
and let me know how you are progressing.

This time he ended with "sincerely yours." Less than seven months later
another letter revealed there had been problems, but Schwab dealt with
them sympathetically: "Dear Albert, I have your letter of February 20th,
and was very sorry to learn of your illness. Glad to know, however, that
you have recovered and are able to attend to business. Sincerely hope you
will be able to establish a good practice, and you have my best wishes for
success in this direction. Will always be glad to hear from you. With kind
regards, I am, Yours very truly, CM Schwab."[43] A man who could write
like that amid all the distractions of Homestead at that time possessed
some very positive human qualities.

Not all reconciliation was so easy. On 5 November 1898 Andrew Carnegie opened a new library at Homestead. Schwab was on the platform
and introduced his senior partner in what was reported as a "neat" speech.
The donor ended his own colorful remarks with an eloquently expressed

wish that the inauguration would finally dispel the recollections of the black days of 1892:

> The memories which Homestead has called up to this time have sometimes saddened us, and we hope that this occasion might fill our minds with such a beautiful picture as to enable us to banish the cruel memories of the past for ever. . . . [A]ll the regretful thoughts, all the unpleasant memories are henceforth and forever in the deep bosom of the ocean buried. Henceforth we are to think of Homestead as we see it today. This building, which I now dedicate, may it indeed be between capital and labor an emblem of peace, reconciliation, mutual confidence, harmony and union. Today Mrs Carnegie and I carry away with us, enshrined in our hearts, the happy faces of 10,000 friends.[44]

His hopes were no doubt genuine, but the evidence of many independent writers was that in the mill down by the river Schwab's regime, however much it had increased efficiency, had certainly not produced a congenial or happy place of work.

During the early part of Schwab's superintendency, the journalist Hamlin Garland had been told by a Homestead worker, "The worst part of the whole business is it brutalizes a man. You can't help it. You start to be a man, but you become more and more a machine. . . . It's like any severe labor; it drags you down mentally and morally just as it does physically." Five years later, an abler writer, the twenty-eight-year-old Theodore Dreiser, described the splendid works but horrifying working place into whose shaping Schwab had poured so much energy:

> It is a vast collection of long, low buildings, built of iron, brick and glass, and begrimed by the soot of many nights and days. Hundreds of tall black chimneys rise in pairs and groups at irregular distances. Thousands of open windows pour forth light and fumes. Miles of railroad tracks interlace and thread the many openings and hundreds of cars and engines move to and fro in restless activity. There is a pall of smoke over all, a roar of stamping and grinding machines, a puffing and whistling of engines and a clang of bells. The place is full of the hurry of life and the strenuous propulsion of thought.[45]

Amid this industrial turmoil, thousands of workers struggled to earn sustenance for their families. Two years before Dreiser wrote this description Schwab had moved on, but by pushing for its growth and productivity,

The Homestead Steel Works in 1897.
Courtesy of the United States Steel Corporation.

and in less desirable ways too, he had stamped his personality on Homestead. In turn, it left its mark on him.

The Presidency of Carnegie Steel

Early in 1897, after he had been general superintendent at Homestead as well as in overall control of Edgar Thomson for little more than four years, Charlie Schwab was chosen for the top post in the Carnegie Steel Company. At the time he was a week short of his thirty-fifth birthday. His new annual salary was to be fifty thousand dollars, and he also had a stake in the company's capital. In addition, on a number of occasions Carnegie ensured that he received a bonus of one million dollars for his year's work. His promotion in 1897 had resulted from a reduction in the power of Henry Clay Frick and the subsequent failure of his successor to give satisfaction.

As early as summer 1893 there were rumors that Frick would resign as executive chairman, with one report suggesting he would be replaced by the thirty-six-year-old John G. Leishman, who had joined the Carnegie associates in 1886 as vice president of Carnegie Brothers. Another source identified Schwab as Frick's successor.[46] Both suggestions proved premature. At the end of 1894, under great strain, Frick had a violent clash with Carnegie and resigned the chairmanship. Shortly afterward he was reinstated but officially only as chairman of the board of managers and therefore with reduced executive powers. The office of president was created, with the intention that whoever held the office would be in overall command—subject, as always, to approval from the majority stockholder. Leishman was appointed to this new post. He was easier to get along with than Frick but proved conspicuously less able, and, having suffered the mortal blow of losing Carnegie's confidence, after two years he resigned. Carnegie had already chosen Schwab to be his successor.

For a time it had been thought that Leishman's position might be bolstered if Schwab were appointed vice president, the nominally senior man dealing with financial affairs and the latter a production expert. Schwab was unhappy with this arrangement. He visited Carnegie's New York home to emphasize that he did not want the post: "I do not want to be vice-president, because in that position I would be second man and I would be no good, but as manager of all these works I am very happy and I prefer to stay manager."[47] (If this quotation accurately reflects Schwab's reaction, it throws some light on what was to happen four and a half years later in an even more momentous issue of precedence.) Carnegie seems to have promised Schwab that he would not be a deputy, explaining to Frick, "[H]e [Schwab] always favored in his heart, the Headship of the Company." Rather than being the deputy in a city office, "[h]e preferred being first at Homestead—No Vice Presidency business for him." Leishman had not lived up to their expectations, but Schwab was exceptional: "As you know, I always have felt just as you all have that he is our ablest man." The letter went on in terms that might have been appropriate if Schwab were being called to lead the Knights of the Round Table: "He accepts the call joyously because he knows he has it in him. No doubts—no hesitation—truly he is a wonderful man—and only 34—18 years of it in our service however—that counts." He anticipated the results of Schwab's stewardship: "We will find our property more valuable than ever in my opinion."[48] On Friday, 12 February, a meeting of the Carnegie Steel board was followed by an announcement of the changes in top management. As was the case with John Potter in October 1892, the board indicated that no one was at fault or had failed: "Mr. Leishman has been urging his partners for some time to relieve him from the harassing duties of the presidency of the company, owing to the state of his health."[49] In the new organization production and financial control would be separated. From 1 April Schwab would control manufacturing operations. Alexander R. Peacock as first vice president and Lawrence Phipps, nephew of Carnegie's oldest friend and second largest stockholder, as second vice president, would manage finance. William Ellis Corey, who had managed the armor plate department since 1893, took over as general superintendent at Homestead.

Carnegie's confidence in their new president was to be fully justified. Carnegie Steel further improved its standing as the largest, most competitive, and most profitable steel operation in the United States (see table 3 in appendix B). During the eighteen years up to and including 1896, covering the whole period of Schwab's association with Carnegie operations from the time he drove stakes and held a surveyor's staff in the yards at Edgar Thomson to within his last few months as general superintendent at Homestead, net profits had totaled $53.2 million; over the next three years they were $39 million. It would be wrong to attribute this astounding result directly to Schwab's leadership. For one thing it was a period of exceptional growth in the industry and of fairly high prices. In addition, within the company they were now reaping the rewards for the investments and extensions in mines, transportation facilities, and manufacturing plant that they had made during the mid- and early 1890s. Frick had left the top executive position two years before, but the company continued to benefit from what his business genius had achieved, and he still played an important part. Even so, Schwab's role in this climactic period of Carnegie Steel success was important. Two of their well-tried means of securing success were unceasing improvement of physical plant and better methods of operation. Schwab was a master of both. It was the responsibility of their sales department to secure the larger orders that would justify continuing along these lines.

Schwab followed a variety of routes in the search for even higher efficiency. Building on his practice at Homestead, he streamlined the exchange of information between the various plants. It had been customary for superintendents of the mills to come into the general offices in the Carnegie Building in downtown Pittsburgh on Saturday afternoons. Typically, Schwab wished not only to make this regular occasion more relaxed but also to save time. A few days after he took control he wrote to the chairman about his new scheme: "It is a waste of time both to the superintendents and myself to have them spend as much of their time at this office as they do on such afternoons, in view of the fact that I visit the mills so frequently. At the same time it is important that they should be together once a week, or once every two weeks. Therefore, I think it would be better to have them come in here at 12.30, having luncheon at the office; discuss matters until about 2.30, giving the superintendents an opportunity to return to the mill if necessary, which is often the case." He asked for Frick's advice, but he made clear that he had decided what he wanted to do. Six months later Carnegie responded enthusiastically when asked what he thought of the new arrangement: "I think your Superintendents' Saturday meetings one of the best ideas that has ever entered your fertile brain. I see how many points of trouble are met and solved, giving unity of action among the various works."[50]

Another way to higher productivity and lower costs involved providing incentives for key members of the staff to make even greater efforts. Schwab pushed on with the established system of distributing small shares in the partnership at the beginning of each year. Late in November 1897 he put forward to Frick "as my recommendations" four names, each for a one-ninth of 1 percent interest in the company. Although the company's nominal capitalization was then a wholly artificial and unrealistically low $25 million, even on that basis each of these small shares was worth almost $28,000. One of the men rewarded was Schwab's brother Joe, now general superintendent at Duquesne. As Schwab pointed out, Joe had reduced the cost of producing billets there by $0.60 in the last five months. (Such a reduction was important, as the average Pittsburgh price of billets was $18.83 a ton in 1896 but only $15.08 the following year.) Schwab's comments on another of his own suggestions showed him asserting his position against his long-term senior. He wrote to Frick that E. F. Wood, assistant general superintendent at Homestead, "no doubt stands foremost in the rank of American Metallurgists. . . . It should also be borne in mind, and it is now a matter of record on our Minutes, when Mr. Corey was appointed General Superintendent of the Homestead Works, on the first of last March, Mr. Wood was promised an interest in the firm. The value of his services warrants such an inducement, and as far as Mr. Woods is concerned, I have really promised him this interest with the full consent of Mr. Carnegie and members of the Board."[51]

Another aspect of Schwab's rise to power at Carnegie Steel, both as general superintendent of Homestead and Edgar Thomson and as president, involved family relations. Much later he would claim, "I never allow any of my relatives to work or to be connected with any of my organizations in any capacity." In fact members of his family occupied major executive positions under him at Carnegie Steel and later on. A leading example was Rana Schwab's younger brother. Alva C. Dinkey first took a humble post as telegraph operator at the Edgar Thomson works in 1882 or 1883, just as Schwab's own meteoric rise began. For a time, Dinkey left the firm for other jobs in the Pittsburgh area, where he gained vital experience in electrical engineering. He returned in 1891 and played an important part in electrifying the Carnegie rolling mills. Hooks and tongs were so effectively replaced by the electric powering of feeding tables and other units of plant that in one mill he reduced a work force of twenty-five to only four men. In 1901 he was appointed Homestead general superintendent and later, head of Carnegie Steel.[52] Although it may well have been an advantage in the early or mid-1890s to have a family member in a senior position in the Carnegie firm, there is no evidence that Dinkey's subsequent advancement was not due to his own abilities. With Schwab's younger brother, the same principles may have applied, but the results were less happy.

Joseph Schwab was two years younger than Charlie, who in 1883 helped him to get his first job as a draftsman at Edgar Thomson. He moved on to civil engineering and then into the blooming mill. From 1886 he superintended the Homestead structural mills while his brother was general superintendent. By 1897 he had been appointed general superintendent at Duquesne. Three years later he seems to have tried to use his familial relationship for his own benefit, when he wrote to the president, "As you know the present General Superintendent's residence at Duquesne will be so close to the new blooming mill now being erected that it will be almost impossible to live there on account of the excessive noise. As per instructions I have had plans prepared for a new residence to be erected on the property recently purchased for that purpose. The estimated cost of building is $22,000 and I wish to have your approval for this expenditure." This time his brother was not readily compliant, deciding that a decision should be deferred.[53] Joe became a partner and later his brother's assistant in even bigger operations. In all these moves his own competence was important, but so too must have been the brotherly support. Eventually he left the industry to become a stock market speculator and, much more overtly than Charlie, to live the "sybarite" life the latter was often accused of enjoying.

At the other end of the scale, that of the plant workers, under the Schwab presidency wage rates were further reduced for the "tonnage men" in order to compensate for the increased output secured by outlay on more productive plant. Reviewing the situation in the December following his appointment, Schwab described some of the earnings of these "tonnage men" as "beyond all reason"—at Homestead some roller men in the beam mills earned $12 daily, and in the Union mills plate rollers might take home as much as $15. He wanted to cut the average wage for roller men to $6. At the two works and for tonnage men alone he figured that $240,000 to $300,000 could be saved each year without causing trouble with the workers. There was considerable further conflict with labor. One issue was company pressure for more Sunday work. Another was the continuing fight to prevent unionization. For example, in May 1899 Corey reported that some men in the Homestead open hearth shop were trying to form a lodge of the Amalgamated Association of Iron and Steel Workers. After looking into the matter, he discharged four of the leading men, and when further information was received, he expected to dismiss at least six more. In Schwab's words, it "showed the importance of watching closely for such movements and taking vigorous steps against them from the first." On the other hand, in its paternalistic way the company looked after loyal workers. In August 1898 Schwab reported to the board of managers, "Last week one of our oldest employees, John L. Jones, who has been in our service nearly 26 years, died, leaving a large family with but few resources, outside of a small amount of life insurance. Mr. Jones, in time of labor troubles or strikes, has been one of our most valuable men. I would recommend that his family be given $1,000 and his salary to December 1898." There was unanimous agreement.[54]

The necessary counterpart to the struggle to reduce the burden of wages was continuing capital investment. These capital improvements brought all-round expansion but further increased the importance of Homestead within the organization. A new finishing plant was installed there, including a major plate mill purchased and moved from Bethlehem, but extensions above all centered on open hearth capacity. In 1896 the monthly average output of open hearth steel at Homestead was 30,400 tons; by March 1899 it reached 90,000 tons. In April 1892 the Homestead melting shops accounted for 14.3 percent of the steel of all types made at the three major Pittsburgh plants; seven years later their share was 37.4 percent. By early 1901 the open hearth furnaces at Homestead accounted for only a shade less than half of Carnegie Steel tonnage.

Under Schwab the company continued the integration of operations others had already achieved. By mid-1898 some hot metal from the recently built Duquesne blast furnaces was being supplied to Homestead and a Union Railroad bridge was completed over the Monongahela so that iron could be brought from Edgar Thomson. In February that year another important step was taken, though it was one about which Schwab was initially as doubtful as Carnegie: the purchase of the Carrie Furnaces across the river from Homestead. Frick initiated this move. After the acquisition yet another hot metal bridge was built. Steel making costs were reduced further, though it is not known by how much.[55]

An indication of the high efficiency and competitiveness of Carnegie Steel under Schwab was its position in the rail trade. In 1889, the year of Jones's death, Edgar Thomson rolled 18.4 percent of the nation's rails, a far higher proportion than ever before. In the middle three years of the 1890s it averaged 24.5 percent. In February 1897 pooling arrangements in the trade broke down and rails that until then had sold at $27.50 a ton were soon being offered by Carnegie Steel at a price as low as $17. Writing to Frick on 15 May 1899 Schwab suggested they could make rails for less than $12 a ton–the average selling price that year was $28.12 a ton, FOB mills. Over a number of years this letter from Schwab to Frick became notorious. It was widely cited as evidence that Carnegie Steel and probably some other leading companies were making excessive profits at public expense. More wisely, some commentators recognized that the $12 figure was unreal, representing processing costs alone and making no allowance for overhead or depreciation. When asked about it years later, James Gayley searched his own recollections: "I never did believe he could do it. I asked him once how he proposed to do it and he just smiled." Carnegie provided another perspective on such an episode, when, long after retirement from business, laughing at an elaborate statement of costs submitted by Schwab for a tariff hearing, he observed, "There are more ways of figuring cost than of killing a cat." To the same government inquiry Schwab made clear that his figure had been only the mill cost, making no allowance for general charges, including interest and depreciation "and similar charges which were always made by the auditing department in making up the yearly report." His much quoted letter to Frick "was written as an enthusiastic and optimistic young man seeking preferment in a great company."[56]

Schwab became the representative for Carnegie Steel in top level negotiations with other companies to control the market, especially for rails. For the 1897 season Carnegie Steel and Illinois Steel were together allotted a 53.5 percent share of the pool orders. [Illinois state law did not allow in-state companies to take part in pooling arrangements, so Carnegie Steel took the allocation for both.] Lackawanna Steel received 19 percent, Pennsylvania, Cambria, and Bethlehem each got 8.25 percent, and 2.75 percent went to Maryland Steel, Pennsylvania's tidewater subsidiary. This arrangement broke down in February 1897. That year Edgar Thomson rolled a shade over 29 percent of all the steel rails made in the United States, its highest proportion ever. During September Schwab met John W. Gates of Illinois Steel and Walter Scranton of Lackawanna to try to reestablish cooperation. He now proved his abilities as a negotiator. A central consideration he brought to the talks was the principle he had elaborated some years before concerning the economics of production at Homestead—the need to operate at high capacity so as to obtain good figures for unit costs. On Friday evening, 24 September, he reported his hard-won progress to Frick: "Gates, Scranton, and myself started in at 10:30 this morning. Things looked bad for a while. After several hours['] talk without accomplishing anything, I took Gates into the back room and had an hour's earnest talk." The result was an agreement between the three men that showed very clearly how ruthless competition had become. Lackawanna and Cambria would have the same share as in the broken arrangements for 1897 but Carnegie and Illinois would take up all of the rest, amounting to 36 percent of the tonnage for each of them. "With reference to Bethlehem and Penna Steel the idea was to tell them plainly what had been done, that we had agreed to take the business of the country," Schwab wrote. These two firms would be offered incentives to accept this state of affairs. For sales made by the three dominant companies at $18 a ton or less, the excluded producers would receive nothing, but for any sales made at $19 a ton they would be allowed $1 on the share they held in the previous pool—for example, on the 2.75 percent of the total tonnage in the case of Maryland Steel. The allowance would increase to $1.50 per ton on sales at $20 and so on, increasing by $0.50 for every $1 increase in the rail price. "It is believed by Gates and Scranton that they will accept this proposition. If not," Schwab concluded, "go ahead without them keeping price down where necessary in their district to take the business. . . . If a fight is necessary in one district other members must help fight it out."[57]

Negotiations were complicated when Powell Stackhouse of Cambria asked for an allotment of 12 percent rather than 8.25 percent. Gates invited Scranton and Schwab to Chicago to sort the matter out, but Schwab refused to go. Scranton was "awfully broken" over the affair; Schwab reported he had had "some talk with Gates after the meeting adjourned of a very friendly character." Some weeks later Frick felt the need to inform Scranton that Schwab had been given "absolute authority" as a negotiator on behalf of Carnegie Steel and had acted "in the best of faith with you." Three weeks afterward, in the first week of 1898, having met Gates, Scranton, and Stackhouse, Schwab assured Frick, "[T]hese arrangements will enable us to keep up the price of rails for sometime, and also to take as much business as we need this year, at an advanced price." He sent a copy of the draft agreement signed by the four men on that date. It showed not only the extraordinary way in which they were attempting to control the market but also the limited extent to which they were prepared to bind their individual companies: "We, the undersigned, hereby agree that from and including this date we will not quote or sell, directly or indirectly, Standard Steel Rails at less than the following prices for use in the U.S., viz: $18.00, f.o.b. all Pa. Mills, privilege of equalizing freights with Pittsburgh, $20.00, f.o.b. cars Chicago, privilege of equalizing freights with Pittsburgh and Scranton to intermediate territory, $20.00, f.o.b. New York for all Pacific Coast business, a conference and agreement to be made on all lots over 3,000 tons. This agreement to remain in force until ten days' notice shall be given in writing."[58]

Later in 1898 and looking ahead to the following year Schwab was less happy about cooperative action. As was his common practice he reported on the day's proceedings from Holland House, where he stayed when in New York City: "Our meeting to day amounted to nothing. Long discussion as to percentages, etc., without any conclusion. Sum total of percentages submitted by each firm as to what they thought they ought to have, amounted to 124 per cent. You can see that this is a long way off from anything reasonable."[59]

Years afterward, testifying before the Stanley Committee (the U.S. House of Representatives committee investigating U.S. Steel), Schwab was asked about this sort of agreement:

Q. Did these gentlemen's agreements include the fixing of prices?

Schwab: Yes; but pardon me, Mr. Chairman, a gentlemen's agreement was never made, at least not within my knowledge, for any definite period of time.

Q. They were made to be broken on notice?

Schwab: Well, they were usually broken when some one felt like doing it.

Q. And notice given?

Schwab: Not always; no. I think, as a rule the opposite was the case.

Many years later still, by which time Schwab was the only survivor from these pool negotiations, he spoke even more directly about the difficulties, uncertainties, and underhanded methods involved. Quotas were based on capacity, on the territory to be served, and on the location of the rail mill, but discussion was always complicated by distrust and the danger that someone would break away or "chisel" the prices and thereby, as it was elegantly put, demoralize the markets. Gates for Illinois Steel and Schwab on behalf of Carnegie Steel would each struggle for a bigger allotment. Being nearer the biggest centers of consumption in the West, the former was usually given a price 4 percent higher than was the latter. Then, "after the allotment was made Gates and I would get together in a pool of our own and settle matters to our own satisfaction." But as he recalled, either in the bigger group or in direct discussions between the two leading companies, it was necessary to be wary of Gates, who "was as crooked as they came without running contrary to the law. . . . [H]e had no ethics, although he was warm-hearted.⁶⁰

Schwab was also involved in the beam pool. In this product Carnegie Steel was even more dominant, making 48 percent of the tonnage rolled by the six main firms in the first eleven months of 1897. In rails they were competitive enough to invade the natural market areas of Chicago mills; in structurals they could win their way into eastern outlets. The Carnegie operating department was informed that the Pencoyd works, though well located on the edge of Philadelphia, had been able to supply no more than 6 percent of New York's beam business in July 1897. Their own company was quoting competitive rates there. Early in November Schwab negotiated with Willis King of their near Pittsburgh neighbors, Jones and Laughlin, with Stackhouse of Cambria Steel, and with three eastern Pennsylvanian producers: Percival Roberts of Pencoyd and representatives of the Passaic mills and of the Phoenix Iron Works. They arranged to fix percentages, tonnages, and prices with the aim of raising the last. Carnegie Steel received 50 percent of the tonnage. During these negotiations, Schwab tried psychological pressure on his rivals: "I take these people to Homestead this morning as I wish to fully impress them with the extent of our facilities for this class of work." In fact, to maintain their position in the trade they had to make further major investments. Informing the board of managers in July that it was now difficult to sell any other than open hearth structurals, whereas 80 percent of those made at Homestead were of Bessemer steel, he asked for sixteen to eighteen more forty-ton open hearth furnaces.⁶¹

His new duties, like his earlier managerial responsibilities at Homestead, took much out of Schwab. This drain on his physical well-being certainly was the case at times when he was in negotiation with rival concerns. For instance, writing on Wednesday, 29 September 1897, from the Wall Street office to report his difficulties about rail allotments with Gates and Stackhouse, he added, "I am not feeling well this evening and will

Andrew Carnegie in 1896.
Reprinted from *A Carnegie Anthology*
(New York: Privately printed, 1915).

not be home until tomorrow night." A year later, after another frustrating meeting, he reported, "Have been quite ill yesterday and to-day. Hope to be better in the morning." The compensation for these exhausting efforts was the high regard that his colleagues generally had for him. There were, however, occasional disagreements with other members of the board. Reporting the 1897 structural agreement to Frick, Schwab added, "Peacock as usual opposes. I think principally because he did not negotiate, as he can give no real reasons for his objections."[62]

Carnegie too could be sharp, though he speedily returned to warm appreciation, as he showed in connection with a misunderstanding in early fall 1897. On 18 September Carnegie, then overseas, sent the board his "Further thoughts upon Minutes of August 31 1897": "First: may I recall that, had the Board taken immediate action last year, upon a plan urged by its President, that we should now have a million dollars invested in open hearth plant at Braddocks [*sic*]. It was only discussion and views freely given of one or two, which prevented this serious mistake." In response Schwab seems to have pointed out that it was under Leishman's presidency that the misjudgment had been made. A few days later, writing to Schwab, Carnegie was still critical and seemed to take up Frick's accusation of a few years before that Schwab misrepresented things: "Isn't it a pity that the President did not think to explain what he desired to the Board. He would have made a good report if he had taken time and saved a great deal of unfortunate misunderstanding. . . . I cannot understand why you do not watch your figures. Believe me you will never obtain the confidence of your partners unless you are more careful as to your statements in figures." But he then went on to soften the impact of his criticisms: "You are a hustler! Very much surprised to see by the photograph that you have done so much in one week at Open Hearth." Soon afterward he acknowledged that he should have referred to Leishman and that Schwab had in fact counseled delay about installing open hearths at Edgar Thomson.[63] In another letter he wrote, rather playfully, "In short, my dear fellow, I am thoroughly converted where I need conversion and hope you will go ahead with your improvements. . . . Believe me, I am rejoicing equally with yourself at your brilliant success and at the improvements which I am sure you are going to make." He quoted for Schwab's benefit a report he had from Lauder: "'Everything about the business is in first class shape. I do not hear a single word of adverse criticism. There has never been a time on my return that I can recall when everything seemed moving so smoothly.'" This praise led to an outpouring of Carnegie gratitude: "I do hope you will come over to Cannes, and spend as long as possible with us and bring Mrs Schwab along. There is no couple in the world that would be more welcome than you." Although he reveled in this sort of appreciation, Schwab was sometimes willing to stand up to Carnegie. As he gently put it in summer 1898, discussing the pig iron situation, "We look at matters a little differently here from what you do."[64]

Though he was still chairman of the board of managers, inevitably Frick began to be—and to feel—pushed into second place as Schwab asserted his independence. The tone of his report to Frick about the September 1897 negotiations with the other rail makers gives an example of Schwab's sense of his position relative to Frick's. He ended his account, "Will be in the office (Wall Street) tomorrow morning at 10;30 am. If you see any serious objections to above arrangements kindly call me on the phone." Two months later there was a note of sadness in a letter from Frick: "I did not know until I saw in yesterday morning's paper you were going to New York night before last. Presume you did not know it when we went home together in the evening."[65]

A few days later any disturbing thoughts Frick may have already had must have been reinforced by some remarks by Carnegie that clearly constituted a challenge to his own outstanding abilities, achievements, ambition, and character. The subject was shares in the business: "I think Schwab as President should have one half more than the Vice-Presidents, say three percent to their two—he's worth it and more, a genius. Lauder writes our business never in such fine form and all pulling together. Let us get cheap freight rates and defy the world." Frick's response a few days later was generous: "[T]here is no question about Mr. Schwab. Our business was never handled so well."[66] It may be that he felt pressured to endorse Carnegie's high opinion of the president, but his sterling refusal to be either cajoled or bullied in the way that other partners were makes it likely that Frick fully believed in any opinions he expressed. When in autumn 1897 Carnegie pressed Schwab to take a holiday with him in the Mediterranean, he followed up by including their chairman in the invitation: "If Schwab or Frick for any reason need a rest during winter here's the spot—ship them COD."[67] He had obviously written a little earlier on the same theme to Frick, for the latter wrote back, "Think a thirty day trip would do Mr. Schwab a great deal of good and shall urge him to go. A man must have a rest every now and then, if he wants to keep in good shape." Schwab did take his winter holiday in Europe that year, though details are unknown. On 12 January Frick cabled him "Bon voyage" as he set out on the steamship *New York*. Five weeks later a cable to the *Paris* at Southampton conveyed another reassuring message from chairman to president: "Everything in good shape. Business healthy. Bon voyage."[68]

Though there was evidence of Frick's continuing goodwill, shortly after Schwab had left home Carnegie wrote to the chairman in a way that must have made unmistakably clear that he had been superseded in the mind of the man who, with 58 percent of its nominal capital, effectively controlled the company. When at the end of the 1880s Frick had proved his own exceptional worth, Carnegie once told him, "Take supreme care of that head of yours. It is wanted again. Expressing my thankfulness that I have found THE MAN, I am always Yours, AC." In 1893, on his first visit to Pittsburgh after the Homestead strike, Carnegie spoke of Frick publicly as an unrivaled industrial leader: "I am not mistaken in the man, as the future will show. Of his ability, fairness and pluck no one has now the slightest question. His four years' management stamps him as one of the foremost managers in the world; I would not exchange him for any manager I know."[69] Now, no more than five years after that fulsome endorsement, Carnegie drove home a very different message. Some of the old, excessive terms of praise reappeared, but they were attached to another name: "Schwab's visit has made a great impression upon me, and you are no doubt feeling as I do that a great load is off our shoulders. We have got the man and, having him, there is no reason why we should hesitate about going forward and keeping the lead."[70]

For the Carnegie enterprises 1898 was a banner year. Their steel output topped 2 million tons for the first time, amounting to almost a quarter of the national total. Edgar Thomson made 28.4 percent of the nation's rails. At $11.5 million, net profits were 64 percent higher than in 1897, which had also been a record year. Mergers and reconstruction were in the air as the United States moved into one of its outstanding periods of industrial amalgamations. A week before sailing for his European holiday Schwab conducted a tour of the Homestead, Edgar Thomson, and Duquesne works for Judge Elbert H. Gary and two others from the recently formed Federal Steel Company and the newly emerging American Steel and Wire Company of Illinois. He reported to Frick that they were interested "and I am sure very much impressed": "The Judge constantly talked of the possibility of inducing Mr. Carnegie to consolidate with them. Made no reply, but simply listened to what he had to say. Tells me he has some ideas about valuation to take up with you when he sees you." That spring there were more suggestions of a link, some including other firms as well. By fall and the following winter even Carnegie appeared to be warming to the idea.[71] Meanwhile, Schwab's presidency went well, and contacts with the chairman apparently remained cordial. When Schwab was at the Mammoth Hot Springs Hotel at the northern end of Yellowstone National Park in August, he received a letter from Frick that seemed to point to cordial relations: "Find everything in good shape and outlook bright. Weather delightfully cool today. Hope you are enjoying yourself. Do not hurry home if you are." When he was back in Europe early in 1899 Schwab's exchanges with Frick were still happy. Late in January the latter sent a cryptic cable to Southampton to await the steamer *St. Louis:* "Matters in status quo. All going well. Outlook bright." A few days later Schwab replied from their London office, "We arrived safely yesterday, after a very rough voyage; we were only able to run half-speed the last three days on account of heavy seas. We are all well, but I can assure you I felt the need of some rest after leaving Pittsburgh."[72] By the year's end the two men would be at apparently irreconcilable loggerheads.

Major industrial combinations of all kinds had a record year in 1899, amounting to $2.26 billion or 170.4 percent more than the combined total of the previous four years.[73] The steel industry was prominent, the American Steel and Wire Company of New Jersey having been organized in January, National Steel in February, American Steel Hoop in April, and National Tube two months later. Together these four combinations represented a capitalization of $265 million, much of it not backed by assets, being in the expressive terminology of company finance, "water." During early spring it seemed that, rather than combine with others, Carnegie Steel would be reconstructed with a major change of ownership. This reconstruction would mean that Andrew Carnegie would be bought out, with Henry Clay Frick and Henry Phipps replacing him as principal owners of both Carnegie Steel and the H. C. Frick Coke Company. It also involved a group then prominent in many of the major changes in industrial organization: the Moore syndicate, with brothers W. H. Moore and J. H. Moore at its center. On 10 May 1899 Frick outlined the scheme to Schwab. Except for Carnegie, the new board would be the same as the old, with Frick as chairman and Schwab as president. He added, "Please show this to all interested and tell them to do no talking."[74] Two days later, the death of financier R. P. Flowers brought on disturbances in the financial markets that helped ruin the scheme. Over the next few months a rift developed and gradually deepened between Carnegie and Frick. Other members of the board were drawn in, including Schwab, who was an important player in an acrimonious dispute over the pricing of coke from the H. C. Frick Coke Company delivered to Carnegie Steel blast furnaces. Even so, through late September Schwab managed to maintain friendly relations with Frick. This effort at harmony came out most clearly in a letter he wrote on 26 September reporting on the new rail agreement. In the letter he also thanked Frick for a picture he had sent. He went on effusively, the words he used, if sincere, being excessive and, if untrue, a gross sort of deception:

> Dear Mr. Frick permit me to write what I would find it difficult to say to you, because you would not listen, and say that while I fully appreciate the value of such a picture it counts as naught compared with the consciousness of having won your friendship and regard. I regard that with more satisfaction than anything else in life—even fortune—you have been so eminently fair and good to me that I can never forget it, and be assured if I have anything of value in me your method of treatment will bring it out to its fullest extent. Working with and for you is a great pleasure, and I am yours to command al-

Henry Clay Frick, c. 1900.
Reprinted from I. Tarbell, *The Life of Elbert H. Gary:
The Story of Steel* (New York: Appleton, 1925).

ways. I do not write this as a formal and set letter but as a spontane-
ous expression of my true feeling.[75]

Less than ten weeks later it became clear that concern for his own fortune
was stronger than his commitment to Henry Clay Frick.

By fall 1899 a crisis in Carnegie Steel affairs was approaching, and
members of the board had to decide which of the contending parties they
supported. The evidence is that, whatever cause or provocation Frick had
provided, a campaign against him was carefully planned behind his back.
On Saturday, 25 November, his sixty-fourth birthday, Andrew Carnegie
wrote a typically disjointed letter telling his cousin "Dod" Lauder that his
encouragement had helped him make up his mind about reorganization
at the top:

> You voice my views exactly. Frick goes out of chairmanship of board
> next election or before. . . . Now I have long felt that Chairmanship
> was a mistake. It overshadows President and you know how Frick
> got Phipps to urge me to make Chairman the Executive Officer and
> I told him NO NEVER. I was with Schwab always. Schwab has be-

haved far too kindly to Frick, but this was best after all. You may tell Schwab he will be the man and the only man and that next election chairmanship will be abolished. Now CMS must see that his men stand firm for this policy, must express opinion No chairmanship and be loyal to CMS. CMS can manage all this nicely—Everyone likes him at heart, not like Frick. . . . My resolve is taken and cannot be shaken. I have given to Schwab and his brother and a few others control in my will and in life shall stand by him—"Who wouldna fecht for Charlie." Yours Naig. You may show this to Schwab and let him lay his plans accordingly.[76]

Next day, Sunday, Carnegie wrote to the president and managers of Carnegie Steel. His note was in pencil, so that, as Schwab later suggested, his own secretary should not know of their difficulties. It threw down the gauntlet for open conflict, ending with expressions of paternal feelings for them all, "which it is unreasonable to expect can embrace Mr. Frick who is well calculated to play the paternal himself . . . an able man possessed of many virtues who cannot however harmonize with me, nor I, it seems, with him, somehow or other, much to my regret."[77]

Because of the position he occupied and the role planned for him, Schwab was a key player in this dramatic stage of the company's development. After an apparently normal meeting of managers on Monday, 27 November, he reported to Carnegie that Frick had "seemed cheerful and happy. . . . Don't think he has any idea of resigning." He added that if Carnegie made clear his wishes to them, "the Board would not hesitate to do as you wish."[78] A day or two later Schwab traveled to New York for a meeting of rail makers. While there he called on Carnegie. On the morning of Sunday, 3 December, immediately after arriving back in Pittsburgh, he wrote to Frick, telling him that Carnegie would be coming to Pittsburgh that day and intended to ask the board and partners to remove him from the chairmanship. Schwab made clear it was a case of every man looking to his own interest and that, as Carnegie had a commanding share in the company, all junior members and partners would fall in with his wishes. If they failed to do so, "[a]ny concerted action would be ultimately useless, and result in their downfall. Am satisfied that no action on my part would have any effect in the end. We must declare ourselves. Under these circumstances, there is nothing left for us to do but obey. . . . My long association with you and your kindly and generous treatment of me makes it very hard to act as I shall be obliged to do. But I cannot possibly see any good to you or any one else by doing otherwise. It would probably ruin me and not help you."[79] Although he intended to send his letter to Frick, he had second thoughts and with considerable courage decided instead to deliver it personally to him at home. The result was a fearful outburst of Frick's anger. Next day Carnegie visited Frick, and on Tuesday the latter sent in his resignation from the board. After a break over Christmas and the New Year, on 10 and 11 January 1900, the members of the partnership were asked to sign a resolution asking Frick to turn over to them his 6 percent share in Carnegie Steel on the basis of its nominal capital, a figure far below any realistic valuation. Thirty-two partners endorsed the resolution and signed the document in two columns. The first column was headed by the signature of Andrew Carnegie, the second by that of Charlie Schwab.

Triumph or Deception?

For Charlie Schwab 1900 was an exceptional year, in some ways the dizzying peak of his working life. He was now the undisputed head of the largest and supposedly most successful and profitable of all steel companies, controlling and coordinating mines, ovens, railroads, and works that employed about forty-five thousand people (see table 4 in appendix B).[80] That year his company would produce 29 percent of the nation's steel and more than one in ten of every ton of steel made worldwide. His salary was around $100,000, but he was paid bonuses totaling many times as much. His preeminent position in world industry was, as a *Pittsburgh Dispatch* headline put it, the culmination of "A Workman's Marvelous Rise." After already being president of Carnegie Steel Company for three years he at last decided to move from Braddock. His new home was "Highmont," in Pittsburgh's east end, a house owned until the previous year by Jacob J. Vandergrift, who, having started out as a river boat captain, had transported and refined oil and constructed what is said to have been the first natural gas pipeline before setting up the Apollo Iron and Steel Company and building the model town that was given his name. Highmont, said to be one of the finest houses in Pittsburgh, with six acres of land, had cost Vandergrift about $150,000; Schwab bought the estate, with not only the house but also rugs, tapestries, paintings, and so forth, for $250,000. He spent a good deal of money on further improvements, including the installation of a gallery in which to display his pictures. (Highmont was to be his home for only a few months, however. By March 1903 he had sold it to his former colleague, Daniel M. Clemson, for some $300,000.)[81]

The beginning and the end of 1900 were marked by two dinners, one a celebration of achievements and the second initiating a new, even vaster venture. In the months between there were times of booming trade and longer periods of hard struggle, expansion, and high commercial success but also apparently some scheming in order to present Carnegie Steel in an attractive light in order, literally, to sell it. In pursuit of the last there may have been serious misrepresentation of the facts. In all these aspects of the year Schwab played a key part.

On Sunday, 7 January 1900, Pittsburgh newspapers reported a celebration by the new top management: "Surrounded by a perfect wood of food- and fruit-bearing trees with their dangling products, a party sat down in the Hotel Schenley to perhaps the most extravagant banquet ever served in Pittsburgh last evening. Surrounded by their wives and every evidence of the tropics, the heads of department of the Carnegie Steel Company enjoyed a dinner extraordinary at the Hotel Schenley at which the steel king himself was expected at every moment."[82] At that time the company and most of Carnegie's former partners were in the midst of the dispute with Frick. Beyond that obstacle lay the uncertainties and possibilities of the first year of Schwab's unquestioned leadership.

During the first two weeks of 1900 Frick was displaced from his remaining positions of power. At a specially contrived meeting held in the town of Scottdale three days after the Schenley dinner, he lost control of the H. C. Frick Coke Company. Next day he was irreconcilably alienated in a violent confrontation that ended a visit by Andrew Carnegie to his Pittsburgh office. By Thursday, 11 January, the request for surrender of his interests in Carnegie Steel had been signed. Predictably outraged, Frick filed a suit against Andrew Carnegie and the partners who supported him. They prepared replies to his suit. Through these uncertain times Carnegie tried to present a brave face and support their new head. In February, writing from the "Florida Special Pullman," he breezily addressed Schwab as "Pard," assuring him, "We have them, never fear." In fact the outcome was uncertain, and in any case there was the prospect that court proceedings would result in commercially sensitive material being laid bare for public scrutiny. Such circumstances encouraged search for a compromise. A breakthrough came at a meeting at Carnegie's New York home on 17 March. Further talks in Atlantic City four days later produced an agreement, and a new firm, The Carnegie Company, was formed as a holding company to incorporate both Carnegie Steel and H. C. Frick Coke. Of its capital Carnegie held $174 million, Phipps, $35 million, and Frick, $31 million. Within a week Carnegie had received a congratulatory cable from John W. Gates in San Francisco. Gates, now head of the American Steel and Wire Company, recognized that the settlement represented a decisive shift in the balance of power in Carnegie Steel: "Heartiest congratulations on successful termination of what would certainly have been a bitter long personal litigation. Please insist on Charles M. Schwab for president. No more loyal, capable, honest or energetic man ever lived and none more capable or loyal to your interests. Ellwood [I. L. Ellwood, his partner] heartily concurs, J. W. Gates." Frick was excluded from all active participation in management, and though Carnegie remained a distant superego, Schwab was the unquestioned seat of day-to-day power. Yet, although he was the controlling genius of the organization, Schwab's share of its capital was only $19 million. Sometime in spring 1900 Carnegie informed Schwab that he was transferring to him 2 percent of his interest in Carnegie Steel as a gift, and he added, "I hope you will remain as president until you are an old man."[83] The next few months would be ones of high achievement, but as they passed the president remained under heavy pressures.

As well as directing operations Schwab headed planning for extensions into new fields of production, including possible major steel making operations away from their Pittsburgh center. Photographs of him at this time show a young and vigorous man, but his face was rather pudgy and pallid. Undaunted, the image makers of the time managed to transform him, physique and all, into an industrial superman: "Physically he is short, full face, keen brown eyes, quick step, frank speech, courteous but firm." His punishing daily regimen attracted fulsome praise. Early each morning he inspected part of the works and then at 10 o'clock was in his office to deal with the mail—efficiently, "for he comprehends, decides and acts quickly." After reviewing the mail he met departmental heads. Once a week he inspected a whole works. His Saturday lunches now had forty department heads in attendance. He explained to the press, "Not a word of business is permitted during the meal; but after everything is cleared away we discuss matters in hand and exchange opinions. . . . On Monday the gentlemen who have lunched with me call their head men together and have similar meetings." His awesome powers were said not to compromise his ease in human relationships: "He is a common man among all the others—a fellow associate with all, with no one under him. So far as he is master, it is only through greater knowledge, capacity and experience. . . . He masters details, decides and acts promptly, assured of success."[84] Schwab clearly benefited from highly favorable press reporting, and it seems that, from this time forward at least, he had public relations assistance. There is some evidence of this assistance in an article on Carnegie Steel published under his name in January 1901. In no sense does it underrate his abilities or his intelligence to suspect that some of the expressions used in the article were not ones he normally employed—as, for instance, the words "fat satrapy" to castigate the superintendency of the Pittsburgh division of the Pennsylvania Railroad or the description of their plant as a "Cyclops worthy of the Homeric archetype." He might well have referred to the coking coal and iron ore riches "without which America would not be the leading producer of iron and steel in the world" but it is surely unlikely he would have added "or Pittsburg[h] the *officina gentium*."[85]

Throughout 1900 extension and improvements of plants continued. Homestead was now the biggest and most valuable of the Carnegie works. That March the balance sheets valued Homestead at $16.6 million, Edgar Thomson at $10.4 million, and Duquesne at $7.9 million. Adding the Carrie Furnaces, its source of molten iron, extended Homestead's lead. By the year's end Duquesne and Edgar Thomson were each million-ton plants; Homestead crude steel capacity was 1.9 million tons. For the first few months of 1900 trade conditions were favorable and prices well up on the 1899 average, but then the general business situation worsened so that, one by one, prices for various products fell below those of the previous year—after May for bars and billets, after August for beams, and at least by October, for rails. On 7 July Corey reported the need to close a number of departments at Homestead within a week for want of orders. By the end of the month business generally had fallen off 40 percent as compared with June and "promises even worse"; already the Duquesne furnaces had stocks of 32,000 tons of pig iron. As general trading conditions worsened, the major finishing groups—American Steel and Wire, American Tin Plate, American Sheet Steel, American Steel Hoop, and National Tube, which bought much of their steel in semifinished form from either Carnegie, Federal Steel, or National Steel—were beginning to integrate backward to make more of the material they consumed. Some of them were building blast furnaces and acquiring mineral reserves. Together trade recession and loss of outlets for semifinished steel presented serious challenges even for a company as efficient as Carnegie Steel. Some of their competitors were even harder hit. To the Operating Committee in May Peacock reported, "Jones & Laughlin are practically shut down. The Illinois Steel Co. [now part of Federal Steel], aside from the rail mill, are shut down. The National Steel Company are running about one-half of their different plants." Inevitably Carnegie Steel felt the impact. Deciding to follow its traditional route of going for business whatever the price, it suffered a sharp contraction in earnings. They reached a peak in March, then fell month on month for half a year, reaching a low in September at little over one-tenth the March level. In October Henry Bope of the sales department described general market conditions as unchanged, but earnings had now turned sharply upward, only to fall to a new low in November.[86]

In addition to the price cut, under Schwab's leadership and with active prodding from Carnegie plans were drawn up to expand geographically and to finish more of the semifinished steel they had previously sold. Market extension could be secured through lower freight rates and through control of railroads, the latter a field in which Carnegie's youthful experience was helpful. Through fall 1900 they were looking into prospects for getting an independent railroad to the East Coast, perhaps by controlling the old Western Maryland Railway, a Jay Gould road, perhaps by a new route farther north linking with the Reading Railroad. Carnegie had high hopes from the extensions of the Gould's Wabash system. At the same time there were ideas for company boats carrying steel from Conneaut, Ohio, to Chicago—"even if the costs are high." Increases in overseas business seemed promising. On 2 February Carnegie sent Schwab a penciled note: "Good prospects Foreign trade—Things getting good for us in Britain—Labor scarce, coal and coke very high and going higher." This note was accompanied by a press clipping on price advances in some British iron and steel districts. Steps were taken to open export markets on a larger scale through Millard Hunsiker, who had represented their interests in London for most of the previous six years. That fall four oceangoing steamers were chartered from the Algoma Central Steamship Company to carry steel from Conneaut to Britain. A few weeks later three thousand tons of Carnegie plate and angles arrived on Clydeside on the steamer *Dunstan*. In spite of the cost of the Pittsburgh-to-Philadelphia rail haul and transatlantic freight charges, the delivered price was some 10 shillings ($2.40) a ton below the price of shipbuilding materials in the United Kingdom.[87]

Through the months of good trade and those of worsening conditions alike, Carnegie Steel was taking the offensive in new plant and new finishing lines. On April 23 the Howard Axle Works, which claimed to be the world's largest, was brought into production close by Homestead. Late in July, by which time American Steel and Wire was planning a new integrated steel plant, Carnegie Steel announced the largest wire rod mill yet built. It contemplated installing sheet and hoop mills. In August, when a group from Bethlehem Steel visited Homestead, it found the remainder of its Bessemer shop was being torn out, and the works now had forty-four open hearth furnaces, a dozen of which were working on molten metal from Duquesne furnaces. The length of the plate mill bought from Bethlehem had been extended by 50 percent.[88]

Notwithstanding his age, Carnegie was full of energy and bubbling with ideas. Old business convictions or theories, some borrowed half-digested from Charles Darwin or Herbert Spencer, surfaced once again, as when he cabled his partners in July: "[L]et me say that all is coming just as expected. There is nothing surprising; a struggle is inevitable and it is a question of survival of the fittest."[89] But he was three thousand miles away; the labor of transforming his dreams or broad development schemes into engineering drawings and to construction schedules was borne by the president, who was now struggling to steer current operations through difficult conditions.

As always there were opportunities for Schwab to obtain a change of scene from the blackness of Pittsburgh, but they too could be affected by business preoccupations. Trips to New York were usually either to see Andrew Carnegie or to negotiate with competitors. To save time, Schwab showed what to Carnegie seemed an unwise commitment to overnight travel. Twice within ten days in January he communicated his anxiety about such night journeys, on the second occasion suggesting an alternative: "Try a day trip Saturday am. Really it is enjoyable." Wider travels too involved company business. An example was a Great Lakes visit made in late July. Led by Schwab the party included George Lauder, James Gayley, and Daniel Clemson of Carnegie Steel, Thomas Lynch from H. C. Frick Coke, and James H. Reed of the Pittsburgh, Bessemer and Lake Erie Railroad. They toured some of the "connected" properties of the steel company, inspecting ore handling at Conneaut and from Duluth traveling by special train to the Oliver Iron Mining Company properties on the Mesabi and Vermilion Ranges of Minnesota. On their return they visited the Lorain yards of the American Shipbuilding Company in Ohio for the launch of the Pittsburgh Steamship Company's new lake steamer, *Princeton*.[90] It must have been an interesting but scarcely restful trip.

Aware of the strain under which his president and other partners were working, Carnegie continued to offer refuge at his splendid "castle" in the Scottish Highlands. In early June, as trade faltered, he told Schwab, "All very well here and Skibo finer than expected. Tell any of the managers that in case of a collapse they can be cured here upon most reasonable terms." A month later, with conditions worsening, he repeated his invitation: "[S]ay to any of the partners that there is rest for the weary here. I think they will need some. Come over."[91]

However genuine Carnegie's concern for his senior colleagues' health, it was frequently overwhelmed by his insistence that they should not miss any business opportunities and, therefore, by his exhortations to more effort. This persistent pressure was apparent in three springtime letters to Schwab, each separated by a few weeks. They conveyed different messages and were distinguished by marked contrasts in tone and even in form of address. A mid-April letter was solicitous, cheering, and unusually intimate—he even seems to have included an early example of what three years later would involve him in the spelling reform movement:

> My Friend, Please tell Dr. Ward obliged for his note assuring me you are all right only rest needed Now please postpone all questions until your return and be sure to come here and spend a day or two clear before sailing. I promise not to trouble you. Don't you try to deal with affairs that can better wait, as all can wait. Plenty of time next fall to adjust status new partners. . . . Do be sensible as I am—I am going to take a holiday and not bother about business. Follow a good example when you see it. P.S Just you larf.—This day week you are on the sea. A.C.

Five weeks later, writing from the Langham Hotel in London to "Dear Mr. Schwab," his mood was harder: "Cannot understand April $3,220, [thousands] when March was $4,350 after deducting coke, a difference of $1,100, equal to $4 per ton on 250,000 tons probably sold in April. Of course April has two working days less, equal to £300,000. Still there is unaccounted for $800,000, equal to $3 per ton. Can you give me any probable reason for this? We are off for Skibo on Monday. So glad to hear you are yourself again. very truly yours, A.C." Two weeks after he arrived at his Scottish retreat, and following a cable from Schwab about the downturn in business, he responded with a variant of his fighting advice to "My dear Mr. President." He told Schwab what he already knew: if he could not arrange percentages with other firms, "a struggle must ensue among producers for orders." In such circumstances, "[t]he sooner you scoop the market the better. It has never failed that the lowest price given has proved to be a high price at time of delivery on a falling market. When you want to catch a falling stone it won't do to follow it. You must cut under it, and so it is with a falling market."[92] Equally characteristic of its author was a late August letter to Schwab from Henry Phipps. Trade was worsening and prices tumbling. It was, Phipps wrote, a note "to express the hope that you will not allow the present troubles to unduly depress you. . . . Please bear in mind—save your health—don't worry. . . . In smaller affairs for full 30

Charles M. Schwab, c. 1899.
Reprinted from H. N. Casson, *The Romance of Steel*
(New York: A. S. Barnes, 1907).

years I went through several severe depressions and anxieties from which
you are happily free. With best wishes for courage, confidence etc., I am
yours sincerely, H. Phipps."[93] (The words "happily free" perhaps referred
to Schwab's lack of dependent children.)

Schwab visited Europe at least twice in 1900, in mid-May and in early
September. Here, too, mundane concerns could take precedence over rec-
reation. On the second trip a group of partners, including Thomas Morrison, George Lauder, and William H. Singer, stayed at Skibo. Reported as
being "for social purposes," their visit also took in important items of business. Andrew Mellon, who was then involved along with Frick and William H. Donner in an important new rod and wire mill along the Monongahela at what became Donora, was invited to Skibo for talks, for this
new mill would threaten the rod mill that Carnegie Steel had announced

a few weeks before. There was even a possibility Carnegie Steel might purchase Donora. Mellon reached Skibo on Sunday, 30 August. Schwab arrived next day. That evening Carnegie, Lauder, and Schwab discussed the matter with Mellon. Schwab objected to a takeover, arguing that the Donora location was not good, construction costs would be high, and the plant was too small. He seems to have spent the whole of the next day in conclave with Carnegie and Lauder.[94]

Schwab's heavy work schedule in this period of his life did not prevent him from involvement in what seems to have been his first extramarital affair. His sister-in-law, Minnie Dinkey, was recuperating from typhoid in the Schwabs' Pittsburgh home when Charlie Schwab had an affair with her nurse, the outcome of which was the birth of a daughter. He seems to have provided for her reasonably well. Although he assured Rana that this was a unique infidelity and would not be repeated, he proved unable to fulfill his promise. Except for one or two cases mentioned by Hessen, the details are unknown, but one episode in 1900 showed both his propensities in this direction and the way in which his frequent business travels provided opportunities. In May, Andrew Mellon, himself then playing the uncharacteristic role of suitor, having just become engaged to Nora Mc-Mullen, wrote home to Frick, "Hunsiker [Carnegie's London representative] met Schwab at Southampton but has seen very little of him since reaching London. He was to have joined us in a poker game last night but later sent word he could not come. Yesterday afternoon Hunsiker and I passed him in a hansom with a fine looking lady. Hunsiker has been anxious to learn who she can be."[95]

By the middle of the year Schwab was in the late stages of designing a major tube making plant, a new field of operations for Carnegie Steel. Sometime in late 1898 or early 1899 the idea of building this mill and associated iron and steel capacity next to the Conneaut ore docks and the lake terminus of the company's Pittsburgh, Bessemer and Lake Erie Railroad had been debated by the board of managers of Carnegie Steel; author James H. Bridge suggested that the idea came from Frick. On 17 February 1899 the National Tube Company was formed, and within four days Carnegie's reaction to the new company had been communicated to the board of managers of Carnegie Steel as an endorsement for an eventual Conneaut works: "I have not heard of anything which strikes me so favorably—from ore to pipe." Within a year National Tube claimed it controlled 90 percent of the nation's tube capacity, though it made only about 75 percent. Lacking steel making capacity on a scale anywhere near comparable to that of its mills, National Tube started by buying most of what it used, largely from Carnegie Steel, but by late 1899 it had begun to build an integrated works at Wheeling. Like other finishing groups, during 1900 it reduced purchases of semifinished steel. In addition to the commercial logic of having capacity next to the lake terminus of the Pittsburgh, Bessemer and Lake Erie Railroad, and the combative stance of its controlling partner, it was the process of backward integration by National Tube that induced Carnegie Steel to set in train the tube project it had long contemplated. Schwab later maintained that they entered new trades if they seemed a natural progression for their business, but messages from Carnegie to his partners made clear the move was offensive. On 4 June 1900, as steel prices trended downward, he wrote a confident reply to a Schwab cable of two days before: "I should not allow present drop to postpone our going into Tubes. This is a dead sure thing for us, a clear track all the way. The tube people do not give us trade any more as they used to. We have only to build the works to make a satisfactory division of the tube business with the one party in it, the Trust. . . . Don't be scared into postponing, the cost of works will now be less, and by the time you are ready to make tubes chances are the market will be good." Two months later, with prices tumbling, he was still in favor of action: "[S]o as to keep others out, have you given notice our intention is make tubes [?]." During the year Schwab spent much—though how much is unknown—time toiling over plans for the tube works. After examining possible alternate sites near Pittsburgh, including Liberty on the lower Youghiogheny River, Peters Creek on the Monongahela River, and Tarentum in the lower Allegheny valley, on Sunday, 11 November, Schwab and Carnegie met and decided that Conneaut, Ohio, was the place for the plant. Just over eight weeks later, on 9 January 1901, plans were announced for expenditure of up to $12 million to construct the world's largest tube making plant on a site east of the Conneaut harbor. It would have two, possibly four, blast furnaces and twenty fifty-ton open hearth furnaces. Room was available there for mills making tinplate, wire, nails, and other products if they were later needed. If they shipped goods by water during the navigation season from April to December, Schwab reckoned that freight costs to lakeside markets might be not more than a third those by rail.[96] Site preparation began.

By the time Carnegie Steel revealed plans for Conneaut, all-round expansion of capacity was under way in the industry. Federal Steel was integrating forward with more finishing capacity. The main rolling mill groups were integrating backward into steel and iron making. It seemed that there would be greater overcapacity and even more painful, cutthroat trading. Many individuals were now trying to find an escape from this looming crisis. Notwithstanding all other demands on his time, Schwab played a key and unquestionably the most colorful role in this process.

The financial results for Carnegie Steel in 1900 were claimed to be extraordinary. Earnings nearly doubled from 1898 to 1899; next year they were recorded as almost doubling again. After March 1900 the profits of the H. C. Frick Coke Company were included. Over the years almost all historians of Carnegie Steel—including the present writer—have quoted 1900 profits as $40 million. Such an excellent performance achieved in the face of the difficult trading conditions of most of the second half of the year was taken as yet another piece of evidence of the unrivaled efficiency of the whole Carnegie Steel operation. It is true that in 1911 the Bureau of Corporations wrote of valuations of the Carnegie Company as providing "very liberally—for earning power," but such a cautionary note was unusual throughout the next century. In 2004 Charles R. Morris took the very logical step of checking the $40 million figure by recording the monthly figures—and making careful assessments of the contributions made by H. C. Frick Coke and the Oliver Iron Mining Company. He concluded that the real figure for profits was just short of $28 million. Three contemporary sources seem to clash with this conclusion. When in January 1901 Carnegie wrote a penciled valuation of his company, one of the three categories listed was "Profit of past year and estimated profit for coming year $80,000,000." A few years later, in his autobiography, Carnegie indicated that 1900 net earnings had been $40 million. Bridge, whose purpose was largely to celebrate the contribution made by Frick and others, which he thought had been underrated, also stated that 1900 earnings had reached a record $40 million. The value of this evidence is questionable. Carnegie had a good reason to inflate the earnings of his company—it made it more desirable to a potential buyer. The same motivation did not apply in the case of Bridge; Morris suggests that he may have learned the figure from Frick. A weakness in such an argument is that neither Bridge nor Frick was easily distracted from identifying falsehood, and neither had reason to exaggerate the 1900 profits. Another piece of evidence is particularly interesting, for it was obviously not intended for public scrutiny and yet gets away from the $40 million figure.[97]

Seventy-nine years after the events traced in this chapter, in the Schwab Memorial Library in Bethlehem, a note handwritten by Schwab sometime in mid-December 1900 was found to contain his estimates for the 1900 earnings of companies that he already envisaged might be brought into a massive new consolidation—"on a common basis of capi-

talization of companies." There are some minor variations from the figures in the document he was to send to Carnegie—and probably also to
J. P. Morgan—about a month later. In this first estimate Schwab put the
1900 earnings of Federal Steel at $11 million, National Steel at $8 million, National Tube at $13 million, American Steel and Wire at $7 million,
American Tin Plate at $5 million, American Sheet Steel at $4 million, and
American Steel Hoop at $2 million. His figure for Carnegie Steel was $38
million.[98] Morris's 2004 computations based on the company's monthly
earnings seem to indicate that even this estimate was a considerable exaggeration of the real figure.

On various occasions during 1900 the sale of Carnegie Steel was debated and Schwab was involved. Years later Ida Tarbell had considerable
discussion with Elbert H. Gary when she was writing a biography of him.
It was presumably the judge who told her that soon after the Carnegie interests were reorganized in spring 1900, Schwab paid a visit to the Federal
Steel offices. "'You ought to take over the Carnegie properties,' he told the
Judge, 'ought to buy them.' After considerable discussion, Gary agreed to
talk to Mr. Morgan." Although Gary urged the purchase, Morgan did not
feel able to raise the money. In testimony in the dissolution suit against
U.S. Steel in 1913 Gary stated that Schwab had made two approaches early
in 1900 and another two months later. Schwab maintained that the Tarbell biography was in many ways inaccurate but admitted that he had discussed the sale of Carnegie Steel several times that year.[99]

By December 1900, trade was reviving, prices had strengthened, and
Carnegie Steel profits again increased, though they remained well below
the level of six months before. At this time Schwab played the part that
led to the sale of the company, the long-delayed withdrawal of Andrew
Carnegie from business, and the transformation of the steel industry as a
whole. The inception of these sweeping changes occurred at another major dinner.

3 ❦ U.S. Steel

During the last few weeks of 1900 and the early weeks of the new year the idea for a great agglomeration of iron and steel making and finishing capacity to be given the grand but justifiable title "United States Steel Corporation" was sown, and it quickly germinated, grew, and took form. At the end of the first quarter of 1901 the organization appeared, a full-grown giant on the world stage, ready for work. Charles M. Schwab was intimately involved in the creation of this giant, playing three key roles: as an authority on the structure and prospects of the industry, as the representative of the most important single interest within it, and as a prospective leader for the new corporation. Even so, varying reports, reflecting subsequent rewriting of the course of events, suggest that it is far from easy to find out exactly what transpired and thereby to be sure of Schwab's relative importance in the unfolding of those events. Consequently, it becomes necessary to consider the whole process of the formation of the new company.

At the end of 1900, as always, events were largely shaped by powerful economic forces. Such forces are not readily directed and not controlled by any individual or company. Since the last years of the 1890s there had been a strong merger movement. In the steel industry this movement largely consisted of horizontal integration but also involved the creation of a few major vertically integrated companies such as Federal Steel and National Steel. During 1900 the finished product amalgamations made moves to produce more of their own steel supplies. In response, some of the bigger integrated companies that had supplied them, especially Federal and Carnegie, built or planned plants to convert more of the steel they had previously sold semifinished in the form of slabs, blooms, billets, rods or sheet, and tinplate bars into finished products. Construction of major new plants, such as one that Lackawanna Steel already had under way at Buffalo and the giant complex that Carnegie Steel had long contemplated and early in January 1901 announced for Conneaut, was another factor seeming to point to even more competitive trading. Demand fell from mid-1900 as the potential supply of steel products was being increased. If, as seemed inevitable, the main companies went ahead with most of their plant extensions and associated investments in new mineral capacity, docks, railroads, coke ovens, and so forth, it could be anticipated that ahead there lay still more underutilization of capacity, keener competition, and lower prices. Disruption of the commercial well-being of this vital industrial sector seemed likely to be the paradoxical outcome of what was universally hailed as a decade of remarkable triumph in American engineering and organization. During that period new worldwide standards of excellence for the industry were set.

This general situation was given detail and color by personal features. Andrew Carnegie, though still vigorous, and indeed as far as competitors could see as combative and resourceful as ever, celebrated his sixty-fifth birthday on 25 November 1900. He had made clear he wanted to spend his later years in the pursuit of what he regarded as worthier ends than accumulation of yet more wealth. His former key manager, Henry Clay Frick, had been ousted from the company but was unlikely to retire from business because he was only fifty-one in December 1900, was already becoming involved in some new steel projects, and was reported to be interested in others. At Federal Steel the fifty-four-year-old Elbert H. Gary had made clear he did not think that his company, mainly based in Chicago, should have to defer to Pittsburgh operators. In this instance, too, there was a displaced "prince" looking for a new field of action, though he was a man of very different character and personality from Frick. John Warne Gates had been president of Illinois Steel before it merged with Federal Steel. Although now the leading partner in the American Steel and Wire Company (AS&W) and involved in gathering together the plants that produced the Republic Iron and Steel Company, he was still only forty-five, and his roving, speculative ambitions were on the lookout for even bigger things. Much less well known were the qualities and aims of the Reiss interests who managed National Steel or the leaders of major product groups such as Edmund Converse at National Tube, Daniel Reid, who was associated with three separate product groups—American Tin Plate, American Steel Hoop, and American Sheet Steel—or Percival Roberts at American Bridge. Beyond this inner circle of "industrial" actors were financiers and promoters, a group which had been gaining significance. Prominent among them were the Moore brothers, who had organized National Steel and the Tin Plate, Steel Hoop, and Sheet Steel groups but in spring 1899 had failed in a bid to take over Carnegie Steel, and John Pierpont Morgan, who played a major part in the earlier stages of AS&W and above all in Federal Steel. He had "put together" National Tube by combining a company of that name at McKeesport, Pennsylvania, with the Riverside works near Wheeling, West Virginia, and a few smaller tube making plants. Being also deeply involved with major sections of the railroad industry, Morgan viewed with alarm such potentially destabilizing schemes as Carnegie was not only formulating but also, with nicely calculated self-interest, leaking to the public. Finally, Charles Schwab was generally recognized as the most able of all the leading chief executives in the industry. He was not yet thirty-nine.

This complicated mixture of general, company, and personal conditions, factors, hopes and fears, and a lively consciousness of an impending threat of disruption and loss to the established order in the steel industry created uncertainty but also led to a search for solutions. Wider combination and thorough-going rationalization had been seen as a way to make sense and even profit out of potentially disastrous circumstances. From 1899 there had been tentative moves in these directions. The difficult trading conditions in the latter half of 1900 and expansion plans in various quarters revived interest in the possibility of a radical new order. The first signs that Schwab would play a central part came in the fall. On Tuesday, 6 November, he reported to a Carnegie Steel board meeting that the previous week, while in New York, he had received a message that J. P. Morgan would like to see him. Thinking this invitation concerned their plans for railroad extensions, Schwab did not make contact. Afterward Morgan's assistant, Charles Steele, told Schwab that the financier wanted to discuss the tube business, as Carnegie plans threatened his investment in National Tube. This information precipitated action in making their intentions public. As Schwab told his board that day, "I think when Mr. Carnegie comes out here next week and we have definitely decided as to site, we should make a definite announcement of our intentions." Five weeks later, on Tuesday, 11 December, the board authorized the purchase of the land for the Conneaut works. Next day Schwab took the star role in what author Frederick Lewis Allen later scarcely exaggerated when he called it "one of those events which direct the destinies of a nation."[1] It took the unlikely form of a private dinner party.

There are many accounts of the dinner held on Wednesday, 12 December 1900, in the University Club on Fifth Avenue, New York, but there is no authoritative record either of the proceedings of that evening or of the events of the momentous weeks that followed. The varying contents of and emphases in what does exist indicate in part the well-known fallibility of human beings as witnesses but also point to the ways in which different parties stressed, omitted, or sometimes even chose to misrepresent occasions and discussions in order to provide a particular interpretation of the role played by themselves or others. (An extreme example of defective memory was when Schwab, giving evidence to the Stanley Committee in 1911, spoke of the dinner as being "'in the fall of 1899.'"[2]) The hosts for the dinner were the New York banker J. Edward Simmons, who fifteen years before had been president of the New York Stock Exchange and was still president of the Fourth National Bank of New York, and financier Charles Stewart Smith, a founder of the Fifth Avenue National Bank who was involved in other financial and political interests in the city. Smith was a friend of Carnegie. Sometime before, on a visit to Pittsburgh, Schwab had entertained Simmons and Smith. The New York dinner was ostensibly given in his honor by way of thanks. However, the size and nature of the guest list indicated that it was far more than a simple mark of personal appreciation. In writing to George Lauder on the previous Saturday, Carnegie fully recognized its importance. His brief note ended with an intriguing sentence, one that raises—but fails to answer—the question of whether or not Carnegie already had a very clear idea what his company wanted to accomplish that evening: "Schwab's dinner here remarkable. Mr. Smith tells me every one invited accepted and really the biggest men in New York. He is a favorite indeed and this makes him more valuable for us."[3] It was a considerable gathering. Most accounts report eighty or so men; in 1911 Schwab said it was "a great number—70 or 80"; twenty-five years later he reckoned about one hundred had been present. Apart from Schwab, those invited seem to have included only four men from Carnegie Steel. Their three main stockholders did not hear Schwab speak. Andrew Carnegie arrived just before the dinner but soon excused himself and went off to another engagement. (Even so, as one of the junior partners recorded, "Mr. Carnegie, with his ever ready smile of pleasure when one of his officials received recognition, such as rendered Mr. Schwab, told the whole story in a few words: 'Honor to whom honor is due.'") Henry Phipps received an invitation, but as he explained to Schwab two days later, he had mislaid it and therefore forgot to attend. Understandably, Henry Clay Frick seems not to have been invited. The only Carnegie partners present for the speeches were Judge James H. Reed, head of their Pittsburgh, Bessemer and Lake Erie Railroad, and junior partner Albert Case, who next day sent a list of forty-six of the guests to Carnegie Steel so that it could be included in the Friday issue of the *Pittsburgh Dispatch*. (His list was not only partial but also inaccurate in that it included Phipps.) Remarkably, there seem to have been no representatives from other steel companies. Industrial guests included Henry H. Rogers, vice president of Standard Oil, and among those from railroads there were Paul Morton of the western systems and a member of the Vanderbilt family, Chauncey Depew, who had taken over at the New York Central when Cornelius Vanderbilt died the previous year (neither Morton nor Depew were listed by Case), and Edward H. Harriman. The bankers were much more numerous and included August Belmont, Jacob Schiff, and James Stillman. When the men took their places at the tables, Morgan, as senior representative of the financial interests present, was seated on Schwab's right, while Simmons, the host, sat on his left. It would be interesting to know who had drawn up the list of persons to be invited, but in any case, as biographer Joseph Frazier Wall neatly put it, "If Schwab himself had not done the arranging [of the dinner] clearly he understood the purpose."[4] Essentially—indeed literally—his task was to sell the steel industry to the leading financial interests.

The new University Club was described at this time by a Carnegie steel man as "a gem" in architectural design and furnishings, made more attractive on this evening by "beautiful floral decorations" and the "sweet strains of music." A third sense was beguiled by the "elaborate menu which Mr. Simmons had prepared for his guests." As they ate Schwab talked busily with Morgan.[5] When the meal was over, Edward Simmons made a few remarks before calling on Schwab to deliver the only speech of the evening. The latter recalled that he had been told to speak for only fifteen to twenty minutes because "these are old men and they have to go home early." (In fact the average age of the thirty bankers and other "capitalists" listed by Case and for which details have been traced was 61.9 years; seven were over 70. Understandably they must all have seemed "old" to a speaker of 38 years and 10 months.)[6] Years later Reed mentioned that Schwab started his speech by saying that he could not talk about anything but steel—"I remember that because he always starts every speech that way." Then, as biographer Burton Jesse Hendrick wrote using almost biblical imagery, "The speaker took the assembled bankers up to the mountain top and spread before their startled eyes the splendor of his universe of steel." He outlined the glorious possibilities inherent in the currently difficult situation; as he put it to the Stanley Committee, "I explained the great advantage to be gained by the organization of such a corporation as United States Steel." Over the preceding few years the industry had lowered its production costs—the actual costs of processing from a metallurgical and mechanical point of view—to a level he believed (erroneously, as events proved) could never be materially further reduced. But further cost savings might be secured if instead of many companies making the same products, they could join together and introduce plant specialization. In extreme cases a rolling mill might turn out only one product and as far as possible run on one or only a few specifications day after day. Within such an umbrella organization it should be possible to increase the efficiency of all by fostering competition between the managements of various plants and by further integration of processes. Steel distribution should be organized so that deliveries were made from the plant nearest to a center of consumption, cutting out cross hauling and reducing costs. Expansion of the export trade was desirable. Economies obtained in these ways would bring with them lower prices and thereby increase steel consumption.[7]

Wall records that Schwab's speech lasted for less than half an hour, while Hessen writes that he went on for forty-five minutes and Allen reports that it took an hour.[8] Surprisingly for an after-dinner speech, and particularly if it was as short as some accounts reckoned, it is said that Schwab was interrupted frequently by questions—and warmly welcomed them because he had, ready to mind, all the facts of the industry. Years later he recalled that a few questions came from Morgan and many from Harriman.[9] In fact, as the list of those present and, still more, the form of his address both suggest, the occasion was more an industrial promotion than a conventional after-dinner speech. It was exceptional too in its immediate impact. Usually Morgan went straight home after attending a dinner, but on this occasion he drew Schwab over to a window seat where he engaged him in further discussion—in Eugene Grace's account for a few moments and according to Hessen for a half hour.[10]

When the evening was over Schwab returned to Pittsburgh, where an important part of his work was hurrying forward the plans for the new tube works on the shores of Lake Erie that would seriously challenge Morgan's own interests. Schwab assured Carnegie their new plant would undercut costs of manufacture at National Tube by at least ten dollars a ton—one-ninth of the maximum price for tubes reached early in 1900. To throw down the gauntlet in this manner was, as a newspaper put it, "plunging the steel industry into a war which could prove disastrous to some of the weaker combatants and costly and weary to the strongest."[11] It was also a spur for anyone concerned with maintaining industrial stability to take action.

Writing less than seven years after these events, and after speaking to a number of individuals in a good position to know the truth, Herbert N. Casson recorded that, a few days after the dinner, Schwab and John W. Gates, who had spoken about a big steel consolidation on and off for three years, went to see Morgan and in a night-long meeting outlined for him "the big possibilities of the steel business." The implication is that they took the initiative in setting up the meeting. When asked some years later why he had helped in the formation of the United States Steel Corporation, Gates made the disarmingly frank reply, "To convert a lot of doubtful assets into cash."[12] (Yet in testimony to the Stanley Committee only a few weeks before his death, in an obviously flawed recollection, he gave a radically different account of the whole thing. On that occasion he attributed the origin of Morgan's move toward consolidation to a dinner meeting of Morgan and the railroad magnate James J. Hill, at which, after discussing the implications of Carnegie's railroad plans, Morgan moved on to the effect of the Carnegie tube works—which Gates placed not at Conneaut but at Ashtabula, Ohio. Hill suggested that Morgan speak to Gates. Hill acted as intermediary. When Morgan saw Gates, his inclination was to approach Carnegie through Frick, but Gates warned him against this path and agreed instead to arrange for Morgan to meet Schwab.)[13]

Hessen's account was also based on Gates's testimony but, more logically, did not omit mention of the dinner of 12 December. According to him, it was some three weeks after the dinner, that is, in the last few days of 1900 or very early in 1901, when Morgan talked with Gates (whose methods he profoundly disliked), telling him he wanted to prevent Carnegie from building at Conneaut. At this time Carnegie was resolutely going ahead; as he wrote to his cousin on New Year's Day, "Am anxious to get these Tube Works fairly launched—we need this sure feeder to what we have."[14] A few days later plans for Conneaut were at last made public. About this time Gates arranged for Schwab to meet Morgan in a Philadelphia hotel. Arriving there, Schwab learned that the financier was unwell and had been unable to keep the appointment. Schwab thereupon traveled on to Morgan's New York home where—apparently notwithstanding the alleged illness—he and Gates spent the whole night in discussion with

Morgan and Robert Bacon, his assistant. Bacon recorded that Morgan was much impressed by Schwab, and at the end of the meeting he asked him to indicate which properties he thought should be included in a giant steel amalgamation. In the last few years of his life Schwab gave his own account of what followed. He listed the companies, their individual plants, and his estimates of what should be paid for them: "I knew exactly what each one was worth. Nobody in the world helped me with that list. I didn't use the ordinary book value, but based my estimates on earning capacity, good will, the physical state of the properties and their *potentialities* as an investment. I left out many companies, including Bethlehem, because they would have provided nothing but duplication, and the ideal corporation would have no duplication of any sort in it."[15] After a few days of work he returned for another all-night session with Morgan, Gates again being present. When it ended Morgan decided he would finance the steel combination Schwab envisioned on condition that Carnegie would sell.

It is quite clear that Carnegie knew something was going on, though the evidence is tauntingly circumstantial rather than explicit. In a letter to Schwab that unfortunately is undated but seems to have been written in late December 1900, he urged the president to hurry on the purchase of land for the Conneaut works but ended his letter with the question, "Is all going well?" On 7 January he sent a telegram that seems to have referred to Morgan and may perhaps have wholly concerned his attitude to their tube mill project, but again the ending was intriguing: "Am down town today on matters. Saw the important man today. Everything looks well. Anything new? Andrew Carnegie." On Friday, 25 January, he responded to Schwab's report on their rivals and on his expansive vision of their future and then remarked, "Surprised at importance Independent Co.s surely some could be bot [bought?] out." Eventually, while Schwab and Carnegie were in the mollifying setting of Saint Andrews Golf Course, Westchester County, Schwab broached the subject of selling "his" company. Wall dates this occasion as the last week of January, and in view of the above it seems a reasonable conclusion.[16] According to Hessen, Carnegie proved open to the idea and that evening decided to sell; others suggest he told Schwab he would give his decision next day. Schwab recalled that Carnegie "received the proposition with a great deal of reluctance, but finally agreed to sell. It is my private opinion that shortly afterwards he very much regretted it."[17] The result of Carnegie's deliberations was a very brief, penciled note of his own valuation of Carnegie Steel, which amounted, including profits made in 1900 and expected for 1901, to just over $487 million. Schwab delivered the scrappy memo to Morgan, who, after a mere glance at the figures, accepted Carnegie's own evaluation. Years later Schwab reckoned Carnegie Steel had been sold cheaply. After reading Carnegie's note, Morgan called in Elbert Gary, who declared in favor of going ahead.[18]

In complete contrast to this account, Ida Tarbell assigned a key role to Gary—whose recollections she drew upon. She suggested it was a few days after the dinner when Morgan and Schwab had the long meeting that prompted Carnegie to pencil his note of a price at which he would willingly sell. Within ten days Schwab had returned to Morgan, they talked over the position of Carnegie Steel and Carnegie's price, and Schwab set out to persuade his host that the steel industry was, as Bacon put it, just bursting into "a new and tremendous field of importance and activity and consumption." She recorded that on a Sunday morning about three weeks after the dinner—that is, probably in the first few days of January—Morgan sent Bacon to see Gary, who spent the remainder of that day sketching out a scheme for amalgamation that he presented to Morgan on Monday. For four weeks before the first public intimations of the broad plan, Gary worked further on this scheme. Then at some stage of the process Morgan called on Julian Kennedy, who, notwithstanding his old connection with Carnegie, had for many years been an independent and widely respected consulting engineer, to undertake an appraisal of the plants that would likely be included. When it was time for the proposed constituent companies to enter into the agreement, the only major hitch was that Gates held out for a higher price for American Steel and Wire. He accepted the price offered only after a direct threat from Morgan that if he refused to do so, the new corporation would build its own wire works. Schwab by contrast maintained that all *his* estimates were accepted and agreed to except for those for American Tin Plate, for which the Moore interests were paid slightly more than he had proposed.[19]

It should be noted that Schwab said that Tarbell's account of Gary's role in the formation of the United States Steel Corporation was untrue in many respects, and certainly the evidence that in fact Carnegie did not give his approval and name his price until late January seems to rule out her whole theory. Schwab's own testimony to the Stanley Committee ten years after these events was rather confusing: "I got the price from Mr. Carnegie and took it to Mr. Morgan, and beyond being consulted with reference to general views, values of properties, probable earnings, and so forth, I had nothing further to do with the organization of the United States Steel Corporation." By the time Carnegie wrote his autobiography, his reliability as a witness had diminished to the point that he wrote, inaccurately, "At this juncture—that is March 1901—Mr. Schwab told me Mr. Morgan had said to him he should really like to know if I wished to retire from business; if so he thought he could arrange it."[20] Put like that, it all appeared a much simpler, smoother, more logical, and more gentlemanly process than it seems to have been in reality.

Inevitably, in Carnegie Steel and in Pittsburgh generally progress toward an amalgamation aroused keen interest, which in turn revealed strengths and weaknesses in the company. The uncertainty and tension seem to have brought about some disruption to the ordered course of business. On Wednesday, 9 January, a regular meeting of the Carnegie Steel Company was held. The minutes of the next regular meeting recorded the signing of the minutes from 9 January—but ninety years later the 9 January minutes were no longer in the records held in the Library of Congress. On the evening of this unrecorded board meeting, and a year after they had first celebrated the post-Frick regime, the officers of the Carnegie company gathered once again in the grand banquet hall of the Schenley Hotel. Each leading officer proposed a toast. Schwab chose a theme well calculated to stimulate or puzzle—"Expectations." As late as 24 January Carnegie was denying—even to close colleagues—rumors that his company was about to be swept into a bigger group. On that day he wrote to George Lauder, "There is no substance in the reports anent great combination. . . . I don't think any of us would be willing to trust our 160 million Bonds in any management but our own—These could easily be made ducks and drakes of—In our hands they can be made A1 and the stock behind them—a couple of years will do this as I see it."[21]

However, at the same time as he was writing in this pugnacious fashion, Carnegie was receiving from Schwab a series of statements comparing their own company with others, a list significantly confined to the companies that the amalgamation was soon to bring together. The letter accompanying these figures was an intriguing, confusing combination of anticipations for an expanded Carnegie Steel and, though more vaguely, for something even bigger. He looked some few years ahead when "they" would produce twice as much per month as they had in 1900, a tonnage a little less than all the other companies soon to be linked had produced that year. In short, Schwab seems to have been considering the new conglomerate a greater Carnegie Steel:

> I really believe that for the next ten years the Carnegie Company will show greater earnings than all the others together. . . . I shall not feel satisfied until we are producing 500,000 tons per month and finish-

ing same. And we'll do it within five years. Look at our ore and coke as compared with the others. If you continue to give me the support you have in the past we'll make a greater industry than even we ever dreamt of. Am anxious to get at Conneaut. Are pushing plans rapidly and will be ready for a start in the spring.

Schwab may also have sent his figures, along with an account of his expansionist thinking, to Morgan as part of his collection of evidence for the necessity for an amalgamation. In any case, the figures showed that although 1900 data—questionable though its accuracy is now seen to be—indicated that Carnegie Steel had a higher utilization of capacity than the other two major integrated companies and had much higher earnings per ton of crude steel, when the financial record of the finishing groups was brought into the account, their own performance had been by no means exceptional. There is in the Carnegie papers at the Library of Congress a note that, although undated, seems from its position in the records to be from the last week in January 1901. It is headed "Schwab/Morgan" and mentions stocks; accompanying it is a note that, though cryptic, seems to prove that by now Carnegie was fully aware of the drift of things and of their implications: "Changes may require new works on other ground near there. Old works [Lorain] useless." Within a few more days the vital decisions had been made.[22]

On Monday, 4 February, a letter was sent to Carnegie at 5 West Fifty-first Street, New York (the Carnegies' new home at 2 East Ninety-first Street was then being completed). It was signed by twenty-nine partners, headed by Schwab, Peacock, and Gayley, and contained their agreement to the combination and a fond farewell to their head.[23] Next day Carnegie informed Lauder about the new arrangement. For other colleagues a time for rest from the burdens of the day had not yet arrived. J. P. Morgan issued an official statement of the formation of the United States Steel Corporation on 25 February. It included a brief valuation of the main companies to be included, except for Carnegie Steel. That day Henry Phipps wrote to Schwab, "I am delighted to hear what you tell me. For the success which you have done so much to bring about I congratulate you most heartily. . . . I shall be pleased when you are freed from the strain of the last few weeks." By 2 March it had been announced that arrangements had been made for the acquisition of nearly all the Carnegie Steel directors' bonds and stock in the erstwhile company.[24]

Over several weeks there was speculation as to who would head the new corporation. On 11 February, referring to rumors of combination, the

Pittsburgh Dispatch indicated that some had suggested that Frick would try to block the arrangement; others were putting his name forward as the likely president. Frick and Schwab were reported to have breakfasted together at the Holland House Hotel in Manhattan on Tuesday, 12 February, but no inkling of their conversation reached the newspapers. It was soon reported in the press that Schwab would be head. Much later it became known that the main condition Morgan had set for going ahead with the amalgamation was that Schwab should accept its presidency. He did so on the condition that he would have full responsibility.[25] Accordingly, when the new United States Steel Corporation began trading on 1 April it was headed by Charles M. Schwab. Six weeks earlier he had celebrated his thirty-ninth birthday. He was full of hope for the future of his new charge, the largest industrial organization in the world.

His new role required that he leave Pittsburgh for the New York head office of U.S. Steel, which meant procuring a New York residence, one suited both to his exalted office and his aspirations. By now he also had both the wealth to purchase or construct such a home and the income to sustain it. For a time he lived in an apartment on Seventy-second Street. In 1901 his salary was $100,000, but he received a bonus of $2 million. He then moved to the Lorraine, an apartment house on Forty-fifth Street, and then to a five-story house at 323 West Seventy-fourth Street. He had decided to build in upper Manhattan, and by autumn 1901 he had spent $865,000 buying an entire block surrounded by Riverside Drive, West End Avenue, and Seventy-third and Seventy-fourth Streets. The New York Orphan Asylum had been occupying this block, but the asylum was torn down and its operations moved elsewhere. Schwab engaged Maurice Herbert, an architect well known in high society, to build a house worthy of the president of the world's biggest company.

Schwab's new home, "Riverside," was built between 1901 and 1905. It cost some $3 million, but the interiors were furnished so lavishly that the final figure for the whole project was in excess of $5 million. Early reports indicated its design would "follow the first period of the French Renaissance," but it was in fact a hybrid, with the main part being modeled on the Chateau of Chenonceaux and the wings patterned after the castles of Blois and Azay-le-Rideau. It fronted on Riverside Drive and had gardens to the rear, with terraces, lawns, and trees all enclosed by an iron fence. One terrace had a life-size bronze statue of a "puddler," a worker engaged in a metal making occupation with which Schwab had never had much connection. The house was provided with the then usual stepped and covered entrances. Inside was another mixture of styles—the large

Riverside, the Schwabs' home in New York City.
Courtesy of the National Canal Museum, Easton, PA.

smoking room was "fairly" pure Flemish, the parlor of Louis XVI style, the dining room à la Louis XIV, and a library in the mode of Henri IV. A main hall two and half stories in height was dominated by a ceiling-high carved marble fireplace, a large stained glass window with three figures representing, respectively, dramatic music, sacred music, and poetry, and a marble staircase. Halfway up the latter was the console of a pipe organ, costing $100,000, and distinguished not only by its giant size but also because for many years it was considered the finest in New York City. The noted organist Archer Gibson was paid $10,000 a year to play it—and with a few guests the owner would enjoy performances by outstanding artists, including Enrico Caruso and Nelly Melba. The two-story art gallery contained masterpieces by Titian, Hals, Corot, and others and sculptures depicting American metallurgy. As seems to have been common for the homes of the top tier of self-made men, Riverside had a fine library, though as Carnegie once condescendingly remarked, "As far as I have known millionaires, the library is the least used part of what he would probably consider 'furniture' in all his mansion." The dining room was dominated by a ceiling painting, *The Prosperity of America* by Jose Villagos. In another room a domed ceiling decorated with angels prompted a child visitor to inquire with the disarming but penetrating simplicity of her years whether this was heaven. The decor everywhere was "heavy" and elaborate. Predictably, the senses were widely regaled, glass chandeliers spreading light and pipes conveying the organ notes throughout the building. This most opulent palace of seventy-five rooms was for many years the home of a childless couple who resided there for no more than three or four winter months. Upkeep of Riverside cost forty-five hundred dollars a month; it became a matter for self-congratulation that, by means of incentives for efficiency, Schwab managed to cut this figure to sixteen hundred dollars.[26]

The Struggle for Leadership

On Monday, 25 February 1901, the charter of the "United States Steel Corporation" was filed at the office of the secretary of state at Trenton, New Jersey. On the same day J. P. Morgan issued an official statement about the new company. A few weeks later a list of twenty-four directors was made public, and the chief officers and members of its two central decision making bodies, an executive committee and a finance committee, were appointed. On Monday, 1 April, the United States Steel Corporation began trading. It was widely assumed that Charles Michael Schwab would dominate the new organization with the force of his personality, which seemed to have given birth to the colossus with the speech he had given at the University Club only a few months before. Unquestionably he believed in his own primacy in the new company. Within six weeks of the start of business he was in Washington to testify before the Industrial Commission. Outlining the organization of U.S. Steel, particularly in relation to its subsidiaries, he stated, "*I* was careful to put in no controlling officers."[27] For the next two years the public perception of Charlie Schwab was that he straddled the peak of the industrial world. In fact his experience as president represented a striking and deeply wounding reversal of that of the previous four. As at Carnegie Steel, there occurred in U.S. Steel a struggle for supremacy between those occupying the two top positions: president and chairman. In the former company he had been given precedence over the chairman. Now his presidential powers would be gradually circumscribed by the chairman of the executive committee, Elbert H.

Gary. Carnegie played a decisive part in Schwab's earlier triumph; Morgan permitted Schwab's displacement at U.S. Steel.

Early in April 1901 the *Bulletin of the American Iron and Steel Association* (*BAISA*) observed, "Mr. Schwab occupies today the most prominent and the most responsible position in connection with the world's industrial development that has ever been held by any man." James Swank, the bulletin's experienced editor, emphasized that unique challenges were now being tackled by a uniquely well-qualified man: "The conditions, indeed, have never before existed which would call for the display of technical skill and executive ability on so large a scale as is now demanded of Mr. Schwab. . . . That Mr. Schwab will in every way meet the expectations of his business associates who have entrusted him with such immense responsibility is the confident belief of all who know the man and have watched his remarkable career." Under the circumstances it seemed fair that he should be the most highly paid business official. Offered a salary of $1 million, he suggested to Morgan that instead he should receive 2 percent of all business income in excess of $70 million in the first year. This arrangement brought him more than $2 million.[28]

Not surprisingly, highly romanticized accounts of Schwab's role in United States Steel began to appear in popular newspapers and monthlies. He was variously represented as mercurial, an imperturbable field marshal, or a superman. In May *BAISA* described his appearance before the Industrial Commission as "plain faced, plain spoken, plainly attired, brilliant eyed, clear headed and nimble witted." That November a report on his work regimen was published. Despite its style, it drew attention to the extraordinary demands of his office:

> Every department of the United States Steel Corporation runs smoothly, simply, noiselessly. Knowing the magnitude of the business transacted at the capitol, in Broadway, a vision of hurrying messengers and of crowds of business men thronging the offices rises before one's mind, but there is no appearance of haste or of crowds. Here are roomy, comfortable, carpeted offices, high above the roar and smoke of the city, where a low-voiced boy asks your business and a secretary comes quietly out of his office to show you in to his chief. Here there seems to be something akin to leisure, for by the time business reaches this height it has assumed a highly condensed form. Mr. Schwab himself, though some humorist who loved the exaggerated and inconsequential has computed his time to be worth $10 a minute, is a calm, steady worker. He is surrounded by a per-

sonal staff of helpers, mostly young men, one a brother, who were associated with him in the Carnegie Company. During office hours he is occupied largely in examining reports, in deciding questions, in answering the few important letters which have sifted through all his assistants, and in holding conferences with the members of his cabinet. Organization is, indeed, the main-spring of success in such a colossal enterprise, and yet it is absolutely necessary to have a man in the executive chair who possesses force and independence, who is ready, if necessity demands, to rise superior to organization, to cut red tape, and do the unexpected thing of genius.[29]

Later accounts gave a favorable assessment of what Schwab achieved. One such biographical note eulogized his presidency:

He filled this responsible office with characteristic ability, applying the methods of the Carnegie management all along the line. If the costs at one furnace or mill were a fraction of a cent higher than those at another, or its products less in proportion to interest and labor charges, it was at once regarded as a weak spot in the system and was given attention. The best men of the technical staff were sent there to study its conditions. Whatever was needed was provided, machinery not up to the standard was scrapped and replaced, managers were shifted, labor stimulated, and the thrill of a new life tingling through its sluggish pulses.[30]

In fact, almost from the start of his presidency Schwab was frustrated in his efforts to direct the enterprise in ways he believed necessary for its fullest success.

There can be no doubt that his achievements at U.S. Steel were considerable. Although he figured that the corporation already controlled about 80 percent of Great Lakes ores, he encouraged acquisition of more reserves. In part this move was made in order to extend and ensure the full integration of operations that had been so successful at Carnegie Steel, but it was also partly to deny control of ore to other companies. In accordance with the vision of improved efficiency sketched at the New York dinner in December 1900, he attempted to rationalize freight shipments and maximize their advantages from the possession of widely spread plants, and he helped integrate formerly separate export sales organizations. Most characteristically, he introduced corporation-wide cost comparisons and consultations to improve practices. Within a few weeks of the start of operations, he was reported to have returned from a visit to the "Valleys" district—the steel producing areas of the Mahoning and Shenango valleys centered on Youngstown, Ohio—with plans for large-scale rationalization there. In fact, though there were numerous plant clo-sures and some transfers, later events revealed that U.S. Steel held on to too many old locations.

Schwab also managed to defeat some proposals from fellow directors that he regarded as undesirable. Chicago business leader Marshall Field, a decisive supporter of Gary in securing the presidency of Federal Steel and now a member of the U.S. Steel board, wanted a structural steel plant for Chicago. He complained to Morgan that Schwab was rude to him over this issue; in conversation years later with Clarence Barron, Schwab claimed his response had been, "Never while I am president; it isn't the place for one."[31] Eventually Chicago was to be seen as a very attractive location for structurals, but in another instance Schwab opposed what would unques-tionably have been a retrograde step. Two directors, John D. Rockefeller and his colleague Henry H. Rogers, had invested in the old and now ob-solescent iron and steel operations in the Troy/Rensselaer area on the Hudson River. They wanted U.S. Steel to buy these plants for $15 million, according to Schwab. Looking back, he said, "I sat down on it and the trade never went through while I was president. Afterwards it did."[32] In fact, the purchase was carried through and approved at the annual meet-ing on 20 April 1903 while he was still president. (One stockholder present had the audacity to inquire what advantages U.S. Steel would gain from the purchase. Gary replied that they had "a very large trade" in Worces-ter and elsewhere in Massachusetts and "it was considered desirable and economical to have as a base of supplies the Troy Steel Products Company adjacent to this territory." The press report of this "only incident out of the routine" concluded with the short sentence, "The answer seemed satisfac-tory to the stockholder."[33])

In spite of Schwab's successes, the performance of the giant group was disappointing, and in important respects it gradually, if unevenly, worsened. On Saturday, 11 May 1901, he told the Industrial Commission that he believed that not only would it continue to dominate capacity but, like Carnegie Steel, it would also operate more efficiently than the rest of the industry. He figured that they controlled between 65 and 75 percent of national production: "It will vary with times. I think in very prosper-ous times the percentage will be smaller; in very dull times it will be very much larger."[34] In fact, not only was there to be a long-term decrease in its share of national production but also, in general and in contrast to the experience at Carnegie Steel, it performed less well than the industry as a whole when trade was poor (see table 5 in appendix B). A decade afterward the Bureau of Corporations attributed this poor performance to the fact that, in times of depression, U.S. Steel tried to maintain prices, while independent companies might cut them to keep up their share of the decreasing business. This was true, but an alternative, if less palatable, explanation was that U.S. Steel, starting in an apparently unassailable position, became less competitive. Over the first years of its existence, its share of national production fell, and though by all previous standards the profits it made were unrivaled, if looked at more closely and in relation to its size U.S. Steel's performance was inferior to that of some of the independent companies from which it had been constituted. For a man of Schwab's background and temperament, accustomed to annual improvements in key indicators, such results were disappointing.

In December 1900 and January 1901 Schwab had calculated the earnings of the main steel concerns that were soon to be amalgamated at about $88 million; in 1902, the corporation's first full year, national steel output was nearly 47 percent higher than in 1900; 1902 earnings at U.S. Steel were $90 million (see table 6 in appendix B). To some extent this relatively poor outcome was a natural result of the disruption of production as the schedules of formerly separate operations had to be realigned, but the amount of such realignment in the early years can easily be exaggerated. Moreover, there had been compensating gains, some of which Schwab had looked toward in his University Club speech. The regular meetings of specialists from various works departments, a tradition begun at Carnegie Steel, were now carried on throughout the whole of U.S. Steel. Schwab later recalled the improvements in iron making that in some respects paralleled the rivalry William R. Jones had fostered fifteen years earlier: "One of the things we did, was to send to each blast furnace manager each month the cost of each of the 100 furnaces in the Steel Corporation, or 90 to be accurate, putting the best furnace at the top, with the name of the manager and the conditions, and the worst at the bottom, with the name of the manager and the conditions, for education and stimulation of the other managers. The result of this was that the first year we made a saving in that department alone of approximately $4 million."[35] However, in some respects it proved difficult to institute radical change. The difficulty was partly because of the corporation's size and partly a consequence of the distance now separating top management from production, but in large part it was also a result of wide differences in personalities and policies.

Because the new corporation was so big, it was inevitable that U.S. Steel would be unwieldy. It was a holding corporation, its constituent production companies in many instances continuing as before, though some were soon merged and in other instances newly acquired units were added to existing subsidiaries. There was an ever present danger of clashes of opinion between the top directors of the corporation, based in New York, the boards of subsidiary companies, situated in one or another of the steel centers, and management at the plant or mine level. There was also division between those who wished to continue the old, devil-take-the-hindmost methods of doing business, an approach that the overwhelming preeminence of U.S. Steel in the industry might have assisted, and on the other hand those who saw a need for less emphasis on survival of the fittest and more on cooperation. An important constraint on freedom of action was that U.S. Steel had to act responsibly, for otherwise a suspicious public and watchful government might call for an investigation and possible dismantling.

One of Schwab's former close associates now regained a measure of the power he had lost in the last fifteen months of Carnegie Steel's existence. J. P. Morgan chose Henry Clay Frick to be a director of U.S. Steel. Given his experience, contacts, and character he eventually became one of the key figures on the board, though not until after Schwab's power had declined. Even so, in May 1901 the latter felt it necessary to explain to Carnegie why, though he had earlier assured him he would not serve in any organization alongside Frick, his promise seemed to have been broken. He pointed out that membership of the board had not been finalized until ten days to two weeks after his election as president, and only then did he learn of Frick's inclusion. Surprised, "especially after what he [Morgan] had said to me and knowing your feeling as well as my own in the matter," Schwab had told Morgan, "this was not according to our undertaking." Assuring Schwab that Frick had agreed not to attend board meetings, Morgan had pleaded for him to stay. "After much reluctance I agreed to do so," Schwab wrote, "but I do wish to say this, that if at the end of the year Frick does not resign from the Board, I shall."[36] Frick remained a member of the U.S. Steel board of directors for more than eighteen years; Schwab had little more than three ahead of him.

In summary, as controller of an agglomeration of natural resources and raw materials, manufacturing plants, transport facilities, and financial resources brought together from many previously independent companies, the top management of the United States Steel Corporation was understandably and inevitably subjected to a variety of internal tensions. As well as the danger of clashes between its center and peripheries, there was conflict between the financial and steel sides, to some extent represented by its executive and finance committees. But in addition, and for Schwab most important of all, because the corporation was a collection of previously independent and competing concerns there was also ample opportunity for clashes between leading personalities and disputes over whether it should be controlled by individuals rather than committees.

The entire range of possible points of disagreement was brought to a focus in a dispute rooted in the different business experiences and in the contrasts of character and personality between the chairman of the executive committee and of the president—between Gary and Schwab. A good deal of the evidence for the course of these disputes is retrospective and partial, indeed partisan. Writing in the mid-1920s, after her earlier "muckraking" style had mellowed into a less critical attitude toward big business, Ida Tarbell, provides useful insights in her biography of Gary, especially in a chapter titled "Who Shall Rule?" As might be expected, Tarbell's account asserts the centrality of and justifications for Gary, with whom she had "interesting and illuminating" conversations. A decade later, in protracted exchanges with journalist Sidney B. Whipple, Schwab presented a very different perspective and was outspoken in his denunciation of those with whom he had disagreed. He spoke harshly about Gary—though earlier and publicly he had loudly praised him. Whipple recorded two particularly interesting comments from Schwab on the man who had displaced him: "Gary and I never agreed much on anything. Gary was a lawyer not a steel man." He compared him with another man who differed greatly from him in character and personality, but whom he respected. Frick was "manly and thoroughly convinced of his own honesty." Gary was not a fighter but "a hedger and swindler." Fortunately, a few sources that permit a more objective assessment of the relationship do exist. A published example is John A. Garraty's biography of financier George Perkins. The fullest and most important record lies in the minute books of the United States Steel Corporation.[37]

A number of individuals made directors or appointed to key committees at U.S. Steel brought with them their old, cutthroat business methods, which proved unacceptable to the new regime Gary gradually put in place, presumably with Morgan's approval. Years later Schwab summed up the difference in two sentences of his testimony to the Stanley Committee: "The Carnegie method was to get all the business it could at any price necessary to get it," and "The policy of the Steel Corporation has not been to stifle or destroy, but by naming a fixed open price, to help stabilize conditions."[38] Understandably, those trained at Carnegie Steel found the transition particularly difficult. Frick, Gayley, and Corey each had to

Elbert H. Gary shortly before the formation
of the United States Steel Corporation.
Reprinted from H. N. Casson, *The Romance of Steel*
(New York: A. S. Barnes, 1907).

adjust to the new, more restrained, open manner of trading. Schwab never found it easy, as he made clear to the Stanley Committee: "When I was president of the Steel Corporation, one of the things that I had to contend with was Judge Gary's opposition to those things that I had been so long accustomed to." When asked how he had managed it, Schwab replied, "I did it without his knowing anything about it."[39]

The old approach was aired at the first two meetings of the executive committee on 9 and 10 April 1901. The committee considered the possibility of raising the price of rails. According to the minutes, "On this question, the President believes it to be a good policy to advance the price now and that, in his judgment, it would attract but little attention." Next day Schwab asked the members what stance they should take regarding a conference being held by the railroads about freight charges on ore from the lakes to the Valleys and Pittsburgh. In this instance he believed it was impossible for them to obtain a more favorable rate than other companies from a given railroad: "Mr. Converse [National Tube] is of the opinion that it is far better to have a high rate, just as high as it can be, if they will give us some definite and distinct rebate or preference in some other way."[40]

The case for autonomy in the subsidiary companies versus centralization of power was also related to decision making in the centers of production rather than in New York. Schwab favored the former approach, as he made clear to the Industrial Commission in early May: "[I]n the making up of the working force of the United States Steel Corporation organization, I was careful to put in no controlling officers, no directing officers, my idea being to make the organization of each subsidiary company as strong within itself as possible—to throw the whole responsibility for the results and the manufacture upon the subsidiary organizations." He received strong backing for his policy from some senior colleagues at the center. Before an important strike began on 1 July 1901, William Edenborn of American Steel and Wire argued strongly that each subsidiary should deal with labor and labor disputes in its own way. Though he now lived in New York, Frick thought that power should reside in the manufacturing districts; as he put it bluntly to Herbert Casson some years later, "It is my opinion that the whole organization of the United States Steel Corporation ought to be in Pittsburgh."[41]

Schwab generally sided with the "steel" men and delegated decision making responsibilities. Even so, from the first executive committee meeting there was a contrary trend to reduce the power of the operating subsidiaries and make them dependent: "It is the opinion of the members of this Committee that the president of this company should arrange by consultation, as soon as may be practicable, to reduce the Directories of the constituent companies to a comparatively small number and that they be taken from the leading and active men engaged in operations at the constituent plants." Although to be managed as before, these subsidiaries "through their proper officers, should frequently consult the president of this company." Gary wanted all proposals for plant improvements to be submitted to the executive committee; Schwab argued that responsibility for minor works must rest with the president of the appropriate subsidiary. Coming to specifics, Gary and Percival Roberts voted that five thousand dollars be the upper limit for authorization at the subsidiary level, while Schwab, Reid, Edmund Converse, and Edenborn favored a ten-thousand-dollar limit. Schwab would leave management of the coke properties in the hands of Thomas Lynch; Gary wanted closer surveillance by the committee.[42]

An important consideration in the power struggle proved to be the division of both personnel and function between the finance and executive committees. The former was designed to have a majority of the members with bank and finance expertise, the latter to be mainly of men with direct experience in manufacturing. The finance committee was chaired in the early months by Morgan's business partner Robert Bacon and later by another of his partners, George Perkins. Its six members included Schwab as president and Gary. Gary was chairman of the eight-member executive committee, on which Charles Steele and Bacon were Morgan representatives. This committee had five "steel" men: Schwab, Edenborn, Converse, Roberts, and Reid.

Strangely perhaps, it was on the executive committee that Schwab suffered his earliest defeat, which involved the central issue. His wish was to be as free as possible from all constraints so that he could run U.S. Steel in much the same way as he had led Carnegie Steel. Morgan was away in Europe when on 1 July Schwab submitted to each executive committee member a suggested amendment to the decision making process. He wanted powers concerning operations to be vested in him and in his corps of assistants. From the chair Gary summarized the issue at stake: "Under the by-laws, as they now exist, do you think the President of the company should really have the affairs of the subsidiary companies in charge, for advice, if you will, by and through his assistants rather than through this committee." He went on to make clear his own position, as recorded in the minutes: "The Chairman stated that it looked to him as if the President has as his Cabinet four men instead of this committee." A sense of the heat generated in this late morning discussion and of the efforts to reduce the friction that caused it comes through the staid sentences of the minute book:

> The President stated that he would not take up ordinary matters of detail with the committee because it was impracticable. The Chairman believed that the head of the financial house [Morgan] had a very different understanding as to how the affairs should be managed, to which the President replied that it was impossible. Mr. Roberts does not believe it should become a personal issue between the President and the committee. . . . he believed it should be brought to the attention of the Board of Directors. The President said that he thought the Chairman should take it up with Mr. Morgan.

The meeting was adjourned with naive aspirations for pacification: "The Chairman stated that what is really wanted is success, peace and harmony."[43]

When the executive committee met again the following afternoon, Percival Roberts moved a resolution that effectively required Schwab to conform to the practice laid down in the by-laws, that is, to operate through the committee rather than directly as chief executive. There was a long discussion, in the course of which Schwab "informed the committee that he wanted to continue his own organization and wants every man to feel that there is a head; in other words, he wants to conduct this organization as similar organizations have been conducted in the past." Gary once again tried to calm matters, but when a vote was taken Schwab was defeated. Next day he unburdened himself to Perkins about this decision: "I am simply heartbroken. . . . I have been hampered, criticized and goaded by incompetent critics, who do not understand the whole steel situation." He threatened resignation.[44] He was to stay on as president for another two years but was increasingly frustrated, was allegedly unwell, and for long periods was away from work. In his absence more power passed to others.

After the defeat of early July Schwab seems, to some extent at least, to have lost the will to fight. For example, only a week later he acquiesced without argument when Roberts suggested that between meetings or during the summer when they would be apart it would be wise to delegate the powers of the executive committee to its chairman. Gary said he was happy with this arrangement if Schwab was, and the latter agreed.[45] Although he had aimed for direct, everyday surveillance and prime decision making powers in the whole of U.S. Steel, he began distancing himself from what was in so many ways his own creation. It marked the beginning of what would eventually become for him a complete change of direction. The first step had already been taken. There would be a long, uncertain phase, and then a much more purposeful retreat.

In May 1901, as what he then called a "flier," Schwab had bought the Bethlehem Steel Company. Now, increasingly disaffected at U.S. Steel, he began to devote more interest to this small operation, though eventually—it is not known when—realizing the unsuitability of a president of U.S. Steel privately owning a competing company, he sold it to Morgan. Then on 26 December 1901 he and Rana Schwab sailed on the French liner *La Savoie* for a holiday in Europe.[46] What might have been a short period of rest and regrouping became an occasion for further crises, however. Schwab went to the Riviera, visited Monte Carlo, and was reported to have gambled in the Casino. Various people were scandalized that the head of the world's greatest company should behave in such a fashion. Carnegie felt betrayed, his dismay being mirrored in the letter he wrote on 19 January to George Lauder: "This folly of Schwab's hurts—papers full of it. . . . His denial is no denial—I feel it keenly. Of course his enemies are jubilant. . . . I should not be surprised if it resulted in Schwab's resigning—He cabled offering to do so when Morgan wired him stop—I cabled and got his reply, sorry he made a mistake and so on."[47] Predictably, Gary was shocked by the president's behavior, for as one account put it Gary was a man who was "quite devoid of humor and approached his work with an almost pathetic seriousness." He was said to not play cards because it was below the dignity of the head of U.S. Steel. Schwab believed that when reports of his visit to Monte Carlo reached headquarters, Gary called on Morgan in the hope of securing his removal from the presidency.[48] Schwab in turn made things worse with some very lame denials. To Perkins he wrote, "I have been coming here for 15 years. . . . I always visit the Casino on account of its orchestra." The excuse he gave for a later visit was even more remarkable: "I have never been in Monte Carlo," and then he capped everything with the statement, "I never gamble!" Morgan was more sanguine about the affair than either Carnegie or Gary. After returning from Europe, Schwab went to assure Morgan he had done nothing to be ashamed of: "I didn't do anything behind closed doors." Morgan is said to have replied, "That is what doors are for."[49]

Schwab came back to the United States on 16 February 1902, two days before his fortieth birthday.[50] He resumed his duties but seemed lackluster in comparison with the dynamic and visionary top executive of a year before. A few weeks later he failed to take back an important development sector from the control of the chairman. The executive committee was discussing a major program for expansion of coking coal production and coke manufacture in the Pocahontas district of West Virginia. Gary had said they were to build twelve hundred ovens "right away," and Thomas Lynch had been coming to see him about it. Steele understood that development of these properties had been more or less in the hands of Gary, but "so far as that is a manufacturing question, it ought to be in the hands of the President." Schwab's uncharacteristic response was, "I think it is a mistake. However I am quite satisfied." He then roused himself: "Everything of that kind has always come to me naturally through Mr. Lynch." But when Gary responded, "I think it does not refer at all to operation," Schwab showed little fight: "The development of coal properties is so closely associated with operation in my opinion, that I do not think you can very well separate them. It does not make the slightest difference to me however." Four weeks later the two clashed over the location of a new tube making facility. Despite his long labors planning the Conneaut mill less than eighteen months previous, Schwab now defended expansion at McKeesport. Gary, with sound reasons, suggested the new facility be in Lorain.[51]

On 20 August 1902 Morgan returned from a holiday in Europe, and Schwab had a long interview with him before he sailed away himself next day. Press reports indicated he was not ill but that "his nervous system has been subjected to very severe strain." The idea that he might resign the presidency was mentioned but denied. On his arrival in Le Havre he received a letter from Carnegie wishing him complete recovery. He traveled by rail to Paris and on to Aix-les-Bains, where he was expected to take a rest cure for a month or maybe two.[52] While still resting there a few weeks later he was at a low ebb when he wrote to Carnegie, "I leave here tonight for Como. Doctor insists upon absolute quiet for the next six weeks. I am no better—in fact, not so well. After Como I expect to go somewhere on the Riviera. Probably Cannes and may take a yacht. . . . I am much discouraged at times, but the Doctors assure me that ultimate recovery will be sure to follow." Less solicitous than Carnegie, Frick, writing to a friend in Scotland, contrasted the general "good shape" of U.S. Steel with that of its head: "It is unfortunate that its President does not stand as well as the President of such an organization should, but the organization contains some very good men."[53]

Month after month, Schwab's illness continued and he remained in Europe. Could a man who had seemed to be the key figure in the whole vast structure of the corporation really be so essential if it continued to operate successfully without him? After all, a few days before leaving for Europe he had assured Perkins that James Gayley "is quite capable of attending to all my duties." In any case, those who had struggled to limit his powers during the summer months of 1901 must have further strengthened their positions in his absence. From a distance he kept in close touch with affairs at home, but important decisions were being made without him. In December 1902 the corporation bought the Union Steel Company, which now operated integrated works at both Sharon and Donora, Pennsylvania, the latter mill being one that two years before, in conclave at Skibo, he had opposed incorporating into Carnegie Steel. On 18 December 1902 Andrew Carnegie entertained twenty-four of his Carnegie Steel associates at a housewarming dinner in his new home at Fifth Avenue and Ninety-first Street. Schwab, so long the crown prince of that group, was absent. On the other hand he took steps to ensure that at Christmas his memory was kept warm in the mill town where his career had begun, as he and Rana donated two thousand dollars to be distributed to the poor of Braddock and adjoining boroughs. As the year ended Joseph Schwab was reported as saying his brother had never thought of resigning the presidency and would be back at his desk in a month. On Christmas Day, in a rare newspaper interview, Frick felt it necessary to deny rumors that he was to succeed to the presidency of U.S. Steel, but less than two weeks later he was appointed to the finance committee and began to be consulted as an authority on a number of important developments.[54] Soon Perkins was canvassing the board for reactions to the idea that if Schwab returned it should be to a less exacting office than that of president, perhaps in a special post as chairman of the board of directors—ironically the sort of honorary position that saved Frick's status in Carnegie Steel early in 1895. Schwab eventually arrived back in New York on the *Kronprinz Wilhelm* on 17 March 1903; he had been away from his office for seven months. The press reported that his health was "completely restored." As Schwab later revealed, he had then asked his fellow directors and J. P. Morgan to accept his resignation, but they would not do so. For a time all seemed to go well, and at the annual meeting of stockholders held on April 20 in Hoboken, New Jersey, he took the chair "with the glow of health in his face, bright of eye, and elastic of movement." Two weeks later, at a full meeting of the board, he was unanimously reelected president for the coming year.[55]

Nine days after his confirmation in the presidency he made a triumphant return to Homestead. The occasion was the dedication of the C. M. Schwab Free Industrial School, built and to be maintained at his expense. The town was in a holiday mood, all business being stopped for the day. Schwab's dedicatory address was greatly appreciated—as one report put it, "[W]hat a contrast between these days and those of 1892." But below the surface things were far from satisfactory. On 10 July, Corey was appointed assistant to Schwab, ostensibly in order to help him in his presidential duties. Soon he was performing the active duties of president. Then, at a regular meeting of the U.S. Steel board on 4 August, Schwab offered his resignation. This time it was accepted. He was to continue as a director and member of the finance committee. When the meeting was over a statement was issued in which he explained that in the immediate future his attention would be concentrated on recovery of his health: "I am suffering from nervous trouble and am threatened with a complete breakdown. . . . I am going back to Atlantic City to rest and try to get well." More than thirty years after these dramatic events, in testimony during the inquiry into alleged tax evasion by Andrew Mellon, Schwab gave the simplest but perhaps most adequate explanation of why he had been frustrated and eventually toppled from the presidency: "There were too many people to consult with and advise with. I craved the old authority I had in the Carnegie Company. In other words, I wanted to be 'It.'"[56]

Behind the façade representing Schwab's resignation as a reluctant response to a medical necessity, the palace revolution that began in early summer 1901 had been completed. There were various signs of the working out of this process, some of them circumstantial, some constituting more direct evidence. When Schwab had returned from Europe in spring, Perkins, who had been looking after his interests in his absence, sent a message telling him to say nothing about his health until they had spoken. He had made certain that plans for proposed changes had been kept quiet and would be discussed after Schwab's return.[57] On 4 August, far more was done than merely replacing an ailing president with a new one. In the course of his statement that day, Schwab said, "As a result of the meetings this afternoon my work has been divided." The official U.S. Steel announcement made clear, in part explicitly and for the rest by implication, that at the top, a full-time dedication to the corporation's interests was replacing something less wholehearted: "The office of chairman of the board of directors was created and Judge EH Gary was elected to that position and will continue to devote his whole time to the business of the corporation." The announcement did not indicate specifically that the executive committee would be abolished, but it revealed that the powers that body had exercised had been dispersed—at the very time at which Gary's standing had so obviously increased: "An advisory committee, to consist of three directors, besides the president, to consider and make recommendations concerning questions of manufacturing, transportation, and operation, was created and EC Converse, William Edenborn, and DG Reid were elected as members of this committee." Corey would devote his entire attention to the practical and technical sides of the business and would receive material aid for this purpose from this advisory committee. The commercial press recognized the significance of these changes for the power of the president: "The new president has entered upon his duties and it may be authoritatively stated with his election the steel corporation has inaugurated a new policy. There will be less centralization of power and increased responsibility in the work of the various committees."[58] This statement failed to spell out that the chairman had now become the dominant power.

Schwab's reported continuing ill health did not prevent him from

working. Even before his resignation he had leased and was having fit-
ted up a suite of offices on the fourth floor of the Empire building at 71
Broadway, the same building in which the U.S. Steel offices were situated.
It was said that when he was well again he would take personal charge of
the affairs of the Bethlehem Steel Company and of other large enterprises
in which he had important financial interests. In the meantime he remained the largest single stockholder in U.S. Steel. Before long he began
to make his presence felt on the finance committee. On 1 September he
wrote to Perkins to complain about the forms of organization adopted for
the Ambridge development of American Bridge and in their Pocahontas
coal properties. A few weeks later he voted against the decision to declare
a dividend of only 0.5 percent on common stock for the quarter, arguing
that from his own past statements, stockholders would assume they would
always be paid 1 percent.[59] Yet, from the start it must have been realized
that a man of his talents, experience, and drive would not long be content
to remain merely a critical member of a U.S. Steel committee.

On 26 July 1904, just short of a year after he gave up the presidency,
Schwab's resignation from the board was presented at the regular quarterly meeting of the directors of the United States Steel Corporation. It
was said that he had made the decision in order to devote more time to
other business interests. Even now he retained large financial interests. It
was a year of recession and of falling stocks, but in late September values
began to advance. The opportunity was irresistible to a man of his character. On 28 September, while in San Francisco, he invested $1.5 million in
U.S. Steel preferred stock; over the previous three months he was said to
have bought $10 million worth of its securities.[60]

Although from the end of 1904 Schwab was actively involved in developments at Bethlehem Steel, he still had occasional close contact with
his old company. For example, late in 1909 he visited George G. Crawford,
president of the Tennessee Coal, Iron and Railroad Company, a U.S. Steel
subsidiary company for two years. He had known Crawford when the latter worked at the Edgar Thomson furnaces in the mid-1890s. Now Crawford took him through the Ensley works at Birmingham, Alabama, and
outlined to him prospective developments in the area. No statement was
issued, "but the general understanding is that advice was given or recommendations made by the prominent steel man."[61]

Publicly, Schwab often praised the leadership that Gary exercised in
the steel industry for almost a quarter century after he himself had left
U.S. Steel. In testimony given in the dissolution suit against the United
States Steel Corporation he seemed to approve of Gary's policy of col-

laborative price fixing to achieve stability; he did not point out how this kind of benevolent despotism had benefited independent companies such as his own. He attended the "Gary Dinners" held over a two-year period from late 1907, when price maintenance was threatened by bad trade and during which Judge Gary harangued his fellow steel makers to hold the line. At the last of the dinners, in October 1909, Schwab was chosen to present a gold vase to Gary on behalf of the industry. In doing so he said, "I am thankful for the opportunity of saying one thing, Judge Gary. You and I were associated in business for some years. We had many differences, and I am glad of this public opportunity to say that with my bounding enthusiasm and optimism I was wrong in most instances—indeed, in all instances—and you were right." The generosity of his remark was spoiled by the excessiveness of its form and the high probability that he did not really mean what he said.[62]

In fact, though Gary was a man eminently suited to establish the respectability of the steel industry after years in which its methods had often been questionable, Schwab never had much in common with him. Often still referred to as "Judge" in light of his former legal career, Gary continued to be olympian, cold, humorless, and cautious, more at home in a law office than a steel mill. Schwab's natural antipathy to such a man was further stimulated by the way in which he had been deprived of power as president of U.S. Steel. Late in life, Schwab put on record his account of their relationship: "Judge Gary, who had no real knowledge of the steel business, forever opposed me on some of the methods and principles that I had seen worked out with Carnegie—methods that had made the Carnegie Company the most successful in the world." He thought it was Gary who was largely responsible for excluding John W. Gates from the U.S. Steel board, but he was clearly guilty of wild exaggeration when he reckoned this move was part of a policy of "keeping on the board men who knew nothing about steel and who were merely financiers and of keeping off the board all those who actually knew anything about the making of steel." He once accused Gary, regarded by a large part of the public as a model of business rectitude, of looking for a $15 million rake-off from a steel company promotion and claimed he had told him, "Judge Gary, you're the biggest liar and hypocrite and the most dishonest man I've ever known."[63]

Even after he left U.S. Steel Schwab remained in close contact with Pittsburgh and continued to command respect there. On Thanksgiving Day 1904 the *Pittsburgh Press* published a piece on "Thanksgiving thoughts" by prominent men. A contribution from Schwab dominated the page. In it he praised the city's brains and brawn and forecast renewed prosperity now that the national election was over. He finished with a homily that may have provided encouragement for thousands and was certainly appropriate advice for himself: "If in the past year you have not been as successful as you wished, do not give up in despair. Be alert to every opportunity that comes in your path and, by perseverance, you may soon achieve your goal."[64] Though he had been forced from the peak of the steel world, he would spend the rest of his working life struggling toward the top again.

Speculation and Corporate Growth

One of the outstanding features of American economic growth was the rapid development of the metallurgical industries during the first half of Schwab's life. He was two years old when production of pig iron first passed 1 million tons. At age forty-one, as he transferred his interests and talents from U.S. Steel to Bethlehem Steel, it was at a new high of 18 million tons. In the remaining almost half of his life production reached highs of more than twice this 1903 figure. At his birth there was effectively no bulk steel industry; before his thirtieth birthday the United States was the world's biggest steel producer. Its leadership was unchallenged during and beyond his lifetime. It was a period uniquely favorable for dreams of apparently unending business expansion in basic industry—and for their realization.

During this period of unprecedented and, relatively speaking, never to be repeated rates of growth, steel making underwent a geographical change on an unparalleled scale. In the advanced European countries and even in the vast Russian empire there were shifts in the distribution of population and therefore in the markets for iron and steel, but generally these were small-scale, slow processes. By contrast the spread of settlement and speed of economic development together transformed the economic geography of the United States in the decades following the Civil War and thereby the distribution of outlets for steel. In 1860 the nine states of New England and the mid-Atlantic region contained 10.7 million of the nation's 31.4 million inhabitants. Another 6.9 million lived in the eastern north-central region, leaving 13.8 million or 43.9 percent in the rest of the country. Forty years later the national total was 76.0 million, of whom only 21.0 million were in the two northeastern divisions and 16.0 million in the eastern north-central region, leaving 39.0 million or 51.3 percent in other census regions. In terms of consumption of iron and steel

the westward shift was even more pronounced. There were various com-
ponents of the changes in demand—wire for western farms and steel in
various forms for agricultural implements and machinery, but by far the
most important was railroads, especially in the form of rails for new track
and renewals. Throughout this period rails were the most important steel
product. In 1860 New England and the middle Atlantic states contained
10,010 of the national total of 30,630 miles of railroad; 12,080 miles were in
the West. By 1896 the mileage of lines in the nation was almost six times
that of 1860. The figure for New England and the middle Atlantic states
was now 28,630 miles, less than three times the 1860 figure; the West now
had 104,270 miles. Steel mills well placed for shipping to western markets
were at an advantage in meeting this shift. Chicago was the ideal location.
Pittsburgh and Johnstown had to struggle to hold their own. For mills east
of the Appalachians the situation was even worse, not simply as a result of
increasing distance from the main areas of new construction but because
of the existence of, to use an expressive term, the "intervening opportunity," that is, the supply from nearer plants. Putting the matter in a wider
context, west of the Appalachians were producers not only enjoying easier
access to the biggest markets but also having the best location for access
to iron ore from the head of the Great Lakes and coke from the northern
parts of the Appalachian plateau. There were of course important markets
for steel in the East—which were sheltered by distance from western competition—as for instance in plate for shipbuilding or iron and later steel
beams for bridge and building construction work, as well as significant
rail consumption in replacement of track or for some extensions. There
were important eastern and overseas sources of iron ore. Generally, however, on both the supply and the demand side, the East was increasingly
at a disadvantage. That situation was summed up by the predicament of
the iron and steel operations at Bethlehem with which Schwab's fortunes
were to be identified for little short of two-thirds of his business life.

From the start, character and personality had been deeply inter-
twined with considerations of raw materials and markets in the development of the eastern iron industry. Indeed, as the Pennsylvania state
geologist, John Peter Lesley, recognized in print and Andrew Carnegie
even more persuasively in practice, human resources were if anything of
greater importance in ensuring business success than natural endowment,
for men could take initiatives or respond positively to challenges. In 1859,
in the course of a masterly survey of the nation's iron industry, Lesley remarked of the eastern counties of Pennsylvania that rather than being especially well endowed by nature, "The reputation of this State for iron has

resulted more from the energetic, persevering German use, for a century of years, of what ores do exist."[65] In 1853–1854 an important step in the development of the region's industry was taken when the wealthy Philadelphia entrepreneur Joseph Wharton became associated with the operation and reorganization of the zinc industry in Bethlehem, on the lower Lehigh River. From zinc Wharton moved on with local men to promote local iron smelting under the title of the Sauconna Iron Company. In 1860 this operation was renamed the Bethlehem Iron Company. Over the next forty years Wharton increased his interests until he became the largest Bethlehem stockholder, playing an important part in determining the way in which the iron company grew. There were other decisive personal influences on its development path and reputation.

A visitor in 1852 described the Saucon valley near Bethlehem as a "veritable paradise," but it was already being transformed by new conditions of transport and the opportunities they provided for manufacturing. In short, like Pittsburgh, though on a much smaller scale, this area was becoming a paradise for entrepreneurs rather than for nature. The Lehigh Coal and Navigation Company had opened the rich anthracite deposits that lay in the hill country to the north of the valley. At the end of the 1830s the same company brought the iron master David Thomas from South Wales to initiate in the coal valleys of eastern Pennsylvania the smelting of iron using anthracite as the furnace fuel. In 1846 the Lehigh Valley Railroad (LVR) was incorporated, and nine years later the first coal train ran from Mauch Chunk to Easton. In 1860, looking for increased business, the LVR's general superintendent and another associate in the Bethlehem iron venture, Robert H. Sayre, brought John Fritz from Johnstown to build the new ironworks—an early example of the transfer of talent from this pioneering center, which little over a decade later would take William R. Jones to the Edgar Thomson works. In six years at Cambria Iron, Fritz had pioneered important innovations, particularly in the rolling mills, which had made it one of the nation's most efficient and commercially successful mills. Fritz remained at Bethlehem for more than thirty years, devoting exceptional talents in its service, though not always with full backing from its directors.

The first Bethlehem blast furnace was blown in July 1860. Completion of a second stack was delayed by the Civil War, and it was not operational until spring 1867. Bethlehem Iron initially produced wrought iron and iron rails, but Sayre had used imported steel rails by 1864 and soon recognized that they were greatly superior and that the future of rail production lay in that direction. After an inspection of European Bessemer practice it was decided that Bethlehem Iron should build a steel works. In one respect the timing was unfortunate, for the date of its first Bessemer blow, 4 October 1873, was less than three weeks after the failure of the banking house of Jay Cooke. On the other hand the switch to steel enabled Bethlehem to sidestep the danger of being trapped by what proved the beginning of a long-term decline and then complete collapse of the iron rail trade. In fact, despite the reputation of the mid-1870s for depression, Bessemer rail production continued to increase.

By 1876 Bethlehem had six blast furnaces and could make twenty thousand tons of iron rails and fifty thousand tons of Bessemer rails a year. Initially, it was well served by iron ore from local and New Jersey mines, with some high-grade ores coming from the Mediterranean. The fuel used was anthracite. Over the years the competitive position of eastern firms was undermined by changing circumstances. These included the growth of iron ore shipments down the Great Lakes and recognition that coke was a superior fuel, even in the East, where it was first mixed with anthracite and soon began to displace it. Year by year a higher percentage of national consumption of steel was in the West. As these changes occurred, national capacity to produce grew more quickly than demand, rail prices fell, and competition became keener. In 1873 the average price of Bessemer rails at Pennsylvania works was $120.50; for 1877, 1878, and 1879 it was only $45.33. Then, after rising for two years, from 1882 onward it was below $40.00. Bethlehem, so recently opened and extended, began to seem a marginal producer. It had to adjust or fail.

In the late 1870s John Fritz produced plans for diversification that included production of structural steel. The board rejected his proposal. Another opportunity was taken up, though not until opposition from the general manager, Garrett Linderman, was removed by his death in 1885. Already Fritz and Wharton had visited European gun and armor plate plants and had resolved to enter these trades as the United States decided to construct a modern navy. In 1886 Bethlehem Iron secured large contracts for gun and armor and over the next few years invested heavily in open hearth steel works and forge and mill capacity to produce these armaments. From the early 1890s Bethlehem divided government orders for armor plate with Carnegie Steel, which also was an active rival for foreign business, especially with the Russian empire. Carnegie did not compete in ordnance. Meanwhile, Bethlehem continued to fare so much less well in its old specialty of rails that it eventually became an almost nonentity in that business. It failed to make a successful entry into the expanding mild steel plate business, boosted as it was by the growth, though uneven, of American merchant shipbuilding. Recognizing that it was well situated to supply a crescent of yards from Boston to Baltimore and beyond, by early 1897 the company was completing an excellent plate mill. However, the Bethlehem board then decided not to go further and sold the mill to Carnegie Steel, whose experts were delighted with their coup. Re-erected at Homestead, it proved a great success.

By the 1890s the problems of eastern steel makers centered on long hauls for both Great Lakes ore and Appalachian plateau coke and difficult access to western markets. On the other hand new opportunities seemed to be opening. There were rich orefields overseas—and even some promising if smaller ones within the East. Byproduct coking not only gave higher yields than the beehive ovens of Connellsville along the Youghiogheny River but also opened up the possibility of using some poorer but nearer coking coals and at the same time providing a supply of gas for steel and mill operations. Above all, new markets were emerging in shipbuilding and in the construction not only of bridges but also of steel-framed commercial buildings, growing rapidly through the 1890s as the "skyscraper" made its way into the vocabulary and into the metropolitan landscape. Looking at the East it was too easy for those schooled in old ways to ignore the fact that there was fire amid the ashes. In the meantime the long-established leading figures in Bethlehem—Wharton, Robert Sayre, Elisha P. Wilbur, and Robert P. Linderman—all wanted to retire from the business.

In 1898 Carnegie reassured himself and other Pittsburgh interests that "steel cannot be manufactured on the Atlantic seaboard under any circumstances in competition with her." Two years later in an article for the "Century Number" of the *New York Evening Post* he spelled out his assessment of the situation in the East more fully. He found support for his thesis even in its successes: "The transfer of the great Lackawanna Iron and Steel Works of Scranton, Pennsylvania[,] to Buffalo, and the splendid triumphs of the Bethlehem Steel Company in Pennsylvania in armor, guns and forgings as specialities [*sic*], which give it a unique and commanding position, are proofs that, for the making of ordinary steel the East is not a favorable location."[66] The achievements he quoted were real, but the deduction he made from them was soon proved false. The drift of circumstances was not as firmly set against the region as he suggested. In its recent past entrepreneurs had failed to tackle problems and had let opportunities slip. Within six months of Carnegie's self-satisfying evaluation of eastern prospects, an entrepreneurial link was made that transformed the situation of Bethlehem Steel. Ironically, the entrepreneurship that transformed the company had been nurtured and honed at the very heart of the Carnegie Steel Company. When Schwab purchased the Bethlehem Steel Company in the spring of 1901, he described the transaction as a "flier." Before long it would become his life's work to make Bethlehem Steel an industry leader.

The first stage in Schwab's association with Bethlehem Steel also involved him in the revival of the shipbuilding industry. Between 1894 and 1897 the annual average gross tonnage of seagoing shipping launched in the United States was just under fifty thousand tons, a mere 3.8 percent of the world total. However, around 1900 there were strong indications that the situation was beginning to change. Naval construction increased as overseas ambitions and responsibilities were extended. At the same time there was a broad realization that the booming economy's international trade might sustain a much larger merchant marine and thus reduce the nation's dependence on foreign shipping. For a time expectations were bolstered further by a belief that Republican administrations might pass a bill for a liberal shipping subsidy. Year after year there was a strong growth in merchant tonnages launched, and the number of shipbuilding companies and their reputations advanced rapidly. Before 1890 only two yards on the Atlantic seaboard had built vessels larger than five thousand tons' displacement; within eighteen years eight shipyards could undertake work of the heaviest type. Six of them had already completed first-class battleships and cruisers, and an American writer suggested that four had capacity and equipment rivaling anything in Europe.[67] As these changes occurred, shipyards became more attractive as market outlets for steel.

In the 1890s Andrew Carnegie began to advocate a large expansion in shipbuilding. In 1898 for instance he wrote to the *Iron Trade Review*, recommending the mid-Atlantic coast as a location for major yards. He cleverly managed to explain why he did not follow his own advice: "If I were a younger man, or, rather, if I did not belong to a concern so enterprising as to employ all my capital and give me pleasurable occupation watching over its progress and success, I should be greatly inclined to enter upon the building of ships somewhere near New York Harbor. There would be no warships or Atlantic liners open for bids in any part of the world which the New York yard would not have something to say about."[68] Two years later, after his ejection from a managerial role in the Carnegie Steel Company, Henry Clay Frick became involved with the major new venture of the New York Shipbuilding Company—which, however, notwithstanding its name, was located at Camden, New Jersey. By this time another shipbuilder, this time a major holding company, was at an early stage of formation. It was to be the means whereby Schwab became a major factor in both naval and merchant shipbuilding. His participation also raised important questions about business ethics.

Sometime during autumn 1899 John W. Young, having had some connection with the Newport News Shipyard, made contact with Lewis Nixon, who had attended both the U.S. Naval Academy and the Royal Naval College at Greenwich, in Great Britain. As a member of the construction corps of the navy Nixon had been involved in the early 1890s in the design of the battleships *Oregon, Indiana,* and *Massachusetts.* After that he worked at Cramp's shipyard in Philadelphia before starting the Crescent Shipyard at Elizabeth, New Jersey, in 1895. Between the fall of 1899 and summer 1901 Nixon and Young put together a new holding trust they called the United States Shipbuilding Company, which would control the Crescent yard, the Samuel L. Moore yard, some smaller Atlantic coast yards, and the major Pacific coast operations of the Union Iron Works. Struggling with serious problems of general business confidence, it was not until late spring 1902 that their company could be floated. By this time the manufacturer and small-scale financier Daniel L. Dresser was also involved in the venture. In addition to those already listed the company now included four more important eastern yards: Harlan and Hollingsworth, Bath Iron Works, Hyde Windlass, and the Eastern Shipbuilding Company.

Fearing that without such major established yards as Newport News and Cramp's in Philadelphia the bonds of U.S. Shipbuilding might fail to attract sufficient investors, the promoters saw a need to boost its standing by association with a famous name. In May 1902, after Nixon approached him, Schwab agreed to invest $500,000 in their new company on condition that it bought its steel from U.S. Steel. But then, on 12 June, when he met Dresser and Nixon for lunch, things took a very different turn. Having had a good deal of experience with the production of shipbuilding material at Homestead Schwab now recommended that the promoters include a steel works within their organization so as to provide their own ship plate. He suggested Bethlehem Steel might be suitable, apparently adding that it would be easy to obtain it. Accordingly, he repurchased the company from Morgan, paying $7.2 million in cash—some $300,000 less than its nominal capital value three years before—and transferred it to the new United States Shipbuilding Company. He asked the new corporation for $9 million in cash as payment for his company, but when this amount proved beyond its means he accepted instead $20 million in stock, half preferred and half common, and $10 million in bonds in the new company. As a result, when U.S. Shipbuilding was incorporated on 17 June 1902, Schwab, because of Bethlehem Steel's role, controlled $30 million of the total $71 million of its capital in stocks and bonds. To the Morgan syndicate he transferred $2.5 million of his stock in U.S. Shipbuilding, to represent its profit on the deal. Remarkably, he additionally managed to secure a guarantee that U.S. Shipbuilding would pay to Bethlehem Steel dividends amounting to $900,000 per annum and that steel manufacture should not be merged or consolidated with the rest of the company.

The charter for the incorporation of the United States Shipbuilding Company in the state of New Jersey provided for ten directors, all of whom were officers in the shipbuilding companies absorbed. When an executive committee of five was formed early in September 1902 Dresser, Nixon, and Henry T. Scott of Union Iron Works represented the interests of the shipyards and E. M. McIlvain and Max Pam, those of the steel company.[69] From the outside U.S. Shipbuilding looked impressive and promising, but it soon became obvious that it was insecure. Its prospectus was false; valuations of yards and expected earnings had been exaggerated. Some years later, looking back to the formation of the company, former U.S. senator James Smith Jr. of New Jersey described the accountant's financial reports on the value and earnings of the subsidiary companies as "a mass of willful misstatements." In one case a yard bought for less than $100,000 was made to represent $2 million worth of stock in the company books.[70]

From time to time Nixon issued reassuring statements, but by spring 1903 there were rumors of difficulties. The earlier national increase in tonnages launched had once more passed over into decline, and U.S. Shipbuilding was suffering operating and financial problems. It was said to have under contract $25 million in government work, but the greater part of it was running behind the time specified for completion. Bankers recognized that the corporation was heavily overcapitalized; the public had been cool and its stock issue failed. By summer it was known it might not be able to pay the six months' interest due on its first mortgage bonds on 1 July. At one stage the organizers had forecast it might earn more than $5 million a year; later projections for earnings in the first year were $2.2 million for the shipyards and $1.5 million for the steel division. In fact Bethlehem Steel earned $2 million, but profits in shipbuilding operations were only $830,000. The steel company refused to advance cash to bale out the yards, but so as to relieve their distress Schwab advanced an additional $2 million as working capital. In return for this loan it was agreed that his second mortgage bonds should be replaced with first mortgage bonds. In case of collapse he would gain control of the whole conglomerate.

By July 1903 the United States Shipbuilding Company was declared insolvent. A receiver was appointed to examine the failure, looking for any fraud in its formation and mismanagement in its affairs. Lewis Nixon resigned as president. Schwab, saying that he had been induced by Nixon and Dresser to sell Bethlehem to their company, indicated he was anxious to take it back from them—even though he was still president of U.S. Steel.[71] The collapse of U.S. Shipbuilding helped along the general trend toward recession of trade and a decline in share values, which brought the common stock of United States Steel down to only 12.50 per share. It also marked the beginning of a process that delivered the group into Schwab's hands. The report from the receiver was delivered in October. It contained, as authors Henry Seager and Charles Gulick put it, a "somewhat exaggerated account of the causes of the failure."[72] Culpable indifference to the interests of their company by Young, Dresser, and others was said to be the main cause of failure, but the shipbuilding interests had been outvoted on their own board by Bethlehem representatives who had ensured that spending continued at the steel plant while its profits could not be used to help save the shipbuilding properties. Understandably, Schwab rejected as untrue and malicious the receiver's charge that he had aimed to wreck the U.S. Shipbuilding Company.

In the course of 1904 a reorganization scheme was arranged. Under it the preferred and common stockholders in U.S. Shipbuilding received nothing, but Bethlehem Steel acquired control of the shipyards at a redemption price of $156.25 for every $1,000 bond. On 25 October the Wilmington, Delaware, operations of Harlan and Hollinsgworth were sold under order of the United States Court. The reorganization committee of the United States Shipbuilding Company acquired the operations for $685,000. Schwab attended the sale. A month before, he was at a public auction in San Francisco at which the Union Iron Works was sold to the same committee for $1.7 million. Speaking there, he assured his listeners that the plant would be enlarged and be the finest in the United States if not the world.[73]

By January 1905 Nixon, Dresser, and Young had gone and a new Bethlehem Steel Corporation had been formed with capital of $30 million. It controlled not only the steel plant but also the U.S. Shipbuilding yards. Schwab and his associates dominated its board. They began weeding out the poorer yards, and by spring that year the new company had disposed of the Bath Iron Works and the Hyde Windlass Company. In December

1904 these two properties had been recorded in the Bethlehem books as representing $600,000 in capital. They were sold for $825,000. The money raised was used to help finance a rapid expansion in steel.

Though the shipbuilding venture left Schwab in control of an important part of American shipbuilding capacity, it dented his reputation. The receiver had sharply criticized him, characterizing him as a man who, "while thoroughly understanding the intricacies of 'higher finance' seemed to have overlooked the requirements of common fairness." The arrangements involving Bethlehem Steel were shown to have been grossly biased, with Max Pam, Schwab's attorney, making sure that although Schwab had nominally sold his interest in Bethlehem to the shipbuilding group, "his client should receive everything, while he parted with nothing!" After the adverse publicity of the failure and inquiries into its causes, it was made known that Schwab was doing his best to make things good. He was said to have sold $2 million worth of high-grade securities so as to pay compensation of $1.9 million in cash to friends he had invited to join him in the failed company. A few days later the press carried a more personal, heart-warming story. The widow of Benjamin Wood, who had been publisher of the *Daily News* in New York, had had great difficulties in trying to run the newspaper after her husband's death, and she had ventured and lost her entire fortune in what was called the "shipbuilding bubble." In her morning mail on 9 August 1904 she received a check for $264,000, in full compensation for her investment. It was signed by Charles M Schwab.[74] Despite his efforts, it is not easy to quarrel with the conclusion of a distinguished economic historian a generation later, that "so low was the business morality of the period that the man who profited most by the transaction was rather admired for his cleverness than condemned for his ruthlessness." At the time, the receiver was more concise—it had been "an artistic swindle."[75]

4 ❦ Bethlehem Steel

Shortly before World War I Schwab said that, since he had no children, his best efforts and enthusiasm had been devoted to the task of "building a big business in Pennsylvania." Over many years he had played a vital part in the rise of Carnegie Steel and thereby helped the trans-Appalachian district of the state to achieve national leadership in iron and steel production; in the new century his exceptional talents were applied to operations and expansion in the eastern parts of the state. In some respects, Bethlehem Steel seemed an unlikely candidate for the eminence he planned for it.

In rail production Bethlehem had become a nonentity; in armor it had already become the leading company. Its only rival in armor plate was Carnegie Steel and in heavy ordnance, Midvale Steel of Philadelphia. The armor trade was thus a duopoly and, as far as home outlets were concerned, also a monopsony. There was interchange of information and, for government contracts, a degree of collusion between the two companies. (A few years later Midvale also began to make armor.) As general superintendent of Homestead, Schwab had long had contact with their rival. At the end of October 1893 Carnegie, Frick, and Schwab were invited to lunch and shown through the works by Bethlehem's president, Robert Linderman, and its eminent metallurgist, Russell W. Davenport. On a return visit to Pittsburgh the following year, Robert Sayre met up with Schwab.[1] A year later, as Bethlehem won its first important overseas orders for armor plate in competition with Carnegie Steel, Schwab also learned of their plans to build four more open hearth furnaces and to expand capacity in commercial grades of steel plate. Shortly before learning of those plans, Schwab widened his general knowledge of eastern conditions, visiting and reporting on two relatively small but by no means negligible competitors there, Phoenix and Pencoyd, operators in another trade central to Homestead success, structural steel.[2]

At this time Carnegie seems to have expressed fears that Schwab might be enticed eastward; in June 1894 Frick wrote to reassure him—though he gave no reason for his conviction: "There is no danger of Schwab leaving us, and I should be sorry to have him do so, but if such should occur you need have no uneasiness of any one of our rivals taking him, particularly Bethlehem." Soon afterward, Schwab seemed to indicate he shared the belief of his colleagues that the East was a seriously disadvantaged competitor. Responding to an inquiry from Frick, he calculated that Pittsburgh's cost advantages relative to producing in the East should be greater in the fuel-intensive open hearth process than in the low-fuel Bessemer process. At current prices he figured the cost of coal per ton of open hearth steel was $0.23 in Pittsburgh, $0.58 in Chicago, and $0.89 in the East. In the last region scrap was more expensive than basic pig iron.[3] Two years later, when margins were extremely close in rails and negotiations had been under way among leading producers, Schwab indicated that he regarded Bethlehem to be a marginal producer in commercial steels. He, John Gates, and Walter Scranton had decided to divide the national rail business between their companies, and Bethlehem Steel and Pennsylvania Steel were to be told "plainly" what had been done. Reporting this decision, Schwab added, "I had thought such arrangements with reference to Bethlehem might be objected to by them on account of Armor arrangements between us, but *we* have really been Bethlehem's mainstay on Armor. We have never gone into guns as we should, and to tell the truth I don't think Bethlehem will kick much as Linderman told me they had 'no business' in rails under $20. They might go in structural steel, but would do so anyway, just as they did in plates."[4] They did not go into structurals and failed in plate. Yet in spite of its past lack of success in commercial steels Bethlehem became the basis on which Schwab set out to realize his dream of creating a great new steel company. How did such a dramatic change come about?

Essentially, the critics had overstressed the disadvantages of the East, a number of new, more favorable circumstances were beginning to come into play, and, decisively, as the next few years proved, an exceptional man could overcome difficulties, see possibilities, and drive on to realize them in a manner completely beyond the grasp of ordinary business leaders. In the first instance, as seen above, there was a sharp increase in U.S. maritime activity and expectation of still greater things to come. The biggest eastern works were ill equipped to seize this opportunity, for they still aspired to compete in rails; at the beginning of the twentieth century the two most recently built rail manufacturing plants, one at Sparrows Point, Maryland, and the new works at Lackawanna, New York, with a combined steel production capacity of more than 1.5 million tons, had all but one-sixth of that tonnage in Bessemer plant and were almost entirely engaged in rail or billet production. There also was the prospect of a bigger share of world markets—U.S. exports of pig iron and of all other iron and steel products were 561,000 tons in 1897 and 1,154,000 tons three years later—though they dropped for a time after that. Bethlehem was well placed to take a share in both spheres of expansion. Schwab's early frustration at U.S. Steel provided a strong personal incentive to look for a possible alternative power base. At the same time recognition of Bethlehem's powerlessness compared with the new giant and continuing half-hearted efforts by its top management meant it might be acquired at a cost that was very reasonable considering the company's long-term potential. Action was not long delayed. Schwab first became involved in May 1901, and on Tuesday, 27 August, less than five months after U.S. Steel began trading, a controlling share of the Bethlehem stock was reported to have been acquired by "interests represented by Mr. Charles M. Schwab, president of the United States Steel Corporation." The aging Joseph Wharton, associated with Bethlehem for many years and until this time the largest owner of its stock, had parted with the whole of it.[5]

Understandably, J. P. Morgan was worried that ownership of Bethlehem—in addition to the distraction of finding ways of spending a huge salary and bonuses from U.S. Steel—might dissipate even Schwab's tremendous energies. Consequently, he was willing to take Bethlehem off his hands. However, when Schwab became involved with the United States Shipbuilding Company, Morgan sold Bethlehem back to him and is said to have helped fuse it with the shipyards.[6] For a time Schwab played only a background role in Bethlehem operations, but even then he was involved with some important decisions. Sometime during fall 1901, Edward Harriman, who a year before had shown such keen interest in Schwab's remarks at the University Club dinner, asked him if he could negotiate a merger between Bethlehem and two or three other steel companies, apparently as an adjunct to a major railroad amalgamation and with an eye not only to Atlantic to Pacific linkages but also to South American development. None of these objectives was realized. On a less visionary front, in mid-November that year an initiative was taken by those at Bethlehem Steel to contact the man who, it must be remembered, was president of the United States Steel Corporation. In a "Memorandum of matters to be taken up with Mr. Schwab," Bethlehem's newly appointed general superintendent, Archibald Johnston, listed plans for a new armor mill and raised questions about contracts and prices for Connellsville coke.[7]

Next March Schwab seems to have used information he received at U.S. Steel for the possible benefit of his own company. He informed Bethlehem's president, Edward M. McIlvain, that he had been talking with the steel car maker Charles Schoen, a friend who was considering building a plant to make car wheels: "Schoen's present intention is to set this machinery up in Pittsburgh. . . . It occurs to me that this could best be done in Bethlehem."[8] On 4 August 1903 Schwab resigned from the presidency of U.S. Steel, though he remained a director for almost a year more. During this time he took another step that seems to have been potentially disloyal to U.S. Steel. Again in a letter to McIlvain, he commented on an opinion about armament expressed by Bethlehem's engineer of ordnance, J. F. Meigs: "I cannot refrain from adding, as strongly as possible, my opinion to that of Mr. Meigs', that it is a very valuable end of our business, and that with careful attention to detail, and the pursuing of a proper policy in Washington, that it can be worked up to great proportions." In mid-April 1904 he wrote McIlvain from his "Private Car Loretto, En Route." The letter ended, "Hope also that business keeps up well with you. Notice there was a gun explosion on the *Missouri* killing a number of people. Trust it was not one of our guns. Let me know about this." A few weeks later he thanked McIlvain for arranging a recent visit he had made to Bethlehem.[9]

After he ceased to be a U.S. Steel director Schwab was free to devote his time, wealth, talents, and energy to building up Bethlehem. As early as Wednesday, 17 August 1904, less than seven weeks after his resignation had been accepted, he made his first "official" visit of inspection to the plant he had owned for nearly three years. After this tour with McIlvain and Johnston, his ambitions were beginning to rise, as he was reported to have said, "I shall make the Bethlehem plant the greatest armor plate and gun factory in the world."[10] A number of serious obstacles stood in the way. One was that government orders varied alarmingly from year to year—work in hand at Bethlehem Steel for the United States was $4.45 million at the end of 1905, $4.06 million a year later, and only $2.63 million at the end of 1907. Clearly it was essential to find commercial products to counterbalance the concentration on armaments and ensure work for the iron and steel departments even when demand for war materials was low. A complementary approach was to seek out foreign armament orders. In any case an early requirement was to extend the raw material base on which any expansion of iron and steel capacity would have to depend. Solutions to these problems were to be far advanced though not fully achieved before the outbreak of the Great War.

There is circumstantial evidence that Schwab was soon at odds with some of the established top officials of Bethlehem Steel in his emphasis on diversification of products. This time, in contrast to the struggles Fritz and Wharton had in persuading their colleagues to make armaments, it was necessary to convince them of the need for commercial products. In his letter of appreciation and praise after his tour of Bethlehem in May 1904, Schwab stressed a need for work "aside from the work for the Government." He wanted more emphasis on finished guns rather than gun forgings and indicated that they should sell them to "any foreign government," but he also urged that engineers be set to work looking into and reporting on prospects in crucible steel, steel castings, locomotive tires, and railway springs. A few months later, when British and international members of the Iron and Steel Institute visited Bethlehem, its emphasis was still strongly on war materials. The visitors saw the forging of a seven-inch gun tube for the U.S. Navy, the casting of a fifty-six-ton armor plate ingot, and the forging of a forty-five-ton Krupp steel ingot into plates for the testing of projectiles.[11]

The new Bethlehem Steel Corporation that purchased all the properties of the old United States Shipbuilding Company was incorporated in mid-December 1904 (see table 7 in appendix B). Its $30 million in capital was equally divided into preferred and common stock. On 17 January 1905 at a New York meeting, in a significant departure from the situation under which he had been forced to operate at U.S. Steel, Schwab was elected both president and chairman of the board. Edward McIlvain became vice president, Adolph E. Borie, second vice president, and Henry S. Snyder, who had been with Bethlehem since 1886, secretary and treasurer. Though he now had a hierarchy of control, Schwab, who owned most of the stock, threw himself into reconstruction and extension of his new company. As he recalled long after, "Then I really went to work. Everything I had ever done in my life was child's play compared with my labor for the next half dozen years. I put everything I had in to Bethlehem." He added, "I borrowed right and left."[12]

Very soon important development plans were made public. In formulating them Schwab was helped by his intimate knowledge of U.S. Steel, its strengths, weaknesses, and lack of development in certain lines. At the end of January 1905 it was announced that some $3.3 million would be spent that year on improvement and extension. A new gun shop, increased capacity for gun carriages, and outlay for shell manufacture were included. The rest of the product development program was confined to established Bethlehem specialties—high grade castings and crucible steel for tires, springs, and so on. As important as these specific expansion programs was a change in organization and ethos, for the arrival of a man of Schwab's experience, reputation, and character brought with it a new pace and tone of work that was felt throughout all departments. Many years later Eugene Grace recalled how speedily the new regime had made an impact on an employee then in his late twenties and in a relatively junior position: "When Mr. Schwab took over at Bethlehem, I was superintendent of yards. . . . I had started with the old company in 1899 and had held various jobs in the plant. But even on the lower rungs I could feel the breeze of the new personality. He radiated vitality. He was tireless. He was warm-hearted and genuine. Not at all the old-school martinet."[13]

That settled ways were being disturbed was not congenial for everyone. Until now at Bethlehem "[t]here had been no general scheme or order, each department going pretty much its own way." Schwab tried to introduce a centralized authority and the sort of emphasis on cost-cutting and financial incentives that had proved so successful at Carnegie Steel. As early as May 1904 he was asking McIlvain for a complete salary list, and later he told him he had carefully gone over the salary information he had been sent and believed there was a need for economy, including some reductions: "Bethlehem is going to have a hard road to hoe, and with every penny, however hard it may seem, we should economize." When Grace returned from Cuba in February 1906 he found that, as he later euphemistically described it, "certain cross-currents had developed." By summer that year Schwab's determination to push through his own policies had forced the resignations of McIlvain and Borie. In the resulting reshaping of the board Schwab remained chairman and Archibald Johnston became president. Grace replaced Johnston as general superintendent. Many years afterward, Grace neatly summarized this palace revolution as a "reorganization" in which "Mr. Schwab retired two older men who did not comprehend the need for more orderly procedure."[14] Bit by bit the whole structure was reshaped, with Schwab applying the lessons he had learned at Carnegie Steel. Rather than introduce newcomers, he increasingly pro-

Eugene Gifford Grace.
Courtesy of the National Canal Museum, Easton, PA.

moted individuals from within—not always a prescription for long-term success. Again drawing on hard-won personal experience, he decided to focus control of the business in the town of Bethlehem, for, as he put it a few years later, referring to his time at U.S. Steel, "I was convinced that no great steel corporation can be managed from New York. . . . I was determined to reorganize the Bethlehem Steel Company and have it managed entirely on the grounds." From the earliest days he introduced a bonus system and provided other rewards for success. For example, the superintendents of the various departments each year picked two persons who would be sent for six weeks to Europe. There they were to spend three weeks studying steel plants, not only to widen their experience but also to give them a respect for foreign ways of doing things. Reflecting Schwab's own practice, the rest of their trip was to be given over to travel and pleasure.[15]

The urgency for economy and increased output at Bethlehem Steel remained. In mid-July 1906 Grace contacted Johnston about their share of the armor for the *South Carolina* and the *Michigan,* the first two American "dreadnoughts," which were laid down that year. The reply he received made direct reference to this urgency: "[I]t is my desire that you should push this work with the intention of making the armor in the least possible time, regardless of the fact that there is such a small quantity to manufacture. If this is not done the costs will run up considerably and this fact must be impressed upon the superintendent of the armor plate department. There must be no disposition to 'string it out' in order to take care of the men, as we cannot afford this." All the time there were schemes for major expansion and product diversification that increased the demand for capital and the need for economy. Some public reports of what was being planned proved false. For instance, before the end of February 1905 there were rumors in New York that Bethlehem had acquired the Tidewater Steel Company of Chester, Pennsylvania, thereby getting control of "a good plate plant."[16] In fact, by that time thinking about new trades was moving powerfully in a very different direction.

The Upward Struggle

Schwab's outstanding achievement in his first decade at Bethlehem Steel was to make it into a major and, above all, the most efficient producer of heavy structural shapes. At Carnegie Steel he had been the partner most closely acquainted with this line of their business, and the major importance of the East Coast market had been fully recognized. As early as spring 1896 Carnegie was suggesting that they should have a yard in New York in which they should stock several thousand tons of beams of all sizes, so as to meet spot demand from building contractors. He thought they might get low freight rates on delivery from their mills by shipping through the Erie Canal, which was then being deepened. A few years later they obtained a low freight rate from the Pennsylvania Railroad.[17] When Schwab conveyed his thoughts about Bethlehem diversification to McIlvain in May 1904, he was already thinking along lines that, a quarter century after John Fritz had tried and failed to persuade his board in the same broad direction, would bring that company into structural steel, this time on a large scale: "I have some very decided views about Bethlehem in structural material, but this can wait over until after my visit to Germany, where we expect to see some mills in connection with this proposition." He was thinking of introducing a radical new technology to the heavy beam trade.[18]

Two years later, in his first annual statement to stockholders, Schwab reviewed the improvements made to the old plant and progress in introducing various, generally small, new lines but then went on to announce a much bigger program. This new scheme would involve a large-scale return to commercial products: "A careful study of the situation at this plant convinced the officers and directors that a still further development was desirable and it was determined to continue the increase of the old plant, particularly in blast furnace capacity, as well as to establish a new plant to be devoted to the manufacture of open hearth steel, structural shapes, rails and billets." The scale of the changes may be appreciated from the fact that whereas the existing plant, the product of almost half a century of growth, covered 170 acres, to accommodate the planned extensions an additional 250 acres would have to be acquired. When the new Saucon works was complete, the annual capacity of Bethlehem for rails and structurals would be 500,000 tons, the latter making up two-thirds of the total.[19] It was in the vanguard in the use of open hearth steel in rail manufacture, and both time and location favored its new trades in heavy structurals.

By the end of the 1890s bridge construction and even more advances in the erection of large and high, steel-framed buildings in particular were causing rapid increases in demand for large structural steel shapes. In ten years to 1902, production of all rolled iron and steel increased 126 percent, iron and steel rails by 90 percent, but for structurals growth was 186 percent. Carnegie Steel and then U.S. Steel dominated this field of production. For almost twenty years Schwab had been closely involved with this product; now he was to revolutionize its production technology and thereby change control and location of the trade. Until then structural units of large dimensions had been fabricated by riveting together smaller beams and plates. After a number of attempts in the late 1880s and 1890s Henry Grey at last succeeded in developing a universal mill to produce large beams—a mill that, because it was equipped with both horizontal and vertical rolls, could roll the entire beam from a large block of semifinished steel, known in this instance as a "blank." As it was rolled rather than put together, its use could save engineers considerable sums in construction. On 15 December 1905 the American Universal Mill Company licensed Bethlehem Steel to install a Grey mill.[20]

The Bethlehem Grey mill rolled its first beams on 9 January 1908. Like the new Saucon rail mill, which had started four months earlier, operations began with "an unusual absence of the difficulties customarily encountered on starting up a new plant." This was good news, for the project had begun to look extremely doubtful in commercial terms. In part this uncertainty was because of the need to change consumer preferences. As Grace remembered, "[T]he old-school engineers who were used to figuring on standard shapes only . . . were very skeptical." It seems to have been Grey who urged Schwab to take the offensive on these prejudices. In summer 1906 he wrote, "What you want is a salesman who knows the advantages that you have—don't let him talk Standard Beams, he is then giving away your powder—don't mistrust the value of the advantages you have by talking Standard Beams—talk the light beams, make them and they will sell themselves after you have put some life into their introduction." Grey reckoned his mill could produce beams equal in carrying capacity to those shown in the Carnegie Steel book of structural shapes, "only without the cost of punching, assembling and riveting, saving about 10 to 20 dollars per ton."[21]

In 1906 and even more so during 1907 many inquiries had come in from engineers anxious to learn about the new product. Even so, in the months following commissioning, there were fears of rival systems moving from paper designs to production by some of their competitors. The possibilities included a mill like Grey's at U.S. Steel, and another designed by a Pennsylvania Steel draftsman who had once worked for Grey, or perhaps the universal mill patented twenty years before by Hugo Sack of Duisburg, Germany, and now being actively promoted in the United States. Another serious problem was that their own capital outlay had far exceeded the estimates for the mill; years later Eugene Grace figured they spent three times the expected amount.[22] The readiness of engineers to adopt the new section, the company's ability to raise the extra capital, and the beginnings of financial returns from sales were all imperiled by the fact that the beam mill came into production during the severe recession of 1907–1908. With his usual public show of buoyancy Schwab tried to talk his way out of the difficulties.

On the day the mill was commissioned, *Iron Age* published an interview with Schwab for the annual review issue of the *New York Times*. He was upbeat: "The ultimate trend will be upwards always, and I do not recall any period of prosperity in the past that, in my opinion, will equal the normal condition of this country in the future. There is no cause for pessimism if the outlook be viewed in the light of common sense and obvious logic."[23] In fact, whatever his hopes for the long term, critical months followed as the running in of the mill coincided with the commercial gloom. In 1908 national raw steel output was only 60 percent of the average of the two previous years; production of structural shapes was less than 56 percent the 1907 figure. Economies were made, as was apparent in a November memo from Schwab, who urged Archibald Johnston, chief armaments salesman, "Now that we are endeavoring, for monetary reasons, to turn everything we can into cash, wish you would make extraordinary efforts with your foreign agents to see if there is any possibility of disposing of any of the guns we have on hand." Most important of all at this critical juncture, Schwab's reputation and network of contacts saved his company from collapse. He induced some of the contractors for the mill to accept notes rather than immediate payment. The Philadelphia and Reading and the Lehigh Valley Railroads agreed to carry Bethlehem freight on credit until it could pay. He borrowed from banking houses controlled by friends. His approach to the Philadelphia banker Edward T. Stotesbury, who was also a director of the Philadelphia and Reading system, gave rise to one of the better stories he told against himself in later years. To his request for money, Stotesbury's response was, "I'll let you have half a million." Schwab replied, "Oh, that's nothing at all. I can get half a million in New York and they don't even know me there." Stotesbury told him, "That's the reason you can get it."[24]

When Schwab approached Andrew Carnegie for urgent help the latter responded by lending Schwab some U.S. Steel bonds to be used as collateral for bank loans. In short, U.S. Steel Corporation credit was used to help finance the mill that would soon undermine its own dominance in structurals. At the end of the year, when Carnegie and Schwab testified in the tariff hearings held by the House Committee on Ways and Means, both of them were convinced of the technical success of the new mill. Andrew Carnegie told the committee members, "We have suffered ourselves to fall behind in adopting improvements, except in the case of the Bethlehem Steel Company." Schwab was assured of their technological superiority but not yet about commercial success: "The new mills, which I have built at Bethlehem[,] have made a radical change in the character of structural steel, so that most of the structural-steel plants of the United States will have to be changed within the next five years." But, when asked at the start of his testimony about his connection with Bethlehem, he replied, "I am an unfortunate stockholder as well as President."[25]

Despite Schwab's doubts, before the end of 1908 the principal officers at U.S. Steel were already becoming concerned about the long-term impact of Schwab's pioneering installation. In striking contrast, by 1909–1910 policy makers at Bethlehem Steel had concluded it was necessary to expand capacity.[26] In 1910 their structural and rail mills each operated to the fullest extent possible given the melting capacity available, and by World War I the company was firmly established as a leading producer of structural steel. It had made only 0.5 percent of the national tonnage in 1905 compared with U.S. Steel's 54.6 percent; nine years later Bethlehem's share had reached 12.5 percent. In 1907, a year before the Saucon mills began production, Allegheny County accounted for 45.8 percent of the nation's structural tonnage; by 1913, a good year, national output had increased by more than half, but the share of Allegheny County was now 38.1 percent.

Success in new commercial products required an extension of steel and pig iron capacity at Bethlehem. At the beginning of 1905, before the first plans of the Schwab era took shape, its annual capacity for pig iron and ferromanganese was 224,000 net tons; within five years this amount had increased to 364,000 tons and, with three new blast furnaces, was expected to reach 750,000 tons by mid-1911. At the end of 1914 iron capacity was 840,000 tons. The expansion was paralleled in consumption of raw materials; over five years from 1907 iron ore tonnages increased from 0.3 to 1.5 million tons.[27] In turn this expansion highlighted a problem that had plagued the company for many years: its inadequate mineral resource base. In the early months of U.S. Steel Schwab had emphasized the desirability of major extensions to coking coal and iron ore reserves; now he had to do the same again for his new company, but from a much weaker foundation and under conditions less favorable in other respects. Bethlehem was too far both from Connellsville coke and from Lake Erie landing points for Great Lakes ore to be able to show low assembly costs for iron making materials. Using raw materials from these points of origin, the Bureau of Corporations calculated 1902–1906 rail transport costs per ton of basic iron at $1.75 for Pittsburgh and $2.07 for "eastern" centers of production. Reserves of ore in the East were inadequate in volume, and even the biggest, the famous Cornwall banks, produced a raw ore of only 42 percent iron. Early in 1907 Schwab spent $400,000 to acquire iron deposits at Boyertown, Berks County, less than thirty miles southwest of Bethlehem. There was no hope that this acquisition could do more than make a small contribution to their needs, but the fact that it was acquired at all showed how serious the problem was.[28]

Bethlehem and Pennsylvania Steel had long used imported ore, their main source being the Bessemer grade deposits at Juragua in the Santiago district of Cuba, which they had exploited together in the 1880s and 1890s, before Bethlehem took full control. Significantly, two of the earliest steps taken by Schwab were to allocate $600,000 for a new ore dock, a new railroad, and general improvements there and to send Grace out to reorganize the mines.[29] Juragua output was sharply increased—from 181,000 tons in 1907 to 367,000 the following year. In January 1908 Schwab visited the mines. He sent a note of appreciation on the progress to the general superintendent there: "No one shall be happier than I to see Juragua developed to the magnitude that I anticipate for it." However, its improved yields fell far short of their needs, and even these levels of production could not be maintained. Shipments in 1909 were 357,000 tons and in 1910, only 300,000 tons. Clearly, it alone could not support the planned major iron expansion.[30]

The constant cry from Schwab's associates was "buy ore," and the search extended widely. New deposits were acquired in Cuba, some of them on the north coast, but the ore there was poor. A contract for Sanford ore from Lake Champlain was negotiated in 1907, the plan being to mix it with Cuban ore.[31] The following year the Bethlehem Iron Mines Company was formed to hold and operate any new properties the company might secure. It contracted for supplies from Port Henry, New York. A development indicative of the desperate situation was the acquisition late in 1909 of large acreages of limonite ores of a reported 54–57 percent iron content in the far northeastern corner of Texas. For a time it was thought this ore might be shipped around the coast from Port Bolivar or Texas City. Trial shipments were made to Philadelphia in summer 1910, but it was obvious that the logistics of such a supply system were far from promising, and the Texas venture never became important. Offers of ore from the vicinity of Birmingham, Alabama, were scarcely more attractive, given both the location and lower grade.[32] From 1909 trading conditions moved more strongly in favor of foreign ores when the Payne-Aldrich Tariff Act reduced the duty payable on imports from $0.40 to $0.15 per gross ton. There was also talk of bringing iron ore from Sweden, but during the year attention moved to South America. Long afterward Schwab recalled, "At one time, in fact, just as a gamble, I bought 'Venezuelan ore lands' and found there was none there."[33] Real success was achieved farther south, fitting in excellently with two other developments: the duty-free status accorded to ore imports in the 1913 Underwood Tariff Act and, most important of all, the opening of the Panama Canal.

By the beginning of the twentieth century it was known that there were important deposits of iron ore in various Chilean provinces, but they were then of no commercial importance. In 1909 the major French steel and armaments firm, Schneider of Le Creusot, was completing a blast furnace plant on Corral Bay in southern Chile. Shortly afterward, attempts were made to interest American firms in Chilean ores. A man named Enriquez wrote to some U.S. iron makers about a deposit he believed contained some 175 million tons of ore workable by open cut. At that time the freight rate around Cape Horn to the East Coast was $4.60 a ton, but as one American mineral merchant recognized, "It is almost impossible to bring it here now . . . when the Panama Canal is opened it will come here, no doubt." On 7 August 1911 Enriquez visited Bethlehem, and it was reported that Schwab was greatly interested by what he had to say.[34] Shortly afterward geological assessment showed that an ore body at El Tofo in central Chile contained 100 million tons of ore with about 67 percent iron content—roughly 15 percent higher than the average of the Great Lakes ores then being shipped. El Tofo had been taken over but only slightly developed by Schneider under the aegis of La Société des Hauts-Fourneaux, Forges et Aciéries de Chili, whose head offices were in Paris. Total shipments through to 1913 amounted to only 40,000 tons. Bethlehem sent C. A. Buck to examine this ore, and after much work, in late 1912 during a trip to Europe Schwab closed a deal for their acquisition. He managed to ensure that the terms were such as to bear lightly on a company still deeply preoccupied with extensions. The purchase was to be spread over fifteen years, with payments of $75,000 in the first year, $100,000 for each of the next two, and $200,000 annually after that. Royalties would be $0.10 per ton to 1928, thereafter rising by $0.025 each year. Ambitious targets were set for production—rising from 1,000 tons a day early in 1914 to 5,000 tons two years later and eventually to 10,000 tons. The targets for ore shipments to Bethlehem were 200,000 tons in 1915 and 1 million the following year.[35]

The Panama Canal duly opened for commercial traffic on 14 August 1914, but soon after that shortages of shipping capacity as a consequence of the war in Europe put back hopes for large imports. Deliveries of Chilean ore in 1914 were 45,000 tons; two years later they were only about 5,000 tons more than that. Various schemes were considered for transporting the ore. One of the first was for Bethlehem to charter and then to acquire its own fleet of oceangoing ore carriers; another plan, hatched in spring 1914, was to purchase six vessels from Scandinavian builders. By 1916 there were plans for the company to build its own carriers either at the yard at Alameda, California, which it had purchased from United Engineering, or at recently acquired East Coast yards.[36] By 1919–1920 Bethlehem was building two 20,000-ton vessels to carry ore from Chile and to ship oil as a return cargo. El Tofo was soon after this able to produce 1 million tons of ore annually, though as late as 1922 only 297,000 tons were delivered to Bethlehem and not until 1924 did Chilean ore output exceed 1 million metric tons.[37] Yet despite delays and complications, the development strategy that Schwab and his colleagues followed had at last pro-

The extended Schwab family in 1910.
Courtesy of the National Canal Museum, Easton, PA.

duced an oceanic-scale counterpart to the much larger mineral flows on the Great Lakes.

Schwab was the originating, leading, continuing, and activating force in the improvement of Bethlehem Steel's standing. It is interesting to speculate on the reasons for such wholehearted involvement when the work of his previous twenty years had provided him with wealth more than sufficient for a full life. Why, when he left U.S. Steel at age forty-two, did he not follow the lead provided by William L. Abbott, who, after he retired in 1892 at forty, lived on in apparently happy retirement for another thirty-eight years? Schwab might have lived a life of ease, cultivated wider interests, or moved into public service. Why then did he devote the best part of the rest of his life to Bethlehem? In the first place it seems clear that, having been frustrated at U.S. Steel, he wanted to vindicate himself as a business leader, and be the outstanding man in the industry now that Carnegie had withdrawn. He was also responding to a challenge, that of reviving a steel region that had long been in decline. Though eager to make more money, the drive to build, the desire for more material power, and the opportunity to realize more of that fascinating worldly vision he claimed had inspired him when he rode the train down into Pittsburgh in summer 1879 was undoubtedly a stronger motivation. To this degree he was like John W. Gates, a gambler. Finally, it seems probable that, despite all his business talents and attractive human qualities, Schwab was a limited man. Carnegie's striving for culture and philanthropy, Frick's artistic inclination and increasingly sophisticated collecting—these pursuits held no interest for Schwab. For want of something better, he was forced to seek distinction by remaining a master builder of businesses. He himself provided abundant evidence of this tack, and though professionals now wrote his colorful speeches, they could not put into his mouth words completely misrepresenting his personal inclinations.

Success in expansion and diversification at Bethlehem Steel was achieved by the labors of many minds and hands. When he began to devote more attention to its interests, Schwab lived for a time at the former Linderman mansion in south Bethlehem, the largest house in the Lehigh valley and another building that resembled a French chateau. As in Braddock, he helped local causes, supporting the Lehigh Valley Symphony Orchestra and becoming patron of the Bach Choir. He continued to retain a house in the area as he labored for the advance of his company's interests, but later he spent most of his time in New York. Coming to Bethlehem Steel in his maturity, with his character, industry-wide reputation, and fortune already made, he did not form such close relationships as he had in Pittsburgh. With the famous engineer John Fritz, who had built so much of the plant yet whose advice had been ignored by the board on a number of vital occasions—mistakes that had meant vital lost opportunities in structurals and in plate—he had a playful, affectionate relationship, the sort of thing possible between a successful businessman in his early forties and a renowned plant engineer twice his age. For instance, in spring 1908, Fritz, hearing that Schwab planned a business trip to Bethlehem, sent a handwritten letter inviting him to be his guest at his home. Schwab replied to "Dear Uncle John" that arrangements had already been made. Two years later Schwab praised Fritz's human qualities at a dinner given for him by the Manufacturers' Club of Philadelphia. Then he explained his predecessor's continuing hold, referring to "the trouble Mr. Fritz had stored up for him, for, in all the proposals the speaker had brought forward at the Bethlehem works, no matter how fortified, the clinching argument of any one who differed with him was that 'Uncle John wouldn't have done it that way.'"[38]

For his Bethlehem management team, Schwab developed a high regard. One of its leading figures was Archibald Johnston, already long involved with the plant's development as the nation's foremost producer of heavy armaments. Johnston was a talented negotiator for foreign business, and he was Schwab's companion on some of the long trips overseas. He was a Moravian and was well endowed with business qualities. Writing during World War I, Arundel Cotter described him as "[a] man of the world, suave, courteous, but ever keeping an eye out for the nimble contract for steel or anything made of steel that is made at Bethlehem[.] Johnston is recognized by competitors as a dangerous man to fight against in foreign trade."[39] Even more important among Schwab's Bethlehem "boys" was a man for whom such a title seemed incongruous, whose talents lay in plant management rather than in winning business, and who, despite Johnston's seniority, Schwab chose to lead the company. Other than in his outstanding abilities, Eugene Gifford Grace was in many ways very different from Schwab.

Grace was twenty-eight when Schwab took full control at Bethlehem, and he had already been with the company for five years. He was to remain there for another fifty-six, and for forty-four of those years he was its effective head, carrying the aspirations and to some extent the methods of the Schwab era through to and beyond World War II. In early years there was much in his position to mirror Schwab's own relationship with Carnegie, but in this instance deep respect between major owner and head of operations was more prominent than warm affection. Indeed, in some ways their relationship was comparable with that of Carnegie and Frick, for Grace was a consummate manager. When he joined the company in 1899 he operated an electric crane, but by 1902, after suggesting ways of reducing waste and removing bottlenecks in the flow of materials, he was promoted to overhaul the works traffic. He was superintendent of the yards and of transportation when Schwab assumed active control, and in September 1905 Schwab chose him to reorganize and expand the Cuban ore supply. When Grace returned from Cuba six months later, Schwab appointed him assistant to the general superintendent, and in summer 1906 he became general superintendent. He was given charge of the installation of the new rolling mills on whose commercial success the company's future depended. Appointed director in early autumn 1908, by April 1913 he was president of the Bethlehem Steel Company. In taking this final step Schwab was apparently strongly encouraged by Johnston. Grace was now only a year older than Schwab had been when he became president of Carnegie Steel. As his record proved, he had a talent for constructive planning and administration, as well as a reputation for hard work. When in 1916 he moved on to presidency of the Bethlehem Steel Corporation, he was said to look no more than thirty, though he was ten years older. He usually arrived at his office at 7:30 or 7:45 a.m. and did not leave until after

6:00 p.m., except for luncheon. Held in a private dining room on the fifth floor of the head office building, this luncheon was not only a meal but also a time for conferring with the fifteen men known as the "partners." Grace was known as no mincer of words, no lover of bores, was hard and tough, but considered consistent and fair. He drove his subordinates but earned their respect by driving himself as hard. Some of his characteristics must have reminded Schwab of the features he had admired in Frick, but he was now the senior and not the junior partner in the relationship. Temperamentally, he and his president were very different. Schwab usually obtained his ends by coaxing and gentle persuasion, methods uncongenial to Grace. Together these very different men were the key players in the transformation of Bethlehem Steel.[40]

Looking back from the mid-1930s Schwab recalled that he had believed steel could be made in the East as cheaply as or cheaper than in Pittsburgh. To prove this theory he had aimed to make Bethlehem "his" company and until 1914 never took a dividend or paid himself a cent from its operations. In 1905, explaining his $12 million expansion plans, he had said, "What I am going to do is to make the Bethlehem Steel works the greatest steel plant in the world. By that I mean the largest, the most modern, the best equipped, the most highly specialized and, I fear, also the most expensive steel works anywhere." In testimony to the Stanley Committee in February 1912 he revealed a deeper, sadder insight into his motivations: "I want it to be understood that my interest in making the Bethlehem works the largest and best in the country is not necessary to me from a financial point of view. I do not desire to get richer. I have no heirs to leave my money to, and my greatest pleasure, and just now my only pleasure in life, is to build a big business in Pennsylvania."[41]

A few weeks later, at the third annual dinner of the Bethlehem Industrial Commission, he gave local pride and his particular species of eloquence free rein. Noting that five years before Bethlehem Steel's business had amounted to $6 million a year but was now $30 million, he expressed the hope that he would see it reach $100 million—which, he added, would mean the distribution of some $35 million a year in wages in the Lehigh valley. He warmed to his theme; the momentum of the nation's economy would continue to carry the works relentlessly forward, whatever outsiders might do: "Mr. Schwab compared all legislation, local and otherwise, to 'waves washing on the sea-shore.' He said that in the end legislators must conform with industrial advancement and progress and that no forces could stop the onward march of the tremendous aggregation of capital in this country. He concluded by saying that industry and progress are going ahead in leaps and bounds, that the steel industry is now in its infancy, and that the world is going to revolve around the United States as a hub, and he sincerely hoped that the city of Bethlehem would be the axle around which the hub revolves."[42]

Such dedication, wedded to success, received its due accolades. As early as fall 1910, the business leaders of Bethlehem gave him a "splendid" testimonial dinner. It was held in the Coliseum Skating Rink, for the occasion transformed into "a fairy woodland"—but with two thousand high-powered electric lights illuminating the two hundred guests. The tables were placed to form the initials "C.M.S." Former congressman J. Davis Brodhead, a Democrat who lived in south Bethlehem, presented the guest of honor with "an elaborate testimonial" to which "Mr. Schwab made a happy response." Both occasion and setting must have reminded the principal guest of the great dinner of winter 1900 at which the leading officials of Carnegie Steel had celebrated their own achievements and well-being in the Hotel Schenley. Making the resemblance more complete, Andrew Carnegie was again expected to attend. Late in the afternoon a letter from him arrived, and in it he wrote, "I regret my inability to be present at the complimentary dinner you are to give to one of my brightest boys, Charlie Schwab, who deserves the tribute. He has given South Bethlehem what is to be within a few months the most up-to-date steel plant in the world." A few weeks afterward Schwab gave a dinner for the managers, superintendents, and assistant superintendents to celebrate their best year to date. Again it was an occasion of some style: "Each of the 200 guests received a Roman gold watch fob with his name engraved thereon. They in turn presented Schwab with a similar fob set with diamonds."[43]

Sixteen months later, the Industrial Commission dinner provided another link with Schwab's earlier days. One of the speakers was one of Schwab's successors as president of the United States Steel Corporation. Celebrating the hero of the evening, James Farrell claimed, "His career is probably the clearest illustration we have in this country today of the heights to which genius can ascend without other aid than indomitable energy, perseverance and brains." A few weeks earlier at a testimonial dinner for Schwab in Philadelphia, Sen. Boies Penrose had made the somewhat ambiguous observation that, were it not for the energy of such creative men as the guest of honor, "many of our natural resources might still be in the ground."[44]

Certainly by this time evidence of Bethlehem's extraordinary new lease on life was incontrovertible, and the man honored at these lavish banquets must have glowed with more than usual pride at endorsements

Bethlehem Steel Works, c. 1920.
Courtesy of the National Canal Museum, Easton, PA.

coming from such quarters. A nonentity at the beginning of the century, by the time of the boom of 1913 Bethlehem Steel was a major company that had grown more than almost all its rivals; from 1905 to 1914 its share of national steel output rose from 0.2 to 2.2 percent, its share in rails from nothing to 6.2 percent, and in structural shapes, from 0.5 to 12.5 percent.[45] More and even greater advances lay ahead.

Armaments and Shipbuilding

From the mid-1880s Bethlehem was the nation's largest specialist maker of heavy armaments. Under Schwab there was little likelihood that production of war matériel would decrease. He had been general superintendent at Homestead, whose armor plate mill was at that time Bethlehem's only domestic rival. The shipyards taken over in December 1904 from the defunct United States Shipbuilding Company were in part engaged in naval work, and there was an obvious logic in Bethlehem providing their armor and ordnance. Schwab made clear he wanted to expand in commercial steel products but never suggested they should run down the armaments business. From the beginning of his association, the management at Bethlehem pressed the claims of their old specialties.

As early as November 1901 Archibald Johnston was in touch with

Schwab about plans for extensions in the armor department. Next spring Edward McIlvain sent him a copy of a letter from his old Carnegie Steel colleague, Millard Hunsiker, regarding a proposed testimonial for the leading British armament manufacturer, Albert Vickers. Two years later McIlvain supported the advocacy of their engineer of ordnance, John F. Meigs, saying that gun manufacture "is a very valuable end of our business, and that with careful attention to detail, and the pursuing of a proper policy in Washington, that it can be worked up to great proportions."[46] In May 1904 Meigs made his own direct plea for attention to war matériel. As was common with armament manufacturers and sales forces all over the world, after a decade of work in Bethlehem's interest, his commitment was of almost missionary zeal and took no account of the fact that what they made and what he touted for sale were the means of mass destruction. Indeed, his was an almost apocalyptic vision:

> The Company stands only partially equipped at the threshold of a great business, for who can doubt that the great powers of the earth must have in the coming years great armaments. We are building in this country today faster than any nation except England, while our facilities are inferior to those of England, Germany, France, Russia, Austria, Italy, and probably Belgium. We are in a most essential respect behind these nations in development—we have not proper powers of building and repairing our material. Thoughtful men connected with the navy realized this within the last year or two. They want a Krupp or Armstrong. Who will step in? Bethlehem or someone else. Bethlehem has now several years['] lead and has a prosperous and paying business in these lines, but she cannot keep her lead without continuous and great effort. . . . My own connection with all this has been close and my attention unremitting. The company has had my unstinted and unwearied service and my pleasure in seeing the work grow has been great. My confidence that it will continue to grow, if the Company makes prompt effort, is unshaken. But I fear that the importance of acting and acting promptly is not duly appreciated.

He wanted them to be able to turn out twice or even two and a half times as much gun work as the company was then producing.[47]

Meigs need not have worried about the commitment of the new owner, who only three days later, writing to the vice president, declared he was "strongly of the opinion that we should make Bethlehem, as Mr. Meigs expresses it 'the Krupp of America' and go in largely for finished armament of all sorts."[48] Over the seventeen months to and including July 1907, less than 4 percent by weight of Bethlehem sales were of noncommercial steel, but in value the armament business remained of great importance. Schwab was eager to extend the range of their activities. In December 1907 he wrote to Johnston—"Dear Arch"—about projectiles: "It seems to me that this is a very desirable business for us."[49] As with all products it was necessary to meet demand, but in this field there were greater possibilities than in most for cultivating and stimulating it. As it was essential to do so on as large a scale as possible, Bethlehem Steel was willing to supply both the United States and overseas governments. Schwab's own talents and contacts were invaluable in both directions.

During his early years at Bethlehem the Midvale Steel Company attempted to become established as a third important producer of armor plate. In December 1903, after a works inspection by the chief of the navy's Bureau of Ordnance, Rear Adm. Charles O'Neil, and assurances that it could deliver within twenty months of being awarded a contract, Midvale received an order for six thousand tons of armor for the battleships *Idaho* and *Mississippi*. To win business themselves and to frustrate Midvale's attempts to gain more of the market, it was important that the two established producers maintain good relations with the Department of the Navy and with members of Congress whose committee work and districts had ties to the navy. Schwab's experience at Carnegie Steel helped him in this respect. For instance, in June 1904 it became known that President Roosevelt would appoint Paul Morton to be secretary of the navy. Although at the time Schwab was in the process of resigning as a director of the United States Steel Corporation, he seized the opportunity to write the secretary-designate an almost groveling letter in the interests of Bethlehem Steel:

> My dear Mr. Morton,
>
> Permit me to congratulate you upon your appointment as Secretary of what I believe is going to be the greatest Navy the world ever saw. It is gratifying to know that a business man, as capable as yourself, is going to be the head of this great branch of our Government.
>
> In this connection, I desire to say that the Bethlehem Steel Company, where most of the Government's Naval supplies have been obtained, should be regarded by you as your Works, to do with as you see fit, for the best interests of the Government. Will gladly make any extensions, go into any new lines or undertake any manufacture that you may desire.

The Bethlehem Company works almost exclusively for the Government, and we have always been anxious that the Government should take an interest in the development of this great Works, which is so necessary to the ultimate completion and development of our Navy.

> Again congratulating you, I remain,
> Respectfully yours,
> [signed] C. M. Schwab[50]

It is difficult to know how Schwab really regarded the politicians who were of special service to the interests of his industry. He had known Morton as a western railroad executive (he was still vice president of the Atchison, Topeka & Santa Fe when Schwab wrote) and as vice president of Colorado Fuel and Iron, the only rail producer in the West. The professional politicians who were useful to Schwab were a mixed and sometimes rather unsavory bunch. Two were prominent Pennsylvania Republicans. Matthew Stanley Quay was a U.S. senator from 1887 to 1899, and then, after being acquitted on a charge of misappropriating public funds, was senator again from 1901 until his death three years later. In 1894, when both houses of Congress were in the hands of "free traders," Quay was said to have shown "courage and tact" in securing rates of duty in the metal schedules of the Wilson Bill that were more than twice those provided for in the bill as it passed the House. Some light is thrown on his character by his reported response to a question put to him when he became a senator. Asked why he did not work for the people, he is said to have replied, "I work for the men the people work for." Quay's successor as state party boss was Boies Penrose, and in return for his support for duty-free entry of foreign iron ore Schwab contributed to his campaign fund. In 1912 the Penrose hold on Pennsylvania was temporarily broken when Progressives denounced him as an archetypal political boss, and he lost his place on the Republican National Committee for four years. When Penrose approached Schwab for help, the latter consulted Frick, who replied, "Always glad to see you, but I am afraid I can do nothing for Penrose. I had the matter up, but owing to the suit [presumably the dissolution suit against U.S. Steel] and other things, I know nothing can be done at this time." Later still, Schwab continued to be associated with politicians of conservative complexion, including Warren Harding; when a memorial service for the recently deceased president was held in Altoona in August 1923 Schwab was one of the speakers. Four months later, presenting the annual medal of the Pennsylvania Society of New York City to Andrew Mellon, Schwab praised Harding's tax reduction policies.[51]

The attempt to persuade Morton that Bethlehem was uniquely suited to supply the navy did not stop Midvale's advance or defeat the Vickers group's aspirations to interfere in American armaments developments. Sometime in 1904 Albert Vickers urged Bethlehem to associate more closely with Midvale. Soon afterward Hunsiker wrote from London, suggesting that Vickers wished to secure control of Midvale in order to have a going concern in the United States to develop their gun business. Schwab, holidaying in Florida, tried to reassure McIlvain. In doing so he revealed how considerable were the powers he believed himself to possess. He suggested there was no likelihood that Vickers would buy Midvale, "and I believe that I could stop it any time we thought it advisable to do so. What we want to make up our minds to is whether we would rather have Vickers as a competitor or Harrah [Charles J. Harrah, president of Midvale]. Vickers with his reputation on guns might do us a lot of harm."[52]

Early in 1905 the secretary of the navy awarded new orders for armor plate: 5,666 tons to Bethlehem and 2,162 tons to Carnegie Steel. It rejected a Midvale bid, though the price of the two established producers was $453 a ton and Midvale's only $398. The reason for rejection was that Midvale had not yet demonstrated its ability to produce more than satisfactory trial plates. By this time indeed 614 tons of the order originally placed with Midvale the previous December had been transferred to Bethlehem without further advertisement. However, on 21 February 1905, in something of a volte-face Morton awarded Midvale an order for 1,000 tons of armor, though it did not have to be filled for almost three years. A few weeks afterward, writing to McIlvain, Schwab tried another approach to win support in Washington: "Senator Smith tells me that Senator Joe Blackburn [a Kentucky Democrat] is out for re-election. He also says that he believes Blackburn was a member of the Senate Naval Committee and could be of much use to us in Naval matters if re-elected, and suggests it might be well for us to make some contribution, as Blackburn, as he says is hard up for funds. Use your best judgment in the matter."[53]

In May 1905 Charles J. Bonaparte replaced Morton as secretary of the navy. A year later moves were made toward another round of contracts. Early in August 1906 in a letter to the Bureau of Ordnance, Archibald Johnston reported how underused their armor capacity was, and, in a striking reversal of the argument that had been used when Bethlehem had first decided to make war matériel, he argued that commercial steels would have brought them greater profit. He put their annual capacity for armor at twelve thousand tons; the last award from the Navy Department had been for eighteen hundred tons, and as this amount represented the entire work in hand for the next calendar year, revenue from it would be the only cover for the capital tied up in the armor plant: "A much smaller investment in an ordinary steel rolling mill would provide production in one month of a greater tonnage of commercial products (such as rails) than has been shipped from our armor plate and gun forging plants during the entire fifteen (15) years of their existence, and result in a far larger return on the capital invested." In addition to direct dealings with the Navy Department, Bethlehem resorted to another questionable means of applying pressure, this time from a source nearer home. Contact was made with Senator Penrose. Sen. Eugene Hale of Maine and Rep. Alston G. Dayton of West Virginia were also involved. Midvale was believed to be behind in its deliveries from the previous award, and Johnston heard this delay had in turn delayed work at Cramp's yard. Johnston chose his words carefully when writing to Penrose: "If you could see your way clear to stir up the department about this, ascertaining the facts in the case, I should be greatly indebted to you." Less than three weeks later he received a reply. It was not reassuring: "[T]he status of the Midvale people is considered fairly good with the officials and they have been granted a one month extension." Worse was to come. In July bids were received from the three companies for armor for the battleships *South Carolina* and *Michigan*. The Carnegie bid price was $370 a ton, Bethlehem's was $381, but Midvale's only $345. Bonaparte decided that the two more experienced producers should share the contract for one of the battleships and Midvale supply the armor for the other—but that they would all be paid at the Midvale price. That autumn Penrose received his reward from those "greatly indebted" to him. At Bethlehem Steel a so-called "Memo Political," dated 8 October 1906, recorded, "At a meeting between Mr. Schwab, Senator Penrose on Saturday the 6th instant, it was determined that the Corporation would contribute toward the coming election expenses to the amount of $5,000."[54]

The alternative, or more usually the necessary counterpart, to an active domestic business in munitions was to sell overseas. Winning foreign orders was an even more uncertain business than negotiations with the Navy Department in Washington, for there were a number of large, well-established competitors. Again Schwab was actively involved on his company's behalf. On 15 July 1904, before his resignation from the U.S. Steel board had been announced, he sailed for Europe on business connected with the manufacture of armor plate. In November McIlvain pressed him to see if the New York banking firm of Kuhn, Loeb and Company would specify that at least part of the loan they were about to make to Japan should be spent in the United States—he cited British precedents for such conditions for lending, which had long involved war materials. In 1911 Sen. Robert La Follette's weekly magazine made charges about "dollar diplomacy" under President Taft, more specifically that U.S. naval secrets had been traded for foreign contracts for Bethlehem Steel. Although Schwab seems not to have been a key player when at least five British private shipbuilders made inquiries at Bethlehem in 1909 about guns and even armor, he had close, but not always harmonious relations with leading representatives of British armament firms. As early as 1905 his old Carnegie Steel colleague, Millard Hunsiker, now representing the main American armament firms in London, informed Frick that Albert Vickers, commercial director of one of the two biggest British armament companies and a leading influence in international business, was complaining that Harrah of Midvale was quoting cut-rate prices for armor to British shipbuilders. Vickers wanted to check Harrah by being empowered to offer him a third of U.S. business. Hunsiker's opinion was interesting: "Personally I think it would be better to have it left until Harrah gets back to America, or CMS may meddle a little too much in it." Another snapshot of Schwab's role on the international stage came from a senior member of another leading British armaments firm, Armstrong-Whitworth. After attending the armor plate makers' convention in Paris early in 1908, when it was in a critical condition, this representative reported, "One of the chief factors in the present armor plate crisis is a dreadful man called Schwab. He is in Paris, and not so unpleasant personally as his reputation."[55]

In 1913 it was Schwab's turn to be frustrated by the course of transatlantic negotiations. Bethlehem Steel had been in talks with the Sheffield quality steel firm of Hadfields about tool steels, projectiles, and armor, in the last of which Hadfields had recently made important advances in especially projectile-resistant steels. In England Schwab met Robert Hadfield—a man who many years before had produced an interesting private report on a visit to Edgar Thomson works at the very time when Schwab had first become associated with that plant. Hadfield was a distinguished metallurgist but an aloof, self-centered individual, temperamentally a world away from Schwab, who was well able to hold his own in negotiations. Schwab was seeking a license to use Hadfield's armor process, but as he reported to Grace, things did not go well: "Interview with Hadfield most indefinite and unsatisfactory. He realizes his strong opportunity with our Government. Does not fear our competition in England, as shells here are placed privately without advertisement or publishing prices. He is chiefly interested in selling us license to make his shells, in which event he would not bid in our market. Have shown no interest in this proposition."[56]

In the middle of the first decade of the century, U.S. government purchases of armor were well below the capacity of Carnegie and Bethlehem Steel. The addition of the Midvale mill made matters worse. In the hope of finding an outlet for otherwise underutilized capacity Schwab made overseas journeys to win foreign business either for armor and ordnance or for warships built by their shipbuilding subsidiaries. The Russian empire seemed to offer possibilities, having been Bethlehem's first overseas customer in the previous decade. In April 1905, a month before Russia's final humiliating defeat in the Russo-Japanese war, Schwab visited Saint Petersburg. (His European travels included a visit to Luxembourg—presumably to look at the Grey beam mill in Differdange.) When he stopped off in Berlin on 1 May he announced that he had obtained contracts from the Russian government but that it would be improper to talk about them further at that time. Soon afterward it was learned he had won a $1 million order for armor for Russian battleships. A few days later, a major part of the existing Russian fleet was destroyed in battle at Tsushima. After the Russian revolution of 1905 it was reported that Schwab had assured the tsar that he could provide him with a new navy in four years.[57] Next year he was again in Russia, and, as before, he was ostensibly in pursuit of orders for guns and ships, but friends said his visit also involved advice and possible financial involvement in the Izhor steel plant (at the great naval armaments establishment at Kolpino near Saint Petersburg). When in 1907 he and Johnston sailed for Europe on the newly commissioned *Lusitania*, it was anticipated that they would arrange with the Russians to build battleships, but later reports suggested that Schwab might be asked to become involved in reorganizing the Russian navy and those parts of the steel industry that supplied it.[58]

Some sense of the "murkiness" of armament negotiations came out in 1905 and subsequently in a series of exchanges about business in the Russian empire in which the remarkable Charles R. Flint played a prominent part. One of the so-called "fathers" of American trusts, Flint was a man with a very colorful past in the armaments trade. In November he wrote to Schwab from Paris, recommending the appointment of a Mr. Berg to be Bethlehem's agent in Europe. (It is not clear whether or not this was Thorsten Berg, once chief engineer at Carnegie Steel and later U.S. Steel technical representative in Europe.) Flint thought that if Bethlehem wanted major business in Russia, they probably would have to combine with an existing concern or build a plant there. He believed that most American shipbuilders, as well as U.S. Steel and Bethlehem, were prepared to cooperate and work through a single representative in Russia but that Cramp's, feeling itself to be in the best position to get orders, would not join. Flint thought Schwab's reputation was of vital importance: "I am, however, thoroughly satisfied that your prestige in Russia owing to the influence which you exerted when there and owing to your high standing as a manufacturer of steel is decidedly better than that of any other American." But this reputation would not make Berg superfluous: "Mr. Berg . . . expects to go to St. Petersburg within a week, and the ordinary salaried agent isn't 'in it' with him for getting business."[59] Less than three years later Johnston questioned Flint's own standing. Returning from Europe on the *Kaiser Wilhelm II* Johnston had met M. S. Freed of the Engineers' Club of New York: "Mr. Freed informed me that Mr. Flint is in very bad repute in Russia and that he and Mr. Lewis Nixon are both supposed to have done us a great deal of harm by representing themselves as our Agent." Schwab had a low opinion of Nixon from United States Shipbuilding days, but he warmly defended Flint, telling Johnston that he could not believe Freed: "I have been in St. Petersburg and seen Mr. Flint's standing there. I know that he has done a great deal of business in Russia. . . . Flint was able to sell sub-marine boats to Russia and other countries abroad when nobody else in this country was able to do so." These sales had been made during the course of the war with Japan.[60]

In 1908 another alluring prospect for armament sales was seen to be opening, this time in China. Once more Flint appears to have been the initial go-between. Late that fall Johnston wrote to tell him that Bethlehem would be glad to entertain the Chinese ambassador, Tang Shou Yi, and that Schwab would send his private rail car to collect him. He suggested that the Union Iron Works would be the best place to build warships for China.[61] As was so often the case in this sort of business things took a long time to develop, but in 1911 Schwab and Johnston traveled to Peking to negotiate battleship orders. The delay proved to have been unfortunate for early in October, while they were there, a revolutionary outbreak occurred in Wuchang. It spread rapidly, and by the end of the month Schwab had to set out on his return journey, the "rebellion" having caused the negotiations to fail. Even so, when in mid-November he and Johnston arrived back in New York on the *Mauretania* he declared the results of their mission satisfactory. Contacts were eventually resumed; in early autumn 1912 Admiral Ching visited Bethlehem and Schwab again went out to China via Europe.[62]

Well before 1914 Bethlehem ranked high among the world's great armament firms. It had delivered guns not only to the U.S. government but also to Mexico—which by that time was in turmoil and in confrontation with the United States—and to Argentina, some of the smaller South American republics, and the Ottoman Empire. It had supplied 75,000 tons of armor plate for the United States, 4,575 tons to the Russia empire, 2,050 for the Italian ship *Giulo Cesare,* and 8,870 tons for Argentina. Bethlehem was on the European/American circuit for nations aspiring to build or extend their navies. Like long-established European armament concerns, it produced elaborately styled brochures as well as programs to mark important events, as in October 1909 on the occasion of a visit by the Honorary Commercial Commissioners of Japan or in July 1913 when the officers of the Brazilian battleship *Minas Geraes,* completed by Armstrong-Whitworth four years before, were given a tour of the Bethlehem works. Though a relative newcomer, Bethlehem even began to sound out and in some cases to penetrate the outlets for war matériel among the great powers. In the competition to build a battleship for the Greek navy, a German builder was given the order for the hull, but Bethlehem, aligned with the Vulkan yard in Stettin, on the Baltic, was chosen to supply its guns. Early in 1909 the Thames Ironworks, last survivor of a once major shipbuilding complex in the London area, sent Bethlehem an inquiry for the armor and armaments for a first-class battleship as well as for destroyers. In addition, inquiries were made, information sent, or tenders submitted for armaments for naval vessels by such famous British yards as Hawthorn Leslie on the Tyne and by three Clydeside firms—Yarrow, Scotts, and Denny. In searching for work in the Ottoman Empire, Bethlehem allied itself with Palmers of Jarrow, Tyneside, a firm having a well-established reputation for building warships but which lacked both armor and ordnance capacity.[63]

In addition to Bethlehem's armor and heavy gun capacity, because of its inheritance from the United States Shipbuilding Company the Bethlehem Steel Corporation was directly involved in merchant and naval shipbuilding. In December 1904 it controlled five shipyards and other plants involved in maritime supply trades. The new company set out to rationalize its uneven assortment of works. By March 1905, in "pursuance of a policy of concentration of operations at certain plants most favorably located and best adapted for development," the two operations in Bath, Maine, were sold. The Crescent yard was dismantled and its site offered for sale. The Carteret works was out of operation, and those parts of the Harlan and Hollingsworth and S. L. Moore operations not considered essential were sold. The remainder of these latter two plants and the Union Iron Works were in continuous operation throughout 1905. They were allocated $429,000 for improvements during the year, but the Bethlehem steel works received $3 million. By March 1906 all except three large cranes had been dismantled at the Eastern Shipbuilding plant and its site was for sale. In short, by summer 1906 Bethlehem had streamlined its operations so that it controlled only two shipyards, those at Wilmington, Delaware, and at San Francisco. Results in shipbuilding were unsatisfactory. Serious losses were made on cruisers built for the U.S. Navy, mainly at Union Iron Works. There is circumstantial evidence that this yard was not the most efficient of builders. Of three first-class cruisers and six armored cruisers laid down for the United States in 1901 or 1902, Union built one and two, respectively. Newport News built one first-class cruiser in three years; Union took four years to complete a comparable project. In the case of both the Union armored cruisers, five years elapsed between laying down and completion. Although it too took five years to complete one of its two cruisers, Newport News completed the other in four, as did Cramp's for its two armored cruisers. Reacting to such circumstances, the report on 1906 operations recorded, "Future ship contracts will only be taken on an assured margin of profit." During 1907 the Crescent and Carteret operations were consolidated with the S. L. Moore Corporation, Harlan and Hollingsworth was idle for the last part of the year, and although Union Iron Works completed seven ships, the company sustained a loss on six of them. Bethlehem Steel now invested in improving Union Iron Works. By 1914 it was reported by a world authority on naval affairs that effectively all of the plant there dated from 1910 or later.[64]

As Bethlehem armor capacity was expanded and Schwab and his colleagues obtained more overseas orders, it was recognized as increasingly desirable that the company should control an Atlantic seaboard yard capable of building the largest warships. Late in 1910 there was a report that Bethlehem had acquired a large interest in Cramp's, but it was never to control that famous yard.[65] Instead, it gradually became more closely involved with the Fore River Shipbuilding Company of Quincy, Massachusetts. Fore River had been established in 1884 to begin operations on the river whose name it bore. In the late 1890s, when building destroyers for the U.S. Navy, the company also decided to undertake the construction of bigger warships. A new yard was established six miles away on a site where such vessels could more easily be launched. At the time of a visit by a Bethlehem group in 1901 this new yard had not yet been completed. In 1903 Fore River began work on the Curtis turbine and also recruited a new president, Adm. Francis Tiffany Bowles, who had been serving as chief constructor of the U.S. Navy. In January 1907 Bowles asked Schwab if Bethlehem would help Fore River to secure foreign warship orders. He had particularly in mind a program of battleship and cruiser building for China, for which he was negotiating through his London representative. Saying he would not deal with Midvale but wanted some cost protection against tenders by other shipbuilders, Bowles asked if Bethlehem would give him lower prices for armor and ordnance. Schwab assured him they would cooperate.[66]

The relationship between the naval shipbuilder and the armaments group developed. In January 1910 Schwab spoke to the Commercial Club of Providence, Rhode Island, on "The Development of the Steel Industry in the United States." His topic did not prevent him from presenting a panegyric, not dissimilar in tone from his letter to Morton a few years before, on warship building in the region. Toward the end of his address he said, "You have in Quincy, Massachusetts, a distinguished naval constructor—Admiral Bowles. Through Admiral Bowles, the United States has been able, for the first time, to take her place in [the] competition of [the] nations of the world. We had his experience, as against that in England, France and Germany, to build great battleships for our Navy. I want to say publicly, this Admiral Bowles of New England is a man whose ingenuity in devising our own battleships, whose standing as an engineer and officer of the Navy of the great American nation, has made this possible."[67] From Bethlehem's perspective the times were appropriate for such a eulogy. Fore River had not done particularly well in seeking for work with the Navy Department, but it had at last secured a big foreign order.

In 1905 the United States authorized construction of its first "dreadnoughts," the "all big-gun" battleships. Cramp's yard laid down the first of these ships in November 1906, and between then and the outbreak of World War I another nine were completed. Of the ten only one, the *North Dakota*, begun in December 1907 and completed in April 1910, was built by Fore River. There was to be a five-year gap between the laying down of the *North Dakota* and that of the company's next dreadnought for the United States, the *Nevada*, but almost three years earlier the Fore River yard was chosen for a large part of the highly competitive naval building program then being undertaken by the so-called "ABC" powers of South America: Argentina, Brazil, and Chile. Argentina sent a naval commission to London to receive bids for two twenty-eight-thousand-ton battleships. When the bids were opened, Fore River was declared the winner for one of the warships, the *Rivadavia*, to the surprise of most commentators and apparently with the misgivings of some senior Argentine naval officers. The New York Shipbuilding Company of Camden, New Jersey, was awarded the contract for the other ship, the *Moreno*. The securing of the order for the *Rivadavia* and the company's experiences in filling it brought Fore River into closer contact with Bethlehem Steel. During winter 1909–1910 Bethlehem received contracts for armor, armaments, ammunition, spare parts, and accessories for ships for Argentina worth some $10 million, largely for work to be undertaken at Quincy but also ordnance and armor for the *Moreno* as well as guns for destroyers to be built in Germany, France, and Britain.[68]

The commercial links between the two companies were gradually strengthened, largely due to the lack of commercial success at Fore River, whatever its technical achievements as a builder. As early as spring 1910 P. D. Cravath, a New York lawyer, wrote to Schwab that a representative of Fore River had told him they would be glad to sell out to Bethlehem: "He said that the company had not been profitable because of the bitter competition between the big shipbuilding plants, but that he and his associates thought that if the company were in strong hands a great deal of money could be made by bringing about better relations between the big shipbuilders." Doubt was expressed as to whether Bethlehem would wish to take over another yard. In reply Schwab recorded their interest in view of possibilities of large foreign contracts in the future, and he obviously regarded Cravath as a go-between: "I would like sometime to have an interview with the gentleman named, especially if he could give a statement of their affairs and some idea as to how the property might be acquired." Even after this exchange, it took almost two years to get to a point of decision. Meanwhile, on 25 August 1912 Schwab and his wife traveled in their private rail car from Bethlehem to Boston and on to Quincy for the launch of the *Rivadavia* next day. Grace was also present.[69] It soon became clear that construction of the Argentine battleship had brought on a crisis at the yard.

The Fore River company had miscalculated the cost of the *Rivadavia*. This error was due in part to the many trials required for the very large turbines with which it was equipped. Bethlehem had guaranteed the contract and therefore shared responsibility for the delays. In late March or early April 1913 Schwab and Johnston went to Quincy to look over the operations. The latter summarized the situation in a letter to J. E. Mathews of the Bethlehem ordnance department. "Of course we have no desire to take over the yard," Johnston wrote, but their Argentine business was essentially with Fore River, and Bowles had rightly said the steel company was very late in delivering their part of contracts. Consequently, Bethlehem was brought to the point at which it had "to consider the purchase of the yard in order to save the South American situation and our own skins at the same time." He felt that it would happen, but in general Johnston was not in favor of the takeover, and this view seems to have led him to exaggerate the problems: "In my opinion the yard is the least desirable of any in the States; not only by reason of its reputation but also by reason of its location, it being out of the path of steamships requiring repairs; but we may be compelled to take an action which might otherwise seem undesirable." The sale was completed in mid-April. Schwab asked Bowles to carry on for the time being, "just as you would have done had no change taken place."[70] A few days later Johnston again contacted Mathews. As the purchase went through, Johnston began to focus his criticism on the Quincy yard's management. His assessment was scathing: "In view of existing conditions, Mr. Schwab deemed it wise to continue Admiral Bowles, at least until the Argentine ships are completed. I fear that the wiles of our smooth friend have completely 'won over' Mr. Schwab. In my estimation, he [Admiral Bowles] can be the sweetest customer I have ever had to deal with."[71] Johnston cannot have been consoled when a week later Mathews pointed out that, since taking over Fore River, Bethlehem's stock had entered a "decided slump." A major redeeming feature was that the purchase had been cheaply made; in return for making more capital available, Bethlehem acquired the shipbuilding company for what was, according to one estimate, one-seventh of its actual value. Even more impressive, the purchase price was repaid in the first year out of the profits made by the yard's new owners.[72]

An additional gain from the acquisition was that the steel works now had a secure outlet for its products. The annual report for 1913 summed up the situation: "The control of the Fore River plant gives to your Corporation facilities for building, on the Atlantic seaboard, complete battleships fully armored and equipped." More colorfully, Charles Harrah of Midvale, who had grounds enough for resentment against Bethlehem, was forced to recognize that his company would lose any business Bowles had directed their way. He wrote to Schwab in a strange if not uncharacteristic mood: "Ah well, I suppose I must take this loss with Christian resignation. I find that life for me has many tribulations, I mean, of course, in addition to my acquaintance with you." In reply Schwab managed a commendable good humor: "You are always so jocose with me that I do not know whether to regard your communication seriously or not; but someday, when I may have the pleasure of seeing you, which has been denied

me for a long time, I can explain to you the necessity for this transaction.
. . . Don't you take any interest in business any more? It would be a pleasure to see you, even though I should expect your usual 'roast' regarding
Johnston and myself." On 30 June 1913 a new Bethlehem subsidiary was
formed—the Fore River Shipbuilding Corporation. Bowles did not survive long as its head. He was hardly likely to be compatible with the new
owners who had strong opinions of their own, for he was "a man of great
force of character, definite and strong opinions and inclined to be uncom-
promising when he had once definitely made up his mind."[73] Next year,
aged only fifty-six, he resigned as president, to be replaced by J. W. Powell, a man Bethlehem had brought in from Cramp's. For a time Bowles left
shipbuilding, the activity in which, either as naval administrator or business leader, he had spent his working life. A few years later he again came
into contact with Schwab in circumstances neither could have anticipated
when he left Fore River.

The *Rivadavia* was completed in 1914. Apparently it was Fore River,
and a further program of building work for Argentina, which soon brought
Schwab into contact with a New England family whose roots were relatively recent and undistinguished in U.S. nineteenth-century history but
whose branches would gain wealth, fame, and honor in the new century—
the Kennedys. Joseph Kennedy, grandson of an Irish immigrant, studied
at Harvard before going into banking. In spring 1917 he was made assistant manager of Fore River, with special responsibility for the housing,
feeding, and movement of its expanded work force. That year, because
they had not been paid for, Schwab refused to release a number of naval
vessels that Fore River had built for Argentina. He sent Kennedy to arbi-
trate the issue with the assistant secretary of the navy, Franklin D. Roosevelt, who assured Kennedy the State Department would collect the payments and asked that the ships be released. When Kennedy refused, he
was threatened that navy tugboats would be sent to collect them. Encouraged by Kennedy, Schwab refused to let the vessels leave, and the tugboats duly arrived, towed the warships downriver to the sea, and handed
them over to the Argentine navy.[74]

Not much more than a year after it was brought into Bethlehem Steel
Corporation, Fore River was to prove an invaluable asset in first meeting
Allied wartime demands and then in supplying the U.S. Navy and merchant shipping needs. In this way a cheaply bought shipyard made its
contribution to a long delayed influx of revenue for Bethlehem Steel. This
income in turn would permit Schwab to realize his dream of creating the

leading steel group in the East, one that, on the national level, would rank second only to the United States Steel Corporation.

By this time Schwab had gained a reputation as a generally genial and approachable leader of industry, a man very different from the hard and remote Frick or Gary. An example of the favorable impression he made came in a local press report of a 1912 visit to Detroit. The *Journal* outlined for its readers both his general appearance and personality: "Charles M. Schwab is a man of large frame, which however carries no surplus flesh. His shoulders and body are broad and the tapering legs seem at first glance a little small until he is in motion. Then his little active movements suggest something of the well-trained athlete." (Within a few years this description was no longer appropriate, for his body had very visibly thickened.) "His face is smooth, his eye keen but with a twinkling play, his manner free and easy, and he has an irrepressible tendency to the unexpected turn in words that makes for a pleasant joke. He has everybody feeling at home in about two seconds, and if he has other engagements, as he usually has, brings a visit to an end so smoothly that the guest feels well satisfied with himself as he departs."[75]

Occasionally, his genius for human relationships was marred by hardness, as in his dealings with labor, or by an element of "cleverness" or, as a later generation would put it, "one-upmanship." One example of how, despite the surface bonhommie, this one-upmanship disclosed his lack of sympathy with millions of ordinary, striving human beings came late in 1904. He received a letter from a stranger in London, at a time at which there was much distress there. The message read, "Knowing as I do your generosity, I have put you down for a £40 or $200 subscription to our miners' widows' fund. Christmas is approaching and we propose to give a fowl and a Christmas pudding to each miner's widow on Christmas Eve. In this good work your donation will help largely." Schwab replied to his unknown correspondent, "Though I know nothing of you or your fund I respond gladly to the call you make upon me. I, too, am interested in a charity similar to yours. It is an American charity, and, since it stands in need of funds for a Christmas treat, I have not hesitated to put you down for a subscription of $200 to it. Thus no money need pass between us." He once told a story of his visit to the Austro-Hungarian empire. In an audience with the aged Franz Josef, Schwab was asked what interest the fairly small steel industry of the emperor's domains could have for a man like him. He made the clever, if not particularly sensitive reply, "At least, your Majesty, it will show me what to avoid." Yet another instance of self-centeredness occurred some time later when he was interested in acquiring a small rerolling operation, belonging to the Rockaway Rolling Mills on the Passaic River a little more than half way from Bethlehem to New York. He arranged a meeting with its owner, Edward K. Ehlers, in a New York hotel, where after talking of the industry, prices, and so on, the conversation got around to what Schwab was willing to pay. Though at that time he was riding high as he built up his new steel empire, the price he offered for the Rockaway mill was judged much too low. When the parties agreed to break off the negotiations, Schwab suggested they share a taxi to the Pennsylvania Station. He was last into the taxi but first out, leaving Ehlers to pay the fare.[76]

5 ❦ World War I

Bethlehem's War

The steel industry reached record outputs in 1912 and even higher levels the following year. Bethlehem Steel did better than most companies. In 1913 national steel production increased 0.16 percent, U.S. Steel's tonnage fell 1.45 percent, and Bethlehem's went up 13.9 percent. On 1 April 1913, Schwab was in an upbeat mood when he addressed stockholders at the annual meeting: "Business is prosperous. The Company has plenty of orders. Everything is moving most satisfactorily and we are pleased with the outlook this year." After such highs, 1914 was a disappointing year, and by April Schwab was much less ebullient than the year before. He now spoke "rather pessimistically" about trade conditions, though he managed to summon up enough optimism to express his belief that the recession would not last as long as previous ones had, as business was now in the hands of "conservative and capable corporation heads." The stockholders approved the spending of about $6 million on extensions and new plant. For a time the anticipated improvement failed to materialize, and by August the Bethlehem mills were operating at only about 60 percent of capacity, some workers were on reduced hours, and others had been laid off.[1]

At this time of industry and company difficulties, Schwab was also at a low ebb, apparently suffering from mental exhaustion and physical complications. There were family difficulties, too. Edward, his youngest

brother, was twenty-nine when in April John Schwab wrote to tell his eldest son how shocked he and Pauline had been to hear of "Ed's financial
'troubles': . . . I was of the opinion that he was getting in shape to make
some money. We both felt so bad that we sat down and had a good cry."
Amid these pressures and distractions Schwab received an expression of
kindly concern for his well-being that contrasted sharply with the harsh
everyday realities of the business scene. It came in a mid-June message
from Father McGettingen of the Holy Infancy Rectory, South Bethlehem.
As he went off on his annual retreat McGettingen wrote, "I assure you that
during those days of meditation and prayer you will daily be remembered
by me. I hope your illness is not of a serious character. The Bethlehems
cannot afford to have their greatest benefactor lose his health." Six weeks
later, Schwab spelled out his problems in a letter to his wife, addressing
her, "My Dear Old Lady." He was not feeling at all well, being greatly
troubled by spells of weakness, feeling faint, and dizziness. If the electrical treatment he was receiving did not work he thought the only thing was
to go to a spa in Europe, somewhere like Carlsbad.[2] As things turned out,
a more radical change of circumstances provided the necessary antidote.
On the day before he wrote his letter to Rana, Austria-Hungary mobilized
its forces on its border with Russia. The next day it declared war on Ser-
bia. The outbreak of what was soon recognized as the "Great War" in Europe transformed the business situation for Bethlehem. Schwab's indispo-
sitions were pushed into the background as he became involved.

Horrified by the outbreak of a conflict that for years he had struggled
to prevent, Andrew Carnegie left his beloved home of Skibo for what
proved to be the last time on 14 September 1914. Two days or so later
he sailed for the United States on the *Mauretania*. The contrast between
his circumstances and those of his most trusted former lieutenant could
scarcely have been starker. Quickly Schwab was caught up in the height-
ened activity that the war was eventually to bring to the whole American
economy. By early October Bethlehem was fitting guns to motor trucks to
be delivered to France and Russia. Then, on Tuesday, 20 October, Schwab
in New York received a message from the Admiralty in London. It asked
him to come over at once. However, if a letter from Walter Page, the U.S.
ambassador to Britain, is to be believed, Schwab was not the first to attempt to obtain orders for matériel, though if that is so, the pioneer cannot be identified. Page wrote home from London on 11 October: "[A]
Pittsburgh manufacturer is now here trying to close a bargain with the
War Office." For his part, in retrospect, Winston Churchill provided what
could scarcely be claimed as even a half true account: "Mr Schwab was at

that time passing through England on his return to the United States." In
any event Schwab's response to the Admiralty could scarcely have been
bettered. At 1:00 a.m. on the day after receiving the cable, Schwab–traveling as "Alexander McDonald"–accompanied by Archibald Johnston,
sailed from New York on the White Star liner *Olympic.* Early press reports
indicated he was taking the sea voyage in the interests of his health.[3]

As the *Olympic* neared the British Isles, reports of submarine activity caused a diversion from the usual route toward Glasgow. Then, as they
steamed along the north coast of Ireland, those on board were given a
vivid picture of the horrors of modern warfare at sea when they came
upon the twenty-three-thousand-ton superdreadnought HMS *Audacious*
slowly sinking after hitting mines. In hope of helping it limp to port the
battleship was taken in tow by the liner but the line snapped in heavy
seas and *Audacious* sank. On reaching Scotland there was some holdup
with the disembarking of passengers, but on 31 October the commander
in chief of the Grand Fleet, Admiral Sir John Jellicoe, wrote to Churchill,
then First Lord of the Admiralty: "I saw Mr Schwab, Head of Bethlehem
Steel works today. . . . I have allowed him to land and have requested him
to call on you in regard to certain propositions he has respecting sale
of ships to British Admiralty and construction of new ships, especially
torpedo boat destroyers and submarines." When he arrived in London
Schwab met Churchill, Lord Kitchener, who was secretary of state for
war, and the elderly, energetic, and unpredictable John Fisher, recalled to
the post of First Sea Lord only a few days before. Fisher was captivated
by their visitor and by the scale of the help he seemed able to promise.
Writing on 3 November to George Lambert, his close colleague at the Admiralty, Fisher, with an inaccuracy not unusual for him, mentioned "the
great Schwab of the American Steel Corporation. . . . [He is] far bigger
than Elswick and Vickers put together."[4]

Orders placed with Bethlehem included major purchases of naval and
army guns and projectiles. Shipments of fourteen-inch guns and mounts
were made six weeks ahead of the time promised. As Schwab recalled
some two and a half years later, Kitchener had asked him to make 1 million shells for the British government in a year. At that time he reckoned
the annual output of all the munitions plants in the United States was only
about 100,000 shells, but even so he accepted the contract and completed
the order in ten months. Soon Bethlehem was shipping 50,000 rounds of
ammunition to Britain and an equal amount to Russia every day. Johnston
later claimed that, according to Fisher, in the first six months Bethlehem
shipped more ammunition to the British than was supplied by all its own

munitions makers. As well as giving such a large boost to Bethlehem activity, Kitchener seems to have provided Schwab with the first long-term framework under which he and his colleagues could begin planning a program for wartime production and expansion, for by that first October of the war, Kitchener was predicting that the conflict might last five years.[5]

At some time during their visit to London the Bethlehem representatives were asked if they could supply submarines. (As noted above, Jellicoe had intimated that Schwab *arrived* with "propositions" about submarine construction.) Fisher later recorded that in October 1914 the Royal Navy had only fifty-one submarines. (Again, his figure is suspect. As early as 1912 the Royal Navy had sixty-five submarines and fourteen more were under construction.[6]) On 1 or 2 November Fisher and Churchill sent for Schwab and asked if he could supply twenty more submarines. He cabled Henry Snyder in Bethlehem, who in turn contacted the Electric Boat Company of New York, a firm well established in submarine construction, before cabling back that they could build ten boats at the Quincy yard and ten at Union Iron Works. Schwab undertook to deliver the first submarine in six months, though until then the record time for construction had been fourteen months. By 7 November the arrangement was agreed with the Admiralty. Then one evening, after a long discussion about the submarine contract, Schwab was sitting with Churchill and Fisher around the octagonal table at the Admiralty. When asked "have you got anything else that will be of use to us?" Schwab told them of the four turrets, each containing two 14-inch guns, built for the Greek battleship *Salamis,* then under construction in Germany. The turrets were almost complete but still in Bethlehem's workshops. Churchill recorded, "We set our hearts on these," and Bethlehem subsequently refused to ship them to Greece and sold them instead to Britain. It was also agreed that it should supply Britain with twelve 9.2-inch guns built for Chile, promising the latter a future delivery of 12-inch guns instead.[7]

Schwab and Johnston left London on 10 November, and by 20 November they had arrived back in New York. The American press was told that Schwab hoped eventually to write an account of the events of the previous few weeks; certainly not much was revealed at the time. In private conversation he was said to have made a thought-provoking, if enigmatic, comment about the sixty-four-year-old British secretary of state for war: "Lord Kitchener is the best president the United States Steel Corporation ever missed." Before the end of the month Bethlehem was working to capacity to fill British orders worth $50 million.[8]

The arrangement for building submarines for Britain was imperiled by investigations into its legality by Secretary of State William Jennings Bryan. Although Schwab visited the State Department, he was unable to prevent the administration from concluding that Bethlehem's manufacture of matériel for Britain would violate U.S. neutrality—a decision that revived memories of the celebrated *Alabama* case, when a private British yard had built a warship for the Confederacy, with disastrous consequences for Federal commerce and Anglo-American relations. At this critical point someone—it is not clear who—suggested the problem might be solved if Bethlehem made the parts for the submarines but had them assembled in Canada, at a Vickers shipyard developed shortly before the war. Vickers was the very armaments group Schwab had beaten in 1901 to gain control of Bethlehem Steel. On Friday, 4 December, Schwab hurried by train to Montreal to examine this yard. Next day he left New York on the *Lusitania*, reached London on 13 December, and there renegotiated the submarine contract to allow for assembly in Canada. Bethlehem was to be allowed $100,000 more for each vessel to cover the extra costs involved, and delivery dates were extended. Schwab arrived home two days before Christmas. As a seasonal gift to his superintendents, he distributed watches—eloquent symbols of the urgency of their labors.

Before leaving England after his first visit, there was one other, personal service Schwab had been able to provide. On 7 November John Fisher had sent Schwab a penciled note and enclosed a letter he was intending to have delivered to President Wilson. It requested his good offices in securing the release of Fisher's daughter and son-in-law from internment in Germany, where the couple had been taking the "cure" at a spa when the war began. Instead of approaching Wilson, which would have put the president in an embarrassing position, Schwab telephoned John Leishman in Paris, and he immediately came over to London. After Schwab took his place as president of Carnegie Steel in 1897, Leishman had embarked on a diplomatic career, and between 1911 and 1913 he had been U.S. ambassador in Berlin. As was so often the case, Leishman needed money and was therefore willing to respond to Schwab's offer of fifty thousand dollars to travel via neutral Holland to Berlin to act on Fisher's behalf. There were complications, but eventually Fisher's daughter and her husband were released. Schwab received the good news from England on Christmas Eve. Thankfulness was now added to the professional admiration that John Fisher, as head of the Admiralty, already had for their American supplier of weapons of war. As he put it to Schwab, he was "Yours till hell freezes."[9]

Work on supplies for the Allies was pushed ahead unremittingly. In the popular eye, Schwab was credited with the success, but it was Grace who engineered its achievement. It went on despite justified complaints from the German and Austrian embassies that Bethlehem was shipping submarines in sections to belligerents. There were rumors that the Germans—and the British, too—were buying Bethlehem Steel stock and that the former had made a $100 million offer to gain control. Gradually, the pressure of the times took its toll on Schwab. By March 1915 he was worn down from overwork was said to have neuritis and to be seeking rest in hope of avoiding a breakdown by spending some time at White Sulphur Springs, West Virginia. Yet in three letters on 14 May he wrote in triumph to Churchill, Fisher, and Jellicoe (in the latter case recalling their meeting under "such extraordinary circumstances") to let them know that the ten Montreal-built submarines would be completed, and tested in every particular, by 10 June, just over five months from the time of the contract. He stressed that they could have done even better in their own yards, and then he offered to take on further work and indicated his willingness to return to London to discuss this possibility. Fisher replied promptly, saying he would "never forget your splendid enthusiasm and zeal." After the war he wrote, "If any man deserved the gratitude of England, Mr Schwab is the man." Jellicoe responded on 5 June 1915 from his flagship HMS *Iron Duke* using more measured terms but particularly praising their supplier's technical achievements: "I think it is really a magnificent piece of work to have completed in five months, and I only wish that we could turn out work as quickly in this country. I wonder if you had the engines ready, because it seems quite extraordinary to me that you have been able to produce them in such a short time." A few weeks later, by which time all the submarines had left Canada, Schwab wrote back, "You wonder if we had the engines ready. No, the engines were not ready, but were started and built after receipt of the order. I often speak to my friends of my very interesting interview with you, and your delightful treatment of me, and look forward to meeting you again, after your troubles are over, if not before."[10]

Churchill, by now moved on from the Admiralty, where friction between men such as himself and Fisher was inevitable, did not reply to Schwab's letter for two months. When he did so, his words were few but characteristic: "You have discharged a great undertaking faithfully and well. No one but you could have done such a thing. It was a great pleasure to me to do business with you. Take good care of yourself now; these are dangerous times and the Germans have good reason to bear you malice and will I trust have better."[11] After the war Schwab would recall that his services to the British war effort had been warmly praised by prominent individuals, including Churchill and Lloyd George, but he seemed to think it regrettable that he had not received official recognition, though it is not clear what form he thought such acknowledgment could have taken.

This program of work for the Allies meant full activity and unprecedented profits for Bethlehem Steel. In August 1914, as war began, it had less than $25 million in unfilled orders; by January they amounted to $100 million. Contracts for ammunition for Britain in the first autumn of the conflict alone were worth about $125 million.[12] Because of its special circumstances, Bethlehem now outdistanced its steel industry rivals. Net income for the United States Steel Corporation in 1914 was not quite 29 percent as high as in 1913; at Bethlehem and its subsidiaries it was 10.2 percent higher. Schwab was so delighted with their results that he sent an advance copy of the annual report for 1914 to Frick, who responded with good grace: "My Dear Mr. Schwab . . . I am obliged for the copy of your annual report for the year ended December 31st 1914. I shall enjoy looking it over carefully." The key to their success lay in a simple statement in the report: "Notwithstanding the generally depressed state of trade throughout this year in commercial lines, the variety of products of your Corporation, which has directly resulted from its policy of extensive development in diversified lines of manufacture, enables it to report the best record in its history." At the annual general meeting a month later Schwab's address was even more explicit, if less sensitive: "[W]hile the year so far has been very bad for the general steel business, the Bethlehem Company has been fortunate in being engaged in the manufacture of lines which are in strong demand." This good fortune continued. Even during 1915 U.S. Steel net income was 6.5 percent less than in 1913; net earnings at Bethlehem Steel were 178.8 percent higher than two years before. On 20 January 1916 it announced payment of a 30 percent dividend on common shares. That year brought more records, net profits from manufacturing being an extraordinary $60 million and net income more than $43 million. After that, though activity continued at high levels through 1917 and 1918, manufacturing profits fell away, though they remained very high compared with prewar levels. From 1916 both output and profits came from major new additions to the corporation, for the early wartime windfalls gave Schwab and his fellow directors unexpected financial wherewithal to undertake major expansion, in part by extensions, partly by acquisition. The steps to these major additions brought Schwab into keen rivalry with former business associates (see table 8 in appendix B).[13]

In mid-October 1915 a group of leading industrialists and financiers headed by William Ellis Corey bought Harrah's long-established Midvale works in Philadelphia. They reconstructed it as the Midvale Steel and Ordnance Company, with Corey as chairman, Alva Dinkey (Schwab's brother-in-law) as president, and William B. Dickson, another close associate at both Carnegie Steel and U.S. Steel, as vice president. Midvale acquired a plant making small arms and the integrated operations of the Coatesville Rolling Mill Company and Worth Brothers, which were not far from the shipyards of the lower Delaware.. This company seemed likely to be a firm nucleus for a new East Coast group that might rival Bethlehem. In February 1916 an important further step was taken when Midvale acquired the Cambria works in Johnstown, reorganized over the previous four years by Jacob L. Replogle, who, until the sale, had held the controlling interest.

Even more impressive in relation to a major regional grouping was the situation and potential of the associated operations of Pennsylvania Steel at Steelton and Maryland Steel at Sparrows Point. At this time new legislation made these attractive prospects more accessible. The Clayton Act of 1914 contained a clause restricting relations between common carriers and construction and supply companies. Limiting the rights of transportation companies to control their suppliers put in question the long-established interest of the Pennsylvania Railroad Company (PRR) in the two steel companies. As early as March 1913, anticipating the legislation, Bethlehem had discussions with the PRR about taking over its steel interests. The cold calculations of business negotiations must have been eased by the fact that Samuel Rea, president of the PRR since January that year, came from Hollidaysburg, less than twenty miles from Loretto, and seems to have been a boyhood acquaintance of Schwab, though seven years his senior. Rea pointed out that Pennsylvania had a "great" ore supply. In turn, though recognizing there were difficulties, Schwab assured Rea, "I am anxious to take over the Pennsylvania property and make it a success for you and ourselves."[14]

Spiraling wartime demand made acquisition or merger that would bring in such important works as Steelton and Sparrows Point attractive to a number of parties, and war profits provided the funds to carry it through. Almost immediately after Midvale Steel and Ordnance was formed it became clear it was interested in these two works. For many years Henry Clay Frick and William H. Donner, with whom Frick had been associated since the Union Steel works project at Donora in 1901, had had financial interests in Pennsylvania. They too wanted to acquire control. Bethlehem was the third party. On 5 October 1915 Schwab met the Pennsylvania Railroad directors for an all-day conference in the Bethlehem offices. There were still problems, and though it seemed for a time that the takeover had been agreed on, the arrangement fell apart. Early next year Bethlehem's acquisition of the two operations was confirmed. The purchase price was about $32 million, but the gain to the purchaser, particularly in earnings potential, was huge. Steel capacity controlled by Bethlehem Steel was more or less doubled. The prize of the purchase was Sparrows Point. It was only ten years since Donner himself had reported adversely on Maryland Steel to Alexander J. Cassatt, president of the Pennsylvania Railroad, concluding that changes in coal freights and the organization of the ore flows on the Great Lakes had so revolutionized the steel business that he did not "think any practical steel man would consider locating a works at seaport today under present known conditions." He reckoned the average cost of hot metal at Sparrows Point was $13.05 a ton as compared with $9.80 in Pittsburgh. But since his report, duties on imported ore had been removed and Bethlehem had acquired El Tofo. Quickly it was recognized that extensions for bars, tinplate, and possibly wire, which had been contemplated for the Bethlehem works, might be better located at this unrivaled break-of-bulk point. Before 1916 ended contracts worth $2 million were awarded for four new blast furnaces, an open hearth plant, and blooming and plate mills. To ensure that Schwab retained control of the extended company, new stock issued in 1916 did not give its new owners voting powers. By this stage of the wartime boom a new scale of thinking was evident throughout Bethlehem Steel. At the beginning of 1915 extensions totaling $20 million to $30 million were under way. When Schwab and Grace spoke at a dinner held by the Harrisburg chamber of commerce on 2 October 1916, they announced plans to spend $90 million on improvements over the next three years. Even so, years later Schwab reckoned a single manager was one of their main gains from this merger, describing their vice president Quincy Bent as "the biggest asset we bought in Pennsylvania Steel." (Bent, who had been a major shareholder in Pennsylvania/Maryland, was to become one of the largest holders of Bethlehem stock; he also pioneered their important "loop course" management training system and served as vice president until 1947.)[15] Wartime expansion by acquisition had not yet run its course. In 1917, purchase of the American Iron and Steel Manufacturing Company of Lebanon, in eastern Pennsylvania, made Bethlehem a major producer of nuts, bolts, and other fasteners.

After April 1917 orders resulting from U.S. participation in the war were added to continuing huge orders from the Allies. Steel works, ordnance shops, and naval and merchant shipyards were pressed to their fullest activity. Well before the end of 1917 90 percent of Bethlehem orders were reported to be from the government.[16] It was in the midst of this unprecedented ferment of activity that Schwab became involved in a sharp conflict with the government over the production of armor. The company had entered 1916 with almost all departments fully employed. A noteworthy exception was armor plate, in which they had completed their work on all government orders. At this time, with the support of the Wilson administration, various interests accused the three armor makers of price fixing to the disadvantage of the nation. As a result the idea, already current in the mid-1890s, of a publicly owned armor plant was revived. In March 1916 in an effort to refute these allegations before the Senate Committee on Naval Affairs, Bethlehem pointed out that the U.S. government was paying only $425 a ton for armor as compared with a price of $503 in Britain, $490 in Germany and Japan, and $460 in France. The company described a claim made in the secretary of the navy's annual report that a government-owned installation capable of producing ten thousand tons of plate a year could, when operated at full capacity, cut the price to $262.79 as "wholly fallacious," pointing out that this figure ignored administrative expenses, interest and working capital, insurance, taxes, and depreciation—the very same range of considerations that almost twenty years earlier had vitiated Schwab's own $12 a ton figure for the lowest attainable cost of making Bessemer rails. In late March Schwab and his associates began campaigning for public support to reject the proposed government armor works. After writing to Congress and offering to open the Bethlehem books to the Trade Commission to prove their charges had not been unreasonable, they produced a 140-page booklet spelling out their opposition and placed advertisements in 3,257 newspapers across the nation. Late that year it was being suggested in some quarters that Schwab should be made secretary of the navy in place of Josephus Daniels, who had favored the proposal for a government mill. Despite all this activity, and against protests that such action would make the Bethlehem plant worthless, Congress approved a naval appropriations bill that provided $11 million for a national armor plant that could produce twenty-thousand tons a year. Construction began at South Charleston, West Virginia. The work was halted by wartime cost inflation but completed by 1921. South Charleston operated for a short time before being closed after it had been shown that its costs were twice those of the privately owned armor plants. When it was reactivated during World War II it operated as a subsidiary of the Homestead works (see table 9 in appendix B).[17]

The successes of wartime brought a vast increase in income for the company and of wealth for its majority owner. In the ten years to and including 1914 Bethlehem Steel net income totaled $22.8 million. Over the next two years it was $61.4 million. At a 1916 dinner in the company's new main offices, there was a conspicuous celebration of increased corporate wealth. The room was decorated with five hundred poinsettias and more than a thousand American Beauty roses. Of the 118 guests, 18 newcomers to the rank of management were given diamond-studded pins shaped in the form of H-beams. Schwab's own rewards took the form of more public displays of conspicuous consumption. He had a hunting lodge in the Maine woods and was already building a grand new country retreat near Loretto. In spring 1917 he was reported to have bought J. M. W. Turner's painting, *Rockets and Blue Light*.[18]

The Emergency Fleet Corporation

Schwab was unique among great executives in controlling at various times the world's largest agglomerations of capacity in two major industries. He was in turn head of U.S. Steel, the world's biggest steel company, and then built Bethlehem Steel into the world's second-ranking producer. For half a year at the end of World War I he directed far and away the largest shipbuilding operation anywhere in the world. In contrast with steel, his achievement in shipbuilding proved short-lived.

Before World War I the United States was already becoming a leading naval power, but it was very definitely of secondary rank both in shipping and in the construction of merchant ships. By the end of the war the latter situation had been transformed, though as events soon showed such a transformation remained possible only under the exceptional conditions of the times. The tonnage of American shipping registered in foreign trade doubled from 1914 to 1916. In the latter year Congress approved the creation of a U.S. Shipping Board, whose duties included advising on how to increase the size of the merchant marine. Bethlehem had long been a major factor in American shipbuilding. Now, as its steel capacity

expanded, so too did its capacity to build ships. In fall 1915 when Bethlehem was negotiating to buy the properties of Pennsylvania Steel it was
remarked that Bethlehem was as interested in acquiring Sparrows Point
for its shipyard, which was capable of building the largest merchant vessels, as for its steel plant. By June the company was building a $1 million
plant at Elizabeth, New Jersey, for naval vessels. Early in 1916, the Union
Iron Works division of Bethlehem purchased its San Francisco Bay neighbor, the Alameda shipyard, from the United Engineering Company. Big
extensions were made at Fore River, including the construction in 1916 of
what was said to be the largest plate and angle shop in the world. Employment at Fore River quickly rose from four thousand to sixteen thousand.[19]
After the United States entered the war this subsidiary provided as many
as six thousand workers to operate a wholly new yard eight miles distant
at Squantum, New Hampshire. The Squantum yard was designed especially to produce destroyers and was developed on a site that was under
water when the operation was inaugurated on 6 October 1917. Squantum
achieved remarkable production schedules, the destroyer *Reid* being delivered only forty-five and a half days after its keel was laid. Bethlehem
also constructed a new yard at Providence, Rhode Island, and works at
Buffalo to produce boilers and turbines for destroyers. It had great successes too in merchant shipbuilding. In fall 1917 the shipbuilding operations were reorganized, with Fore River, Harlan and Hollingsworth, S. L.
Moore, and the Union Iron Works being subsumed under a new name,
the Bethlehem Shipbuilding Company. At the end of that year, when orders in hand in all divisions of the Bethlehem organization reached $454
million, the shipbuilding division represented 60 percent of this total.
From the time the United States entered the war to the end of 1918 Bethlehem accounted for 22 percent of its new merchant shipbuilding tonnage.
The following year it turned out 900,000 tons, more than a quarter of the
national total (see table 10 in appendix B).[20]

For the last nine months of the war Schwab was temporarily detached
from Bethlehem Steel, not even attending board meetings. He had been
seconded to government service as head of a unique public body ded-
icated to mass production of ships. As Henry Ford moved over to the
economies of the automobile assembly line, he frequently deplored what
he saw as the conservatism of the steel industry. Eventually, Ford rather
overconfidently decided to become a large-scale steel maker, hoping
to demonstrate how a modern, rational industry should be conducted.
Moving in the opposite direction, for a brief period Schwab was closely

identified with the apparent triumph of mass production in a branch of manufacturing in which the United States had been a laggard and which employed old-style, craft methods of production that seemed firmly entrenched, the construction of almost every vessel involving a unique array of specifications.

Ten days after the United States entered the war the Shipping Board organized the Emergency Fleet Corporation (EFC) with capital of $50 million to "purchase, construct, equip, lease, charter, maintain and operate merchant ships in the commerce of the United States." Gen. G. W. Goethals, engineer of the Panama Canal, was appointed general manager. Goethals could not agree with the Shipping Board chairman, William Denman, as to the type of ship to be built, and by July 1917 both men had resigned. Denman was succeeded by Edward Hurley, who had played a pioneering role in the pneumatic tool industry. Hurley also assumed the role of president of the Emergency Fleet Corporation. Succeeding Goethals as general manager was Rear Adm. Washington Lee Capps, who had naval construction experience with Cramp's and at the Union Iron Works. Uncertainties continued, and by December Capps too had resigned. At this point Hurley's friend Charles Piez, a fifty-year-old engineer, took over as vice president and general manager at the Fleet Corporation. One of his assistant general managers was sixty-year-old Francis Tiffany Bowles, who since leaving Fore River in 1914 had been in charge of a textile firm.

The Emergency Fleet Corporation claimed a good deal of success. When fighting began in Europe there had been 33 coastal shipyards in the United States; by early 1917, before the nation became a combatant, the number had reached 105. Another account indicates that when the United States entered the war the country had 37 steel shipyards with 162 building ways, and another 24 yards building in wood with 72 ways. By the time the armistice was signed there were 223 shipyards, building in steel and wood, possessing a total of 1,099 ways. But in the terms that really mattered, output, the results of much effort and investment had been disappointing. Output of all merchant vessels was 346,000 gross tons in 1913, 325,000 in 1916, and in 1917, 664,000. That production lagged so far behind the extensions achieved in capacity was because of severe if very understandable problems. The EFC suffered from many of them. Bureaucracy had mushroomed. Beginning with five people in a four-room suite, within twelve months its headquarters staff numbered twenty-four hundred scattered through twenty-one different buildings in Washington. The yards were staffed by recruits drawn from all ranks of life; they were hastily organized and superficially trained. Calls for more output met with a disappointing response; in many places there were signs of labor troubles ahead.[21]

This unsatisfactory state of things was made intolerable by changes in the war situation. On 15 March 1918 the Fourth Congress of Soviets ratified a long disputed treaty of peace with Germany. The Germans began moving troops to the western front and less than a week later launched their great spring offensive, which threatened for a time to drive the British armies back to the sea. The Allies looked to the United States for a rapid and vast increase in the transatlantic flows of men and matériel, but shortages of shipping threatened to limit the response. The War Department had provided for transfer of 95,000 men to France each month, but the target was raised to 300,000. In such a crisis it was essential to bring into the Emergency Fleet operations expertise in managing large and complex industrial operations. The leaders should be capable of heading and hopefully inspiring both shipbuilders and their work forces. Henry Ford was invited to take the leading part and declined. Schwab was asked, but after "earnest discussion" extending over weeks he too refused. Then, apparently partly as a result of a misunderstanding—and despite the bad feeling over armor plate two years before—at President Wilson's personal request he accepted. On 12 April 1918 he was appointed director-general of shipbuilding for the Emergency Fleet Corporation. His arrival was welcomed by those who anticipated dynamism would at last triumph over bureaucracy. As one trade journal put it, "The calling of Mr. Schwab to do the job of building our ships marks an epoch in our prosecution of the war. A shipbuilder to build ships!, and the greatest shipbuilder of all. This was a great thing for the President to do. It was electrifying . . . it was worth a great victory in the field." Schwab received a huge mailbag of congratulatory letters. Those who wrote included old colleagues such as Gayley, Peacock, and "Dod" Lauder, Elbert H. Gary, Jacob L. Replogle, and A. E. Borie (who had been at Bethlehem when Schwab arrived and was now at the Council of National Defense). There was a cable from Winston Churchill, now minister for munitions in Lloyd George's wartime coalition government, who already had reason to appreciate Schwab's effectiveness in getting ships built. Even dearer to Schwab's heart must have been a short letter received immediately after his appointment. It came from Andrew Carnegie, who recognized that "[t]he right man is undoubtedly in the right place and the work will proceed apace." Schwab wrote back to him, "[Y]our approval will help me more than anything else." In contrast to all the letters from business friends or contacts, however genu-

Charles M. Schwab (*center, with cap and spectacles*)
at the Moore shipyard in California, 1918.
Reprinted from *The History of the War* (London: The Times, 1919).

ine in their sentiments, there was also a touchingly simple note from his
father in Loretto. The seventy-nine-year-old John Schwab wrote,

> Dear Charley, I see by the papers that you are to take charge of all the
> shipyards of the government of course it makes us feel proud of you
> to be placed to such a high position and to get it unsolicited but on
> the other hand feel sorry to think you have to work so hard now take
> care of yourself for health is more than all else. We are both well as
> could be expected for people of our age it is only a few days we will
> be married 57 years not many that reach that long together.[22]

Schwab assumed supreme command of 151 shipyards, 85 of which
were engaged in building wooden vessels. In addition to supporting many
expansion programs, the EFC had started to construct three major new
yards before Schwab's arrival. The largest was on the formerly undeveloped site of Hog Island alongside the Delaware estuary, a tract now part
of Philadelphia International Airport. The Bristol shipyard was also in the
Philadelphia area, and the third of the giant yards was on Newark Bay,
New Jersey. Plans for Hog Island provided for ten sets of five building

ways extending a mile and a quarter along the riverbank. Some of these sets were to be permanent, while others were to serve only during the emergency and were therefore built of wood. Hog Island Yard would have seven outfitting piers, each one thousand feet long and capable of dealing with four vessels at a time. The unprecedented scale of the scheme may be appreciated from the claim that the building capacity of this one opera- tion would be greater than that of all the yards in the United Kingdom, the world's leading shipbuilder. Realization of the scheme came about with unprecedented speed. Into summer 1917 Hog Island was a mosquito- infested swamp; scarcely more than a year later it was a thriving industrial community of more than thirty thousand workers. During 1918 its build- ing ways launched more than half the tonnage of new vessels built in Pennsylvania, including the output of Bristol yard. Looking back a decade later a government-commissioned study of recent changes in the national economy stated, "The Hog Island shipyard, with its many feeder plants, was in some respects the largest attempt at mass production that has ever been attempted, and the influence of the effort in calling attention to the advantage of mass production must have been considerable." On the other hand, in the midst of all the pressures in the summer of 1918, Charles Piez was quoted as saying (when visiting Oakland/Alameda, California) that their experience proved that ships could be turned out faster under West Coast conditions and thus there had been no need for Hog Island "wal- lowing in the mud of Delaware Bay." Schwab also believed Hog Island to have been a mistake and that the work should have been parceled out among a large number of yards.[23]

Within twenty-four hours of taking up his appointment Schwab started moving the shipbuilding administration away from what was once unfavorably characterized as "the atmosphere of Washington." Physically and psychologically it was an important step. From a score of Washington offices, administration was concentrated in three buildings in Philadel- phia, the center of the district in which not far short of half of the EFC's ships were then being built.[24] In May, having delegated to others ques- tions about supplies, interdepartmental relations, and the claims for prior- ity deliveries coming from Washington, the new director-general set out to tour his yards, taking an appeal for more production directly to the workers. He seemed to believe his efforts might have an even wider effect. If he could inspire shipbuilders with patriotic fervor it might diffuse more widely through the rank-and-file of American labor. Accordingly, over the next few months he addressed hundreds of thousands of men, praising, encouraging, and urging them on, promoting what was called at the time "a wholesome rivalry" and leaving a large proportion of the workers fired with a new enthusiasm. Following practices he knew worked well in his own industry, he introduced material rewards; for instance, at the beginning of the campaign he offered a ten-thousand-dollar prize to the yard that produced the largest surplus over its program tonnage.[25] He once said that Charles Piez, who remained general manager, was "the man who really did the work," but in fact Schwab was the inspired and inspiring leader of an impressive team. One member of the party that accompanied him on his tours of the shipbuilding centers was their general counsel, C. W. Cuthell. Charles A. Eaton, head of the National Service Section of the Shipping Board, who arranged speakers and the general propaganda designed to encourage the work, was a more unusual colleague. As pastor of Madison Avenue Baptist Church in New York City, he had been present at a dinner at which shipbuilders complained about the reluctance of their employees to work to full capacity. Eaton argued that if the workers were made fully aware of the issues involved in the war they would present no more problems. He was promptly recruited to justify his optimism, and he achieved it by an unusual approach. As one appreciative account put it, whether speaking to intellectuals or to "thousands of grimy workers," Eaton had an "electrifying" effect: "He made of shipbuilding, in the crisis of the war, a religion. . . . He preached everywhere a sturdy Christianity which sent men back to their jobs with renewed energy and in better heart."[26]

Judged by yard extensions and to a lesser extent by output figures the Schwab/Piez/Eaton regime must be judged a success. In July 1918 American shipyards employed fewer than 45,000 persons; within a year they had 300,000. All of them had to be trained and housed. Another 250,000 worked in allied trades. A few years later Piez recorded his own impressions of the qualities Schwab brought to their work. Clearly he realized what a remarkable colleague and companion the fifty-six-year-old steel maker had been: "He is buoyant, always happy, rather emotional. He works on inspiration and instinct. He makes mistakes,—but what a spirit! What resourcefulness in getting back on the right track. He knows men and their reactions."[27]

Schwab's exceptional powers of organization were well known, but his most outstanding quality proved to be his ability to keep the rapidly increasing work force in good spirits. He often said that "[n]o man had ever worked for him, but thousands had worked with him." And though such words sound trite, there was truth in the claim. In visiting yards or industrial centers not directly involved in shipbuilding, he spoke in his inimitable, familiar, folksy ways, telling jokes, exhorting laborers and managers, and stirring the patriotism of thousands both in and beyond the industry. As he later claimed, he really paid little attention to the material and mechanical aspects of the program but aimed to "put new life, new spirit and enthusiasm into the men who were doing the job and get them to work as they had never worked before." A measure of his success was that during the summer of 1918 one source suggested that a visit by him to a shipyard would be followed by a 25 percent increase in its efficiency. He set the employees hard production targets. For instance, speaking at the Standard Shipbuilding Yard a month after his appointment he announced an objective of one ship a day for the next six months and after that an even faster pace.[28] His exhortations to raise productivity were reinforced by an ability to convey to his listeners such noble sentiments that duty and development of personality were more important than material gain, a possibility that in spite of all that had gone before there might be a harmony in industrial relations, and the still vaguer hope of a happier world in the future. Theatrical gestures of patriotism were woven in with the eloquence to inspire ordinary Americans. For instance, it became known that he had committed himself to foster national unity by giving up use of his private car for the duration of the war in favor of public railroad facilities. Sometimes there was straightforward showmanship, as when in one yard a new keel was laid eleven seconds after the previous vessel on the slip had been launched.

One example of his heavy working schedules and of his technique of handling already receptive audiences must suffice. He spent Friday, 28 June 1918, in Chicago. He arrived in the city at an early hour "laughing and happy." He followed Edward Hurley in speaking in the La Salle Hotel where he was as usual eloquent, if rather hazy, in tracing the outlines of his vision of a better future for all: "This war is going to create a democracy such as the world has never seen before. The aristocrat of the future will not be the man of wealth but the man who has done and is doing something worthwhile. I've grown to be a wealthy man but my greatest pleasure does not come from it. It comes from the recollection of the duties I have done well. It's the personal effort that counts." A great cheer came from his audience when he said, "[T]he American flag has never yet been dragged in the dust, the United States has never lost a war and never will." In the evening of the same day, he proved his versatility as a public speaker by addressing an "immense" audience of working men and others in the international amphitheater at the Union Stockyards. Again his emphasis was on a new oneness in the nation as a whole, and once more he helped convey a confident belief in a new dynamism at the heart of the industry.[29]

In the shipyards of the Pacific coast Schwab made a great impact. (His harsh words about shipbuilding in the Bay Area a decade earlier must have been either forgotten or forgiven.) Yards there benefited from important natural advantages but also faced commercial difficulties. Much of the district, and especially yards in southern California, had a marked climatic advantage over eastern operations, but they were some two thousand miles from their sources of shipbuilding steel and many other important inputs. As a result entire gangs of workers were sometimes idle while they and uncompleted vessels waited for plate and angles to arrive by the usual slow freight train services. Schwab called a conference of steel makers to consider the problems of supplying the needs of government programs, and on one occasion, hearing that a western builder was held up for want of steel, he telegraphed for supplies to be forwarded immediately—by express train. There were some great West Coast shipbuilding successes. At his own company's Union Iron Works a twelve-thousand-ton freighter was launched an hour short of twenty-four days after its keel was laid. A final tour de force that must have been dear to the heart of a showman like Schwab came from Hurley's suggestion that throughout the nation an effort be made to launch the greatest possible number of ships on Independence Day. Schwab and his party, which included Rana on this occasion, arrived in San Francisco from Chicago two days before. On Thursday, the Fourth of July 1918, by making liberal use of motor cars and motor launches, they managed to see fourteen of the seventeen launchings on San Francisco Bay between early morning and late evening. The slipways were hung with flags, and each launch was accompanied by bands and by the hoots and screechings of sirens. Twelve of the vessels involved that day were from the area's three yards that Bethlehem Steel controlled. Two weeks later he was in Tacoma, Washington, for the launch of the *Puget Sound* by the Todd Drydock and Construction Company. On that occasion he told a story about Charles Eaton: "You know the doctor tries to make out that Mr. Piez and I don't know anything about shipbuilding. He tells a story on us, that he took us up to the top of a ship under construction the other day and that I looked down into it and said 'Why, the damn thing's hollow!'"[30]

Notwithstanding all the conviviality and jokes, Schwab's time at the Emergency Fleet Corporation tested him. In the first place the position required unfailing commitment. At the end of summer 1918 he sent Carnegie a progress report on his recent labors: "How often I think of you during

Charles M. Schwab with Charles Piez (*left*) and W. H. Todd in 1918.
Reprinted from *The History of the War* (London: The Times, 1919).

these busy days. I have now been connected with the shipbuilding business 4½ months and am getting everything fully organized and in good
shape. . . . I have never worked harder—even in the old days at Homestead.
I am at work from early morning until late at night, and I am not a young
man any more; but we are determined to win this war, no matter what the
cost of effort." In addition to the long hours, day after day of travel, and
the making of innumerable speeches, he had differences with some of his
colleagues. Late in September he felt it necessary to deny rumors that he
was to resign because of disagreements with Hurley.[31]

As stimulator, organizer, and public symbol, Schwab was undoubtedly
an outstanding leader of the shipbuilding program, and he was acclaimed
accordingly. At the outset his steel industry colleagues lauded his appointment to the commanding position in shipbuilding, knowing what he was
capable of achieving. Undeterred by the pressures and priorities of war,
in early June 1918 the American Iron and Steel Association held its annual
banquet at the Waldorf-Astoria. *Iron Age* reported the reception given to
the Emergency Fleet Corporation's new director-general with a vividness
that almost conjures up the scene in the mind's eye: "When Mr. Schwab
arose, the 1,100 guests sprang up as one man and with cheers, handclap-
ping and waving of napkins greeted him. Mr. Schwab stood smiling for
several minutes while the enthusiastic demonstration continued and then
repeatedly motioned with his hands that it was time for his friends to sit
down." As he responded to this sort of reception it was inevitable that

his latent sentimentality came flooding to the surface: "I have appeared before you many times before and have often acted the clown and told you stories which I cannot tell tonight, for tonight I face you with a heart that is full of appreciation of your kindness and I come burdened with the great responsibility and with the thought that the unmeasured confidence which my friends have placed in me I cannot, must not disappoint." For his part Jacob Leonard Replogle, former general manager at Cambria Steel and then director of steel supply for the War Industries Board, assured his audience and their honored guest that he had no doubt as to the extraordinary capacities of the man they had so warmly greeted: "I think he has the most dominating, and at the same time, most winning personality of any man I have ever known, and his enthusiasm and energy will produce such results in shipbuilding as will astonish the world."[32]

Little more than five months later, and only four days after fighting in Europe stopped, Schwab received the plaudits of leading representatives of his new industry at a banquet given by the Naval Architects and Marine Engineers Association in the Bellevue Stratford Hotel, Philadelphia. This time the president of the association introduced him as "a gentleman who has never shown greater spirit, energy and determination than in these last eight months." On this convivial occasion, Schwab was in a euphoric mood and responded in characteristic fashion. He was folksy, funny, and occasionally rather crude. He paid generous tribute to his Emergency Fleet colleagues:

> [T]he highest type of American manhood and patriotism and energy has been centered in the shipbuilders of the United States. They have done their part and done it nobly; they have worked under the most trying circumstances and with the greatest disadvantages, with a cruel winter last year (we have had none like it for many years) which delayed us many months, with a shortage of labor, and with new management and new work. It seemed to me that the conditions were such as to make large production well-nigh impossible. Yet, gentlemen, you will be glad to know that in the month of October we produced 410,000 deadweight tons of ships, and I think that in the month of November we will pass our best prophecy of over 500,000 tons of ships.

He added a personal note: "I am going down to White Sulphur Springs in a day or two for a rest. I have had eight rather strenuous months." Then he could not resist a joke highlighting one of his weaknesses. When he went to the spa "for a little rest," he hoped that none of his listeners would tell such a story about him as Replogle had once told a New York friend: "He came over and said, 'I saw C. M. at White Sulphur Springs,' and the friend asked, 'Was Grace with him.' Replogle replied, 'Well, I don't know her name, but she was mighty good-looking' (laughter)."[33] For a time after this event Schwab continued to bask in the warmth of public esteem. In Bethlehem his national status was recognized in a ceremony held in the high school auditorium in Bethlehem in early summer 1919. Bishop C. L. Moench of the Moravian church presented him with a gold medal, the cost of which had been raised in small subscriptions sold in the town. The medal bore a simple inscription: "To Charles M. Schwab, as an appreciation of invaluable services rendered our nation, from his fellow citizens of the City of Bethlehem, Pennsylvania. 1917–1919."[34]

Early in summer 1919 Schwab lent his private rail car to Andrew and Louise Carnegie so that they could travel in comfort from New York to their summer home of Shadowbrook in the Berkshire Hills of western Massachusetts. The typed note of thanks that Carnegie sent, and which he signed, is his last personally authenticated letter. Schwab framed it and kept it in his office. A few weeks after the presentation of the gold medal in Bethlehem, Schwab wrote from his Appalachian holiday home to John Poynton, Carnegie's personal secretary: "Tell Mr. Carnegie I am resting in dear old Loretta [his new mansion in his hometown was completed that year]. I go up to the summit where we had so often planned he should have his great residence, and I am sorry that he is not near me here, where we could go over our old and happy experiences together. Also please say to him that as each year goes by and we grow older, I feel a deeper affection and sense of gratitude towards him." He mentioned that they were having great celebrations on 20 August when all Cambria County "are assembling to pay me tribute for my humble part in the war."[35] Nine days before Schwab received those honors, Carnegie died in his Massachusetts home.

Carnegie had provided far more than the foundations for Schwab's material success and wealth, and he always remained Schwab's most influential inspiration. In turn Carnegie admired and had real affection for him. Generally theirs had been a happy, even playful relationship, as when Carnegie had written in November 1896 thanking him for a small gift: "Mrs. Carnegie was delighted with the photograph, and begins to believe that you are an extraordinary man. But women are very apt to make mistakes in regard to the good-looking fellows." It was to Carnegie that Schwab sent his apologies for working at U.S. Steel with Frick, whose condemnation of his reported doings at Monte Carlo particularly hurt him,

Charles M. Schwab in 1919. This photograph
was the last one sent to Carnegie.
Courtesy of the United States Steel Corporation.

and it was from Carnegie that he received solicitous inquiries when he
was ill. They continued to correspond and to meet—at the Carnegie Veterans Association and in visits to each other's New York homes. Schwab
had written in December 1908 to thank Carnegie for the kind things he
had said about him and his steel operations in testimony in Washington.
The sentiments he expressed in that letter may seem excessive, but there
is no reason to doubt that they were completely genuine or that they did
not continue to apply: "Believe me, my dear Mr. Carnegie, I am as anxious
to please you in every act in life now as ever I was and I shall do nothing
in the future that I do not carefully consider before doing as to whether it
pleases you or not. If ever one man loved and revered another man, I am
that man." With his letter to John Poynton in summer 1919 he sent another
photograph of himself, this time inscribed in his own hand: "To my Dearest Friend and 'Master' with the sincere love of 'His Boy' July 24th 1919
CM Schwab." Shortly afterward Schwab's tribute to his late "master" was

unqualified: "It would be difficult for me to find words to express my love and admiration for Mr. Carnegie, my friend, partner and associate for 40 years. He was the greatest man I ever knew, and he had a heart so filled with tender sentiments, especially with reference to his associates, as to make him beloved as well as admired by all those who came in business or social contact with him." He was greatly gratified when he was invited to ride with the family at the funeral, for as he put it, Carnegie had always regarded him as a son. In November he delivered the main address at the Carnegie memorial service held in Pittsburgh. Next March, in a speech at Princeton, he described Carnegie as "my dearest friend that I have ever had in life." Much later, although fully maintaining the deep attachment to Carnegie, Schwab had over time gained enough perspective to recognize that his hero did have at least two faults: vanity and pride in being supreme.[36]

With most of his other former associates at Carnegie Steel Schwab had kept in contact through the Carnegie Veterans Association. As long as Carnegie remained in good health, this organization held its annual dinner at his home. In later years, as numbers dwindled, Schwab was host. A few old colleagues were excluded from the fellowship. The most conspicuous absentee was Henry Clay Frick. Schwab's attitude to him was ambivalent. Though he found him "a curious and puzzling man," he admired his business abilities: "[H]e knew nothing about the technical part of steel" (perhaps an unfair assessment), but "he was a thinking machine . . . accurate, cutting straight to the point." He also had "good foresight and was an excellent bargainer." But he reckoned Frick had no friends and was incapable of demonstrating friendship, an opinion that ignored the few but close companions in Frick's life and failed to do justice to the staunch support he had given Schwab at critical times after his transfer to Homestead in 1892. In 1903, although said to be alienated from each other on the U.S. Steel board, Frick made a gift to him of Frits Thaulow's pastel study of Pittsburgh, probably *Steel Mills along the Monongahela River.* Schwab's hard words also failed to mention that from the early years of the new century, when they both lived and worked in New York, he and Rana were not infrequent guests at the Fricks' Fifth Avenue mansion. Frick died in December 1919, less than four months after Carnegie.[37]

Schwab could also diagnose the weak points of other close colleagues. His former associate at Edgar Thomson, James Gayley, he described as a splendid metallurgist and important inventor but not a businessman. He had enjoyed life but failed to take it seriously. After receiving $1.75 million from the sale of Carnegie Steel and then serving as U.S. Steel vice president in charge of raw materials and transportation, Gayley resigned in 1908 and took up other business in the industry, but by the time he died in 1920 he was worth no more than about $500,000.[38] One of his close friendships was with William E. Corey, a man four years younger and in some respects his alter ego, except that he lacked some of Schwab's more attractive features. Corey began work at Edgar Thomson in 1882, when Schwab was becoming an increasingly useful assistant there to Bill Jones. Over the next twenty years Corey followed Schwab step by step up the ladder of promotion at Carnegie Steel before succeeding him as chairman of U.S. Steel in 1903. Four years later Corey caused a scandal that for a time threatened his U.S. Steel presidency when he married a music hall entertainer. Schwab, with no material interest to gain in the matter, proved a sound friend who spent two hours pleading, fruitlessly, with Corey to become reconciled to his first wife before he embarked on a second, wild marriage.

One of Schwab's contributions to the wartime drive for production had been his appeal to working men. He could persuade them that, whatever the apparent gulf between them in wealth and social standing, he understood them, was not after all so different from them, and was in a position to deal with their fears. Apparently, he was correct in the assumption that their collective memory was so short that they would not recall his well-established attitudes to labor. A British press report (preserved in Schwab's clippings book) described his method of playing on worker emotion, a procedure not so different from that which would be used to less worthy ends in the next few decades by the totalitarian regimes of the Old World. Speaking at the launch of a refrigerator ship that had taken forty days to build, he turned to the workers and cried, "'Now, go to it boys, and give 'em hell!' 'We will!' they shouted. 'Out and build another ship in 40 days!', exhorted Mr. Schwab. 'We'll do it in 30!', the workmen chorused in reply."[39]

In early fall 1918 he sent out an appeal to shipyard workers through the columns of the *Emergency Fleet News*. It was a piece of personalized management-labor communication, effectively a prototype "fireside chat": "This is intended to be a heart-to-heart talk with the shipbuilders of America. I wish that it were possible to take each man by the hand and sit down with him for half an hour and discuss his problems and my problems. I would like to tell him how much the people of the United States appreciate what he is doing to back up our boys in France. And I should like him to know how important it is that there be no let-down, no uneasiness over the future of our shipbuilding operations." He mentioned that after studying the situation Edward Hurley had concluded there would be important needs for shipping in the future: "Mr. Hurley says that it is wrong to assume that when peace comes again, and the war needs for ships have been met, our great new shipyards will have nothing to do. That is a mistaken assumption." Describing the U.S. shipbuilding industry as "this lusty infant," Schwab ended with his own stirring personal commitment: "I have backed the American workman before and I am ready to back him again in this competition for the world's trade in building ships."[40] On 11 November, only a short time after this column was printed, an armistice was signed. Less than four weeks later, on 7 December 1918, Charles M. Schwab telegraphed President Wilson, already on his way to Europe on the liner *George Washington,* tendering his resignation from the Emergency Fleet Corporation. It was reluctantly accepted. Charles Piez took control for the next six months.

In terms of plant, capacity, and output the results of the expansion of the American shipbuilding industry were impressive, though they remained below expectations. By fall 1918 there were 214 coastal yards, and shipbuilding capacity was an astounding 6 million tons, a figure twice that of the rest of the world. Output lagged well behind, even at its peak never utilizing as much as two-thirds of the capacity. The gross tonnage of merchant shipping launched nationwide reached 1.3 million tons in 1918 and increased through the postwar boom to 3.3 million in 1919 and nearly 3.9 million tons in 1920, the last figure being just short of twice the tonnage turned out that year by British yards, itself a record. Some who celebrated these triumphs not surprisingly failed to appreciate the impermanence of what so excited them, and they sometimes showed a lack of knowledge of the wider shipbuilding world, like the author of an article published in midsummer 1918 who announced, "Output of the Delaware River Yards now exceeds that of the Clyde in England."[41] Yet this massive expansion had served the purposes for which it was designed: to provide the shipping to deliver unprecedented amounts of matériel and numbers of men to the Allied cause and, after the armistice, to help rebuild the world's merchant marine. But whatever it achieved in output, new construction methods, and organization, it was not commercially efficient and, notwithstanding Hurley's study of the situation and Schwab's optimistic predictions, was not long sustained.

Efficiency was spoiled in part by the opportunism of some unsuitable entrepreneurs who had been attracted by the inducements. It was realized at the time that the haste of construction often marred the quality of the work and reduced the operational efficiency and life expectancy of some of the ships built.[42] The "cost plus" system that was used encouraged waste and extravagance. As one critical academic economist put it a few years later, when the "fever of construction" had subsided, it was found that "the United States had paid $4 billion to create a fleet of less tonnage and lower earning capacity than the one which the British had constructed for a fourth of that amount" (though over a much longer period).[43]

In 1920 the United States was still the world's leading builder of merchant ships, but by late that year shipbuilding, like the rest of the industrial economy, was rapidly sliding into severe depression. The assurances of long-term work given two years earlier to Emergency Fleet workers were proving ill founded. Indeed after 1921 the tonnage of shipping built in the United States did not even reach the 1913 level throughout the rest of this generally prosperous decade. At the time of the third anniversary of the armistice, as this collapse accelerated, Schwab was honored at a dinner hosted by the Pacific Coast Shipbuilders Association at the Waldorf-Astoria. They presented him with a bronze sculpture by Haig Patigian. On its four panels were figures typifying, respectively, industry, commerce, patriotism, and progress. Topping the sculpture was Pegasus, "symbolic of success and achievement."[44] Such symbolism was at odds with the temper of the times. Ships were now being sold off for a fraction of their construction cost, and the illustrious records set during the war already seemed scarcely credible. In 1914 the United States built about 4.5 percent of the world's shipping tonnage; in March 1923 its share was 6.1 percent, and it was difficult to believe that between those dates building capacity had peaked at roughly twice that of the rest of the world and that in 1919 it launched well over half of its tonnages. In terms of merchant shipping owned, the United States had made much more solid headway (see table 11 in appendix B).[45]

There was to be a short, unpleasant sequel to Schwab's director-generalship at the Emergency Fleet Corporation. Early in 1921 he received a subpoena to appear before the House's Special Naval Committee, then investigating the United States Shipping Board, in order to explain irregularities disclosed when the accounts of the Bethlehem Shipbuilding Company were audited.[46] For wartime services, he, like other business leaders who had provided their expertise for the war effort, had been paid no more than a symbolic dollar a year, and he had made clear that he had never even charged for traveling expenses. The government auditor challenged the validity of such claims of disinterested involvement, in view of the fact that he had withdrawn $60,000 from Bethlehem's coffers to cover personal expenses and that in turn this amount had been charged by the company as costs in the accounts of vessels it was constructing for the government. Angrily refuting the imputation and claiming that Col. Eugene Abadie, who had conducted an audit for the House Committee on Shipping Board Operations, had ruined his reputation, Schwab was visibly under great strain. He suddenly stopped speaking and burst into tears. Two months later the House Special Committee exonerated him.[47] This exoneration was not quite the end of the affair, however. As late as spring 1925 his former colleagues Edward Hurley and Bainbridge Colby were still defending his Emergency Fleet record in a government suit against the Bethlehem Shipbuilding Corporation for alleged overpayments on war contracts. The government claimed $15 million from Bethlehem on the grounds that Schwab had failed to keep the profits of his own company down to the cost plus basis—10 percent over construction costs—a practice he had forced other builders to adopt. It also maintained that $4.8 million had been granted to Bethlehem Shipbuilding for the betterment of its Sparrows Point, Alameda, and Harlan and Hollingsworth operations and for an office building in South Bethlehem but that these contracts were "improvident, unreasonable and unconscionable."[48]

Whatever the problems at the Emergency Fleet Corporation or the bitter tastes left by some of the controversy that lingered on for years afterward, there could be no doubt about two things: the great achievements of the team that Schwab led in speedily delivering essential merchant shipping tonnages and the huge satisfaction he felt. Evidence for the latter is to be found in his own nine-volume collection of clippings. These volumes contain elaborate colored title pages reminiscent of medieval manuscripts and a large, hand-painted, multicolored dedication to "Charles M. Schwab as Director General of the Emergency Fleet Corporation of the United States Shipping Board: Bethlehem Steel Corporation 1918–1919." The large tomes contain a great quantity of letters congratulating him on his appointment, press reports on EFC achievements from across the nation, records of his travels and speeches, and messages from individual yards. One moving tribute had come in a letter and accompanying small package delivered to Schwab's office at 11 Broadway in spring 1919 from "the boys" of the engineering department of the Standard Shipbuilding Corporation at Shooters Island, Richmond, New York. It contained a gold pencil and chain, and the accompanying letter explained that they were sending the gift because an illness Schwab had suffered and then the armistice had prevented them from presenting it on his planned visit to them in October. As the chief engineer put it, "A large part of the result obtained was due to the regard they have for you, personally, and I myself know that many difficult corners were successfully negotiated simply by reason of the fact that they could count on you to appreciate whatever they did." Predictably, such remarks opened the floodgates of Schwab's flair for sentimentalism when two days later he replied, "To the Boys of the Engineering Department: I more deeply prize the friendship of the workmen of this country than of any other class of people. My long years of association with them have been of the most satisfactory and happy character, and no time has been more happy than that spent with the boys at Shooters Island, who have always received me in such a friendly, kindly and enthusiastic manner."[49] Despite the warmth of these remarks, the record of his long years of top management scarcely supported his claim to be a friend of working men.

Friend of the Working Man?

In spite of his well-known and probably genuine approachableness and bonhommie, Schwab always seems to have regarded labor as a commodity. In this attitude he was a product of his age; perhaps his attitude also reflected a basic narrowness in his perceptions of the possibilities, purposes, and responsibilities of life, but after all, that too was not uncharacteristic of the times. He applied this materialistic view of work even to those entering at a level well above that of the common laborer. In *Succeeding with What You Have*, a small tract published in his name in 1917, he gave advice to newcomers to industry: "To my mind, the best investment a young man starting out in business can possibly make is to give all his time, all his energies to work—just plain hard work. After a man's position is assured, he can indulge in pleasure if he wishes. He will have lost nothing by waiting—and gained much. He will have made money enough really to afford to spend some, and he will know that he has done his duty by himself and by the world." He took the matter even further: "If a young man entering industry were to ask me for advice, I would say: 'Don't be afraid of imperiling your health by giving a few extra hours to the company that pays your salary! . . . [T]he man who counts his hours and kicks about his salary is a self-elected failure.'" In the same booklet he mentioned "my 20,000 partners," but these bonus system employees at Bethlehem were only his "partners" for so long as they delivered high productivity.[50] To labor generally he was never friendly. Though certainly outwardly more approachable than many of his contemporaries, time and again throughout his career he proved he had little time for workers' rights.

In 1901, Stephen Jeans, secretary of the British Iron Trade Association, visited the United States to collect material for his impressive book, *American Industrial Conditions and Competition,* a study of the steel industry. He contrasted the attitude toward work held by Americans with that in his own country, from the employer's point of view: "The typical American appears to live only to work, and to work at something that will be a life-long career of usefulness to himself as an individual, and to the community as interested in mechanical improvements and economies." Within such an environment, enterprise flourished: "The British workman, transplanted on American soil, becomes a different man. He finds himself at once drawn into a strong current of pushful, active, virile and aggressive life, and he must go with the stream." At home there was failure to manage workers properly and to weed out and sack inefficient men, but Jeans figured that American workers were content because of the great opportunities open to them. He met Schwab, who expressed the opinion that the two greatest difficulties in Britain were high transport costs and the attitude to labor.[51] In America, the prevailing approach to trade unions ensured that individualism rather than collectivism remained a powerful force. Schwab was always adamant against unionization.

Schwab's systematic campaign to prevent union organization and to dominate the work force at Homestead has already been considered. The first strike in the fledgling United States Steel Corporation occurred in mid-July 1901, less than four months after it began trading and at a time when his power as president was already under attack. By then the once great Amalgamated Association of Iron and Steel Workers was a greatly diminished force; according to Ida Tarbell, by 1901 only a little more than 3 percent of workers in iron, steel, and tinplate manufacturing nationwide were union members. Within the corporation's top management, Schwab and other former Carnegie Steel leaders favored the same implacable approach to labor as Frick had used nine years before. Though Gary was emphatically not more favorably disposed to the general interests of workers, as time was to prove, at this time he did counsel a more moderate, "politically sensitive" approach. Labor was once more defeated, and U.S. Steel adopted a general open shop policy. Schwab was not at the board meeting on 1 October, when, in a splendid display of euphemisms, his fellow directors recorded their "warm appreciation of the wisdom, ability and kindly tact" shown by him and others in the dispute: "It will . . . have results of permanent value not only to this Corporation but to all the labor interests with which it is connected." That he was fully in accord with the policies followed was proved a few weeks later when, reporting visits to a number of works, Schwab said he had "found the labor situation throughout in a very satisfactory condition indeed as a result of the recent strike."[52] Even so, as early as September, he came up with a conciliatory gesture: a profit-sharing arrangement for employees.

His inherent animosity to labor was carried over to Bethlehem Steel and revealed itself in May 1907 when, after visiting the shipbuilding operations of the Union Iron Works in San Francisco, he denounced the rising wages and falling hours there and painted a dark picture of their consequences:

> Our concern will never take a battleship or any other kind of a ship to be built in San Francisco as long as the labor conditions are maintained as at present. We lost $2,500,000 on the last three battleships contracted for and have lost more money in our works in San Francisco than we have made at our other works throughout the different parts of the country [a puzzling statement, since Bethlehem Steel Corporation's net income in 1906 was $800,000].... I have never seen anything like it anywhere.... When we took control of the Union works ... the men were working ten hours a day, but this did not exist long before it was nine hours a day. It is not so much the time as it is greatly because of their inferior and inefficient workmanship that we object, as the same standard has not been maintained. I want to state in the interest of your city that unless labor conditions change here all manufacturing must stop.[53]

At this time, the size of the labor force of the Bethlehem Steel Corporation changed rapidly as it hired and fired workers to match the trade cycle. In the depression of 1907–1908 employee numbers were reduced from 9,783 at the end of December 1907 to 8,615 a year later. Working conditions were hard, often dangerous, and wages low. As had been the case in Carnegie Steel, Bethlehem kept an eye on the industrial and political opinions of employees. By 1910 the company was again solidly profitable, but it would not pay increased wages, and those who refused to work overtime when asked might be dismissed.[54] The leader of the major strike that year, the machinist David Williams, was blacklisted when it was over, and though he was still a young man he never worked again as a machinist. There was even a system of worker surveillance operating between companies. For example, during summer 1909 the vice president of U.S. Steel's Indiana Steel subsidiary wrote to Archibald Johnston, "I have your kind favor of August 20th in reference to two men who left your works to secure employment at Gary with the object of organizing a union. I will investigate this matter and see if these men have secured employment and I wish to thank you very much for giving me this information."[55]

When in 1910 Schwab had to tackle a major labor dispute at the Bethlehem steel works, his conduct made clear that he remained as intractable as Carnegie Steel management had been. The Bethlehem strike attracted national attention, though its place in labor history has understandably been much less prominent than the earlier, bloodier confrontation at Homestead. A report by the commissioner of labor provides a convenient summary of the strike. It began on 4 February 1910 with the summary dismissal of three machinists, apparently because they recorded their opposition to Sunday working hours. As the commissioner put it, "None of the employees of the Bethlehem Steel works were members of any labor organization, and were not therefore in a position readily to formulate expressions of particular grievances." From 4 to 24 February about 800 members of the work force were on strike, but the numbers increased as more became known about the hard conditions of work, the poor rewards received, and as the American Federation of Labor became involved. It was said that 2,233 men were working twelve-hour shifts at the works, either daytime or overnight; hundreds were paid only 12.5 cents an hour. Skilled operators received 14 to 22 cents. During the strike there were riots, violence (in part by the Pennsylvania State Constabulary), and the death of one of the men. Schwab issued a statement that closely mirrored sentiments Frick had expressed eighteen years before at Homestead and that at first sight seemed to fit so uncomfortably with his own image: "It must be understood that under no circumstances will we deal with men on strike or a body of men representing organized labor."[56]

For their part the workers undoubtedly made some wild statements. In part these comments reflected the influence of politically motivated and subversive agitators, but others must have resulted from their own frustration and desperation. There must have been some basis in fact for many of their charges even if they made them in an exaggerated and bitter manner. Writing to the governor of Pennsylvania, a group of workers denounced the sheriff of Easton for requesting the drafting of state constabulary into the Bethlehem area, for these officers had acted as "hired strike breakers" and "immediately upon their arrival began a campaign of slugging, arrests, murder, assault and riot without cause, the viciousness and brutality of which beggars description."[57]

Five weeks later, in a statement of grievances submitted to President

Taft, the Committee of the Striking Workmen presented a more reasoned case, pointing out "[t]hat the Bethlehem Steel Company enjoys the benefits of a high protective tariff and is the recipient of valuable government contracts amounting to millions of dollars annually, from which it retains enormous profits. In spite of these advantages it exacts a maximum of toil for a wholly inadequate wage and constantly strives to lower the standard of living to the barest point of subsistence." The company had "discharged many men who failed or refused to work these excessive hours or labor on Sundays and legal holidays." Presumably well aware of Schwab's care to maintain a favorable standing with the Catholic Church through his generous gifts in Loretto, the men quoted a South Bethlehem priest, Father Fretz: "I have labored among my people in this community for nineteen years and I know that the Bethlehem Steel Company is a human slaughterhouse." Although the effectiveness of this blunt statement might appear to be reduced because Fretz's experience covered a longer period than that of Schwab's control in the local area, it should be recorded that in 1909 twenty-one men had been killed at work and 10 percent of all those employed had had some sort of accident. One of the committee's statements to Taft would reawaken Schwab's painful memories of the Homestead armor scandal: "We charge that during the night work and overtime, defective work is surreptitiously and artificially treated, patched and welded, thereby escaping the vigilance of inspectors who are not required to work overtime by the Government." On this occasion there were no further injurious consequences from this charge. Another contrast with the situation in a bigger industrial complex such as Pittsburgh was that the strikers' position was weakened by the total dependence of the local community on the continuance of the Bethlehem works. This situation ensured pressure to keep it operating. The men argued that a delegation of local business leaders who had visited Taft on 6 April had been broadly sympathetic to their cause until Schwab threatened to close the works if they did not switch their support to him.[58]

The company also hired "scab" labor. Meanwhile, as was so often the case, the situation of the workers was weakened because they lacked adequate financial resources, and in the early weeks of the strike the time of year was unfavorable for a long struggle. Occasionally Schwab allowed passion to overpower statesmanship. At the start of the dispute he was reported to have told some of his loyal workers, "When they get hungry enough, they'll come back." In mid-February, finding a picket line when he left his office, he asked those involved to confirm they were strikers and then rather pettily called back, "Well, I can stand it." By the end of the month he was threatening that if the men did not return to work the company would sublet $2 million in contracts to their armaments rival, Carnegie Steel. On another occasion, in a public display of emotion of which a man as implacably opposed to organized labor as Henry Clay Frick would have been ashamed, he rode up and down Third Street in an open car, shaking his fists at striking men and shouting, "I can stand it, how about you?"[59] On 18 May the strike committee agreed to call an end to the dispute. It had lasted 104 days, and, though his company had been victorious, Schwab had not come out of it creditably.

In the later history of Bethlehem Steel, Schwab sometimes managed to appear to be moving toward a more liberal attitude to the aspirations of labor, but in practice he was now so set in his ways that he assumed it essential for companies to preserve an unquestioned dominance of work conditions and remuneration. Yet he had a talent for eye-catching gestures. In 1915 for instance, when his company pulled off the remarkable achievement of building submarines for Britain in five and a half months, he divided the premium Bethlehem received for early delivery among the workers. In the emotion-charged atmosphere of wartime and during the early postwar euphoria, he seemed to catch the popular mood in the celebration of the common man, but even then his statements were always fine generalities, innocuous statements of intent that, even apart from not following them through, he usually managed to qualify in ways that largely canceled out any good they might have foreshadowed.

By the early post–World War I years he seemed to have entered a mellow phase in his public attitude to labor. Yet even though quoted as saying that the postwar years would see the emergence of "a world for the worker," in the middle months of 1919 when employees in the iron and steel industry demanded higher wages and an eight-hour day he declared, "I will not permit myself to be in a position of having labor dictate to management."[60] In May 1920, he told those attending a meeting of the American Zinc Institute in Chicago, "There are thousands of contented workmen in this country who enjoy a happiness that the owners of palaces can never have," but there was no suggestion that the latter should share any more of their material well-being with the former.[61] A year later, when severe depression was affecting the industrial world, he talked about "today's problems" at a special meeting held by the Chamber of Commerce of the State of New York in recognition of his wartime services. His speech proceeded from worthy, homely platitudes to a promising anticipation of a new industrial order, but then he qualified the vision by canceling out any great expectation of progress for the many:

> In my long experience with men and things, I have found that the best work and the best effort of every man who is worth while comes under the approval of his fellow men; that you will never get the best that is in any man . . . except under the stimulus of approval of the men whom he regards as his friends about him. . . . . Labor should have its fair share of the results of industry. Labor should be recognized as entitled to consult with management in the mutual interest. Labor cannot be driven, and business cannot be successful unless the men employed in it are enthusiastic and loyal. That loyalty cannot be obtained with a big stick; it must be based upon fair dealing and sympathy.

But labor could not be allowed to go beyond its just limits so as to extort more, as a result of which "labor kills the goose that lays the golden egg."[62]

Interviewed in 1923 in London, Schwab again identified efficiency of labor as the key to industrial success anywhere. "Cooperation" was a good thing, but working people must be kept in their places: "Personally, I believe that labor unions, as they are conducted today, have been detrimental to the rapid advancement of industry, being too radical and arbitrary in their methods. Capital interested in enterprise must have a reasonable return, and cooperation must become effective and progressive. We need closer cooperation."[63] He did not spell out which party would have to shift its position in order to increase that cooperation, but it was clear enough what he meant. That year, as he traveled to Europe in the comfort of the SS *Olympic,* in conversation with the columnist Clarence W. Barron he revealed how sentiment and reality were at odds in his view of labor matters and how much he was out of step with the drift of the times. He told Barron, "My feeling is that the average working man is a better man than the rest of us. He is a good, loyal citizen and family man. During the war it made me hot to hear hired speakers address working men and urge them to be patriotic. The working men knew they were just as patriotic—if not more so—than the speaker. *They only want to be led and shown how.*" But he also explained that he had never had unions in his works in the thirty years since Homestead: "We make our own labor unions. We organize our labor into units of 300 and then the representatives of these 300 meet together every week. Then every fortnight they meet together with the head men."[64] This practice may have been convenient for Bethlehem Steel Corporation, but whether the men regarded it as sufficient improvement was not made known. In October 1923 the Engineers' Club of Philadelphia gave a dinner in his honor. One of the speakers was Mayor J. H. Moore of Philadelphia, who as a journalist had reported the Homestead strike thirty-one years before. He observed that such a conflict might never have occurred if, as he put it, a man of their guest's supreme genius in human relations in industry had been at the helm. Schwab spoke about what he called "human engineering." Again he recognized some of the interests of labor but viewed the need for fuller consideration of such interests as a necessary step toward the better functioning of the industrial machine: "The people who labor are human beings, full of sentiment, hopes and aspirations, and therefore the fundamental problem of all industry is to so relate the human elements that the whole process will go forward without hitch or trouble."[65]

Rather than his sort of spectacular but localized and arbitrary giving, most employees, whether in the mills or in the pressurized working atmosphere of wartime shipyards, would probably have preferred a regular regime of better wages and working conditions. Unfortunately, to have provided that would have undermined the whole working regime of the times. Schwab was to live on into years when it was to become clear that workers did not want "to be led" and in which the "human element" was no longer content to remain a mere enabler for "the whole process." Even so, the right of workers to join national trade unions was not recognized at Bethlehem Steel until two years after his death and then only because without such recognition a socially liberal government might have diverted elsewhere some of the flood of orders resulting from a second and greater war.

Whatever their practice, many of the business tycoons attempted to improve their public image—and perhaps also their self-image—through philanthropy. Carnegie's immense program of grants for the building of libraries was the outstanding example of a concern for the wider well-being of ordinary working people that helped soften the public's long-term memory of his labor policies. Late in life Frick took steps to make sure that the art collection that had given him such pleasure should be accessible to the general public. Although in many ways a generous man, Schwab had no well-thought-out program of philanthropy and therefore no means of hiding either his harshness toward workers or his own self-indulgence. When he did give, sentiment rather than reason and impulse rather than plan seems to have directed the pattern. He made donations to colleges and universities. In summer 1902, having been elected a trustee of State College in Centre County, Pennsylvania, he presented it with a chapel costing $65,000, in his name and his wife's.[66] The emotionalism that motivated much of his giving was best shown in the lavishness of his gifts to the Catholic church in Loretto, which served a parish of seventy square miles of rough mountainous country containing a Roman Catholic population estimated in 1901 at about thirteen hundred. Soon after they built their first home in the area, the Schwabs donated a new church. On 10 October 1899 the papal delegate to the United States was one of the dignitaries attending the unveiling of a statue of the prince-priest, Father Gallitzin, the so-called "Apostle of the Alleghenies" who a century before had settled in Loretto. The statue was a gift from Schwab, who now promised a new church to replace the existing one and followed this public statement with a letter to the current priest, Father Kittell, explaining that he and Rana had long had this project in mind. They wanted work to start at once. The new place of worship, said to be "fit for a metropolis," with its furnishings costing $172,000, was ready to be formally presented to the parish two years later. On this occasion Carnegie made an exception to the rules that usually guided his giving and donated the $8,000 organ. In a mood of unrestrained generosity, Schwab said to Kittell, "If there is anything else needed, Father, just get it and send the bill to me."[67]

Similar expansiveness was shown in relation to his and Rana's home-towns. In 1900 the population of Williamsburg was 935. Apart from small-scale rural service functions it had only a dynamite works. Schwab, who occasionally visited, expressed a wish to help the local community. Meeting the leading citizens he asked if they wanted their streets paved, a better water supply, or perhaps would like him to sponsor an extension of manufacturing. They chose the last, and Schwab arranged for the financing of the Williamsburg Paper Manufacturing Company. When the mill was inaugurated on 14 October 1905 he came to town in his private rail car, accompanied by his father and mother, took part in a parade through the streets led by the C. M. Schwab Band, and spoke at the opening ceremony. He assisted in locating the Lehigh Silk Mill in Williamsburg and owned a majority of the stock in its First National Bank, in which John Schwab was installed to represent his son's interests. The artificially stimulated new local business activity brought in new workers, and by 1910 Williamsburg had increased in population to 1,523. Spurred on by this increase, Schwab bought a local farm and became involved in a project to provide housing. Along the same lines, the Schwabs built a church in honor of Rana's family in Carbon County between the little communities of Ashfield and Andreas and in 1903 presented to the bigger settlement of Weatherley a large high school costing $75,000. A century later the latter commemoration of Rana Schwab still survived, a huge, overbearing legacy from the age of the moguls.[68]

6 ❦ The Process of Retiring

When Arundel Cotter wrote his brief history of the United States Steel Corporation in 1921 he made some highly complimentary comments about Schwab: "There is something about him—fascination, personal magnetism, call it what you will—that captivates almost everyone with whom he comes into contact. His infectious laugh disarms hostility and criticism. His great ability compels admiration. . . . Schwab is the Peter Pan of American industry. His is the spirit of perennial youth." As Cotter was recording his captivation, another man, Willis L. King, better placed to make a balanced judgment, was writing his own account of the great men he had known in the steel industry. It contained a more penetrating analysis of Schwab. King, of Jones and Laughlin, Carnegie Steel's only big rival in Pittsburgh, claimed to have known Schwab intimately for thirty-three or thirty-four years. He recognized both his general achievements and those at Bethlehem Steel:

> I am at a loss to place him other than as a "phenomenon." Bright, enterprising, rather more lucky than great, with some weaknesses which would be fatal to most men but on which he seems to thrive. Without fear of debt he borrows to the limit. His interest charges per ton of steel are probably four or five times more than any of his competitors. [The generalizing statistical arrays of accountants make comparisons difficult, but in 1920 U.S. Steel had interest charges of

$1.36 per ton of steel produced, Bethlehem Steel, of $3.45.] ... All the
important men participate in the profits to an extent hardly justified
by good business ethics. By his boyish enthusiasm, winning personality, and gift of speech, he draws all men to him, and I have been
under his spell no less than others; [b]ut I have felt for many years
that there was something lacking, and which, for want of a better
name, I shall call "Stability," and which I fear may be his undoing.
... I count our long friendship one of the most pleasing incidents in
my business life.[1]

After almost forty years of outstanding achievements, Schwab was entering his last phase as a leading force in the industry.

When his service to the Emergency Fleet Corporation ended, he returned to the industry in which he had made his long-term reputation.
But things had moved on, for World War I had transformed Bethlehem
Steel and Schwab's place in it. The company had entered the war as a successful steel maker and shipbuilder, when it had had only one steel plant.
Until 1914 he had taken little or no financial return from his dominant
share in its capital stock, sometimes having to endorse its applications personally in order for it to borrow. Now the Bethlehem Steel Corporation
was a multiplant company that within a few years would record an annual profit more than eight times the 1913 level. Schwab was only fifty-six
when the war ended and a national hero; some of the earlier, less pleasant
associations of his name and reputation were, for a time at least, forgotten in the euphoria. As chairman he was still nominal head of Bethlehem
Steel. Effectively, however, its destinies were now controlled by forty-two-
year-old Eugene Grace. Having built up a high quality team at Bethlehem,
Schwab was now withdrawing from the front rank in its decision making
processes.

After the armistice, business activity continued at a high level for almost two years. Schwab was eager to find out for himself the state of Europe after more than four years of total warfare. In early January 1919 he
embarked on the USS *Washington*. His fellow passengers included Franklin and Eleanor Roosevelt, on their way to the Paris Peace Conference.
On 9 January, as they neared France, Eleanor wrote home to her mother
that on "Sunday night we all attended a concert in the crew's theater and
Franklin spoke well, followed by Mr. Schwab who seems to be a great favorite and certainly makes a good speech. I like him very much and had a
little walk and talk with him today." A few days later he visited the American sector of the western front in the Koblenz area. In spite of his visit,

he remained uncertain about the course and impact of Europe's recovery from wartime destruction. In December 1918 he had declared that the problems of industrial adjustment would be "easily met," but next month, in an interview cabled from Europe by the *Cincinnati Enquirer,* he was quoted as reckoning that "America will not obtain much business from reconstruction work in the devastated regions." At that time he thought they should expect "an era of industrial depression in the United States . . . [with] little business expansion for a long time to come." By the time of the dramatic depreciation of central European currencies in 1920 and 1921, which caused deep distress in the nations concerned, he was sufficiently detached from the horrifying results as to joke about them during an evening meeting of the American Iron and Steel Institute (AISI) in May 1921: "When I was in Europe this year, I went down to Austria and cabled home to Grace one day in a state of great exultation that I had taken orders for steel there for three hundred and ninety million kronen, and I was very happy; but when Grace cabled back that it was $13.81 in American money, I did not think so much of it."[2]

Sometimes he was less amused about the implications of economic change in Europe. During the deep recession of 1920–1921 he told the New York Chamber of Commerce that he had sleepless nights, fearing that after all their wartime sacrifices the Allies were in danger of losing the fruits of victory to the Germans, who had better appreciated the industrial situation. Inevitably he turned the problem into a weapon to be used against their own high operating costs, and his implication was that they must pay particular attention to wages and productivity: "German workmen are efficient; German workmen are eager for work; German workmen are giving a full day's work for a full day's pay; and upon that basis is built all great industrial prosperity in every country."[3] He need not have worried. During the 1920s success in steel depended above all on the domestic economic situation, and through most of those years American demand was buoyant and well protected from foreign incursions. By 1929, far and away the peak year of the decade, production of finished hot rolled products reached 41.1 million tons—imports were 0.4 million tons and exports, 1.95 million tons. The output was 8 million tons above the previous high of 1917.

Even when, as during 1920, business turned sharply downward, Schwab maintained a cheerful public face. He spoke in mid-December at the annual dinner of the Pennsylvania Society of New York, of which he was then president, identifying their current difficulties as a necessary step on the way to greater things; the implications for those in the lower

Charles M. Schwab accompanied by Admiral Lord Jellicoe *(middle)*
of Great Britain at the Brooklyn Naval Yard in 1920.
Courtesy of the National Canal Museum, Easton, PA.

orders of society were not explored: "We are getting rid of the impurities
in our business life. The process is not complete yet. It may take some little time longer. But the patient will in time be cured and when he is cured
the great body of American business will emerge with a vigor and an energy the world has never known before." Two years later, in Boston, he
referred to the many years he had been in industry, telling his audience,
"If I were younger, I would give up all that I have accomplished during
my business career of 43 years to begin again in the lowliest capacity, for
I am convinced that the development of industry in the United States has
only just begun." The next few years seemed to justify his optimism as the
business empire he had built continued to expand.[4]

Massive wartime earnings gave Bethlehem Steel the means to secure
major expansion of capacity beyond that already achieved by acquisition
of the Pennsylvania and Maryland operations. From 1915 through 1921 its
total net profits were about $145 million. Holders of preferred stock re-
ceived $17.5 million, and holders of common stock were paid $27.1 million,
leaving ample funds for plant improvements, extensions, or acquisitions.
Shipbuilding, so prominent during the war, afterward received much less
attention. Building capacity at all Bethlehem shipyards was fully booked
through 1919 and 1920, but after that things went less well. The old disadvantages under which American merchant shipbuilding operated now

reasserted themselves. In 1923 a usually trustworthy foreign source estimated that American construction costs were 40 to 50 percent higher than
those in British yards.[5] By this time, too, the nation's return to relative
isolation in international affairs and the restrictions introduced by the
Washington Naval Treaty of 1922 meant that warship construction had
almost ceased.

A good deal of attention was given to building up mineral supplies for
Bethlehem Steel and to better organization for their delivery. At Sparrows
Point soon after the armistice an important event was the construction
of two twenty-thousand-ton ore/oil carriers to bring ore from El Tofo,
where development work had largely been suspended during the war. By
1922 the company had five of these vessels, hauling ore from Chile and
carrying oil, coal, or coke on the return journey. Control of home mineral
reserves was strengthened. Having purchased forty-six thousand acres of
coal lands from the Elkins Coal and Coke Company of West Virginia in
1919, Bethlehem bought in 1920 the nearby Jamison Coal and Coke Company, which controlled coal that produced less sulfur when burned. Soon
after this purchase the need for more home ore reserves and an urge to
extend both steel capacity and the areas within which Bethlehem operated caused another and even bigger round of company acquisitions.

As early as spring 1908, when both production and price levels were
low, Schwab, who little more than seven years before had been the chief
planner for a major new Carnegie lakeshore works at Conneaut, Ohio, received a letter from a Buffalo real estate operator. It expressed a hope that
he might be interested in the development potential of a major Lake Erie
works: "I think there is, at the present time, a splendid opportunity to
obtain control of the Lackawanna Steel Company. . . . There is no earthly
reason why this plant under the proper management could not make big
money. . . . We have few big men here, and if a man like yourself would
turn his attention to Buffalo he would find it very profitable. . . . If you
would consider the idea of this plant, I would gladly offer you my services,
in getting whatever you may want, on the quiet."[6]

Nothing tangible resulted, but in September 1922 the Bethlehem Steel
Corporation bought the Lackawanna Steel Company for $35 million. The
1.84 million tons it added to Bethlehem's crude steel capacity brought the
total to 4.89 million tons. With the steel plant came more coal properties
in the northern Appalachians and ore reserves in the upper Great Lakes
sufficient to supply the Lackawanna works for fifteen years. The purchase
also improved access to markets in the Midwest and Canada as well as in
New York state and New England. A further stage in consolidation fol-

lowed within two months when Bethlehem agreed to take over all the operations of the Midvale Steel and Ordnance Company except for the steel, armor, and ordnance units in the Nicetown neighborhood of Philadelphia. As well as the relatively small Coatesville and Wilmington works, Bethlehem acquired Midvale's stockholding in the Cambria works and thereby a point of access to the Midwest. Cambria's 50 percent share in the Mahoning pit of the Hull-Rust mine on the Mesabi ore range near Hibbing, Minnesota, added 100 million tons to group ore reserves. Bethlehem steel capacity increased to 7.6 million tons or 15 percent of the national total; it thus ranked second only to U.S. Steel though it was only one-third as large. That Grace negotiated the agreement to acquire Midvale before his chairman had given his formal approval was indicative of Schwab's reduced role. Three days after the takeover was finalized, a report of a speech gave an even more pointed reminder of the semiretired status of the man who, as a boy, had found inspiration in his distant view of activity at the Cambria works: "Mr. Grace indicated in his statement at Johnstown that Charles M. Schwab, whose summer home is at Loretto, Pennsylvania, near Johnstown, will take an active interest in Cambria operations during the summer months." It was pointed out that this new, bigger, widely spread Bethlehem Steel could gain a number of the advantages with which Schwab had argued the case for a great amalgamation in December 1900: a wider product range, more economical access to raw materials, and cost savings by careful allocation of orders and the elimination of cross-hauling.[7] Strangely, at this time his vision of the shape of the future and grasp of the action needed to play a leading part in it began to fail.

He started off well enough, though it was mostly in the form of comment rather than, as earlier, in solid industrial achievements. In late November 1923 he was entertained by the Engineers' Club of Philadelphia. Four hundred men sat down to dinner, and "many ladies, including Mrs. Schwab, looked on from boxes in the balcony." When he spoke, he was eloquent in indicating, celebrating, and identifying himself with the economic triumphs unfolding in the golden decade: "I am an optimist. I foresee for America the greatest prosperity in her history. . . . This is indeed to be the workshop of the world. . . . Don't mind if we are called a materialist people; I am proud of being a son of a material country, because this country has worked for and will work for the material advancement of the world." Four years later he summed up what the industry meant to him in an address in Queens, New York City: "to add to the world's material well-being and its happiness, to make jobs for thousands, to discover individual capability and train for capacity, and to be able to open the doors of opportunity for that capacity to develop in turn for usefulness to the world and to mankind." It was to be a global role that would increase their own wealth, but he had no wider vision of service or goodwill toward humanity. There were great prospects for steel at home, but "then let us take a broader view. Think of the world, the undeveloped possibilities in South America, Africa and Asia and the part America may play in developing the untold resources of those countries."[8]

One field in which he had clearly lost his way was in his assessment of the labor situation. He claimed to be a man of the people, indeed "just a workman." In 1928 when he received the Bessemer Gold Medal from the Iron and Steel Institute in London, he remarked in an after-dinner speech, "I noted some of the workmen from Sheffield here this evening, and when I saw them I felt at once that I was in my own class." As early as summer 1919 he had spoken of the "great social changes which have come in the world by reason of the war." In speeches throughout the decade he seemed to be heralding the rise of the common man. But he—or his speech writers—were always struggling to combine the advancing rights and greater economic importance of ordinary citizens with the need to keep workers under control. In fall 1925 at the University of Chicago he struggled toward such an accommodation: "We have got to devote ourselves to the problem of making men happy not through making life soft and easy, but through so using the implements and the facilities which science has placed at our disposal as to enable men, through their work and out of their work, to realize a larger life and take a greater zest in their workmanship." In fact, he continued to support policies that kept laborers in their place. In the aftermath of the 1919 strike, Bethlehem, like other companies, had adopted an employee representation plan, in which workers in individual plants chose their own delegates to negotiate with management. Through the interwar years, Grace went once a year, for a day, to each of the company's works to arrange wages and other matters for the ensuing year. Such a system of divide and rule was regarded as preferable to a nationwide union; in a revealing phrase Schwab reckoned that with such a union, the employees' interests would be represented by "walking delegates from Kamchatka." His old framework of thinking was also revealed in reaction to the twelve-hour day question, which came to a head in the early 1920s. During an interview by the *New York World,* he said that he thought workers would find an eight-hour shift more taxing than one of twelve hours, because for most of the time in the latter they were not hard at work.[9]

Meanwhile, the extended Bethlehem Steel continued to do well. Following an uncertain recovery from the 1921 depression, over the three years from 1925 to 1927 it operated at an average 75 percent of its crude steel capacity. The only sections not sharing in this high activity were those most closely related to military production, which had in its turn financed the company's postwar expansion. By early 1924 the company was scaling back its armaments business. Speaking in April to a Rotary Club convention in Bethlehem, Schwab was typically immoderate—and meaningless—in his comment on this development. He declared that he would sink his plant in the sea if such an action would end wars.[10] Next year at a conference on education and industry held in Chicago, he pointed out that 99 percent of Bethlehem's contracts were for peacetime products and that the company had scrapped a large armor plant; eighteen months later he even suggested that the manufacture of big guns and ammunition was fast becoming a lost art. Meanwhile, the gap that separated Bethlehem Steel from U.S. Steel was narrowing. Bethlehem's steel output rose from 27 percent the U.S. Steel figure in 1924 to 30 percent in 1927, the year of Judge Gary's death. By 1929 it reached 34 percent. In terms of income before deductions for fixed charges and depreciation, its proportion of the U.S. Steel figure went up rather less impressively, from 21 percent in 1924 to 25 percent in 1929. The company now made efforts to spread out from its heartland in the eastern manufacturing belt. This effort was particularly focused on the booming West, where it built large warehouses in Los Angeles, San Francisco, Seattle, and Portland and followed this construction with acquisitions in 1929 of existing operations that gave it steel capacity and rolling mills in the three main West Coast industrial districts. In spite of an acrimonious dispute with U.S. Steel over the latter's infringement of the Grey beam patents in its new structural mills at Homestead, Bethlehem Steel increased its dominance in this field, now a major and still rapidly growing market sector. Between 1922 and 1930 installed capacity for structural steel rose 45.1 percent nationally, by 14.3 percent in the Pittsburgh/Johnstown district, but by 30.7 percent in the Philadelphia district and 271.4 percent in Buffalo, the last two city districts being areas where Bethlehem was dominant. The company product range was also extended. In 1927 at Sparrows Point it entered the pipe and tube trade, in which it had previously played little part. The company still had one major gap in its product range, and this gap to some extent was due to a lack of vision on the part of Schwab and the top management he had installed.

In the 1920s there began a wholesale switch from heavy steel products to light, flat-rolled steels, which marked the great transition from a largely capital goods economy to one focusing on production of consumer goods.

This transition was to be the major feature of twentieth-century manufacturing. Canning (for convenience foods), domestic appliances, and above all the automobile industry were key elements in this new economy. Expansion in these sectors required growth of the tinplate and sheet steel industries, and this growth was accompanied by change in the processes of manufacture. These changes led to research that produced and industrial enterprise that adopted the wide continuous strip mill. This change, literally of epoch making significance, was pioneered primarily by the American Rolling Mill Company (later ARMCO) and taken up either by existing smaller concerns or by new companies formed expressly to enter the trade. In complete contrast, most long established firms were busy and doing well in traditional lines, and those who controlled them continued to think in old, time-worn categories and to act accordingly. Year after year they let the new technologies pass them by. Only when their old staple trades let them down would they belatedly open their minds and pockets to realize the possibilities of the new (see table 12 in appendix B).

Early in 1926 Schwab was interviewed by a representative of *Iron Age*. He was asked in what products he foresaw the greatest expansion over the next ten years. He replied, "I look for a large increase in steel consumption in every line. . . . We shall see large increases in railroad and building construction, in the oil industry, and in power and all public utilities requirements. Also there will be a marked growth in the great diversity of smaller uses." Yet he and his chief lieutenants were aware both of the far faster growth of the automobile industry than of activity on the railroads, of the wider industrial implications of this growth, and very soon of the introduction into their industry of the new technology for thin flat-rolled products. In May 1928, speaking at the Iron and Steel Institute in London, Schwab singled out three fields of "outstanding practice, which seemed to him to be the coming thing in America." As a British publication reporting on Schwab's speech noted, "The chief change in the years to come would be the continuous rolling of sheets. They [the industry, not Schwab's company] had continuous mills to break them down to a practicable and finished size, and had been able to show an economy of about £2 [about $9.60] per ton in the cost of producing sheets." That year, at the annual meeting of the American Iron and Steel Institute, of which he was then president, Schwab called on George Verity, president of the American Rolling Mill Company, to speak, adding to his invitation, "If some of you do not already know him, you probably will in the years to come."[11] It was a striking sign of the drift of the times that even in the boom of 1929, rates of utilization of mill capacity were low in some, though not in all, of the older or heavier products, but very high in thin flat-rolled steels (see table 13 in appendix B).

As Grace rather than Schwab now controlled the destinies of Bethlehem, the latter now had more time for other interests, including other business. Over the years, as his fortune increased, he had invested quite widely. With his propensity to invest in "fliers," he could not resist the allure of western mining ventures. Even in 1906, at a time when he was pressing for strict economy so as to raise the capital for major Bethlehem extensions, he was reported to have obtained a controlling interest in the Mayflower mine in Nye County, a well-known gold and silver district of southern Nevada bordering on California. Prospects there were regarded as good for a "large, steady producer." A few weeks later he was given options on the Great Western Ore Purchasing and Reduction Company of Inyo County, California, another gold and silver tract, and then on the Lincoln group of copper bearing claims in Nevada. In July 1908, after a period of quiet, a shaft sunk by interests associated with Schwab proved an ore high in copper in the Greenwater Copper Company mining area of Inyo County. The way this find was announced bore the distinguishing marks of his type of business enterprise. The strike was made on 1 June "but was kept as quiet as possible until the Schwab interests could secure control of contiguous territory. Meantime there is again a rush of prospectors into the camp, incited by this reported discovery." Another investment took him into Mexican mining. In 1907 he won control from a Maine group of the Santa Eulalia and San Toy Mining Company, operators of a lead-zinc complex a short distance east of the city of Chihuahua, in northern Mexico. Control of this company was moved to Pittsburgh. This investment proved vulnerable in the uncertain years that followed the overthrow in 1911 of Porfirio Díaz, who had dealt kindly with foreign enterprises. Five years after the revolution began, Pancho Villa attacked and flooded the mines, an event greeted with despondency in Pittsburgh. The owners decided to hire so-called "watchmen" and station them at the mines, which remained more or less in a state of siege for five years. Somehow Schwab managed to extricate himself from this troublesome venture. In the 1920s he was reported to be involved in plans for reorganization of the Comstock mines.[12] Whether at home or beyond the United States, there is no evidence he ever made much money from nonferrous mining.

In 1921 he became a director of the long-established Metropolitan Life Insurance Company and of the Empire Trust Company. This sideline was then a good deal more profitable than Bethlehem Steel, paying in 1920 an

18 percent dividend, averaging 17 percent over the next four years and, for the next five, 16 percent. He was also then on the boards of Chase Manhattan Bank, the Silvex Company, the Empire Safe Deposit Company, and of a concern representing his association with the Grey mill, the American Universal Mill Company. More colorfully, for a decade from 1922, when with E. V. R. Thayer and others he bought a controlling interest, he was closely involved with and for part of the time the major owner of stock in the Stutz Motor Company. Unfortunately, a small-scale producer of high-priced masterpieces of engineering was not well placed to survive the years of deep depression. In 1934 only six Stutz cars were sold, and next year the company disappeared. During the 1920s he was also interested in, or was reported as likely to be involved with, other sectors of the booming automobile industry—in 1923 in the American Motor Body Company, and a year later as chairman of the new Six Wheel Company, formed to make six-wheeled motor buses and trucks. He was a founder, investor, director, and in 1922 chairman of the Chicago Pneumatic Tool Company. While he was in a position to determine matters he insisted that Bethlehem should purchase its pneumatic compressors from Chicago, even though his foremen and bosses strongly preferred Ingersoll-Rand compressors. When he "retired," the company immediately switched over to the managers' preferred brand. Earlier he had been the largest shareholder in American Steel Foundries (ASF), a group formed by an amalgamation of operators in the northern manufacturing belt. In 1904 he sold his ASF securities to concentrate on Bethlehem Steel; Robert Hessen suggests that he did so because of an opportunity for substantial profit. Schwab also invested in alloy minerals, particularly nickel, becoming involved with the International Nickel Company. Few of these outside ventures were successful. He was and remained unquestionably a steel man.[13]

Having reached his sixties, Schwab was passing from active middle age into the early stages of a more leisured pace of life. He continued to travel a great deal and to enjoy the various benefits that accompanied his high reputation in global industrial circles. In spring 1928 he claimed he had crossed the Atlantic eighty times since his first journey to Europe in 1885. He made this statement in London, where he was attending an Iron and Steel Institute function at which he would receive the Bessemer Gold Medal. He had first learned of this award when he was in Europe two months earlier and had since been home for all of two weeks. He journeyed widely across the United States on speaking engagements, becoming as the years passed "a somewhat heavier, somewhat more florid, somewhat less glowing orator at innumerable businessmen's banquets."[14] Yet, whatever the truth of that unflattering assessment, Schwab retained his extraordinary ability to command the attention and affection of the humble as well as the mighty. Nowhere was this knack better illustrated than when he again went to Homestead for a celebration in his honor. It was now thirty-five years since he had first been superintendent there and a quarter century since he had completely left the management of the plant. Of the ten thousand who had worked in those mills in his day no more than about eight hundred were left, but the whole town turned out to pay respects or offer tributes of affection. The mills were closed, the schoolchildren and local organizations paraded, his old carriage was brought out again, and the community went so far as to send to the Midwest in order to bring back his old coachman.[15] It was a remarkable demonstration of regard, and there can have been few other business leaders who could command anything like a comparable response from a community not at all dependent on their goodwill.

Schwab's meteoric career had been accompanied by a long-term and accelerating increase in wealth. In addition to a rising salary, from 1892 he owned Carnegie Steel stock, and his holdings in the company increased until its sale in 1901. When that company was sold and reorganized as United States Steel, Schwab's standing as a man of capital was ensured, and his position had been reinforced by a princely salary, bonuses, and shares in the corporation's profits. On his move to Bethlehem, much of this fortune went into plant development, but it was later recouped from the company's earnings. By the end of World War I he was, according to his own reckoning, worth about $150 million.[16] After the sharp shock of 1920–1921, the rest of that decade was successful and profitable, and at the end of it a *New Yorker* profile put Schwab's fortune at between $200 million and $300 million. It proved to be the peak of his wealth, before unprecedented depression and his own excessive spending took their toll.

During the 1920s, as he became semiretired but his fortune was still rising, he particularly enjoyed a country retreat. One home, however luxurious, was insufficient for a multimillionaire. Carnegie had his summer castle of Skibo in the northern Highlands of Scotland. Frick had a second fine mansion, "Eagle Rock," on the fashionable North Shore in Massachusetts. Predictably, Schwab followed Carnegie's example in returning to his roots. In 1898 he built a country house for his mother in the hills near Loretto, and at about the same time he and Rana acquired a home nearby. Sixteen years later he began work on a forty-room house, set on grounds of one thousand acres. The whole conception was heavily laden with sentiment. Schwab's New York home, Riverside, was in the grand manner of a

An aerial view of Immergrun, Schwab's estate in Pennsylvania.
Courtesy of the National Canal Museum, Easton, PA.

chateau; his new rural home was in the style of an English country estate. At its heart was a crenulated, rambling, red-roofed mansion. Around it were lawns, trees, flowering banks, and a spectacular water feature made up of a long flight of marble stairs divided by fountains, cascades, and reflecting pools. This estate was to be a rural paradise for an emotionally susceptible businessman, comfortably remote from the ugly landscapes of the mill towns and their harsh working conditions, profits from which made the venture possible. The grounds were ornamented with "sensuous statues of pagan gods and goddesses," but efforts were also made to reflect everyday countryside pursuits. On one of his many visits to Europe Schwab was taken with a village in Normandy; as a result he built a copy of it on sixty-six acres of his estate, and his chickens were kept in replicas of French cottages. Whimsical fancy went even further. In celebration of treasured boyhood memories, he paved four miles of the local dirt road over which some forty years before he had driven his father's wagon. Most expressive of what moved him to return to Loretto was the wistful, hopeful name he gave both to the small house built in the late 1890s and to its much grander successor: "Immergrun" (German for "evergreen"). It is doubtful if he was wholly satisfied. As he once put it in a commencement day address, "The happiest days of my life were when I had a modest income and lived with my good wife in a cottage with restful comfort. Now we have many houses—mansions. But we don't own them. They own us."[17]

Luxury travel was the logical accompaniment of luxurious housing. In 1903 he hired a yacht from the Drexel family; three years later W. B. Coxe, president of the Harlan and Hollingsworth Corporation of Wilmington, Delaware, sent him plans of a yacht they had designed for him. The most spectacular example of the comfort his wealth enabled him to enjoy was his private railroad car, *Loretto*. It was used for business, including the carriage of honored visitors, but also provided his own way of escape when pressures in the industrial and commercial worlds became too heavy. He could board it, have it hitched to a main-line train, and travel wherever he wished, perhaps to the West, to Florida, to an Appalachian spa, or, more commonly, over the Pennsylvania tracks either to Williamsburg or to Cresson and then by branch line to Loretto. An earlier private car of the same name was replaced by one that the Pullman Company built in 1917, at a high point in his career. Costing $151,000, this newer *Loretto* was eighty-three feet long and contained a private dining room, sitting room, bedrooms, galley, and servants' area. It was richly appointed, with artist-rendered interior decoration and dark, heavily ornate furniture with mahogany and walnut inlay work. In later decades he also possessed a fleet of automobiles.[18]

In February 1922 Schwab entered his sixties. Family circumstances were now beginning to change rapidly. The day before his birthday his brother Joe died in tragic circumstances. Speculative markets had been uncertain after World War I, and when he tried and failed to corner the market in wheat Joe was financially ruined. He began to drink heavily, and his death was attributed to alcoholism. The parents, John and Pauline Schwab, were still living, and his relationship with both of them seems to have been easy and happy. As he became wealthy, he provided them with financial support and improved accommodation. He found his father employment that did not call too heavily on his energies. In later years they kept in close touch, mainly by telephone. The parents were even included in some of his social arrangements. They enjoyed laughs together, and Hessen reports that John Schwab was especially fond of one joke against himself: the son invited the father to visit the steel works, but when the father arrived the son told a security guard to throw him out, declaring that he had never seen him before. Charlie was devoted to his mother. According to a press report, he once wanted to move a house, but because a tree that Pauline liked stood in the way he arranged for the building to be lifted clear over it. John Schwab died at age eighty-five in 1924. After that Pauline continued to live in a house only a stone's throw from her son's mansion. In later years quilting and sewing took up much of her time, and for every birthday she sent him a new quilt. When she passed away on in March 1936 she was ninety-three.[19]

By the early 1920s Charlie and Rana Schwab had been married for forty years. It is not easy but fortunately is unnecessary to write at length of their life together. Hessen has discussed their childlessness and their long marriage. Carnegie had referred to her as "CM's balance wheel" and commended him to her wise advice, but they never seem to have been really close. Rana was two and a half years older than Schwab, and from an early date she was heavy in build. The unusual nature of their relationship seemed to be summed up in the fact that from its start, though both were then in their early twenties, she commonly called him "Lad" or often "Solomon," and he addressed letters or referred to her as "Old Lady." When in summer 1914 he was unwell and under medical care, he reported to "My Dear Old Lady, . . . I am greatly troubled with weakness, faint spells and dizziness." Apparently he continued to be unfaithful; Hessen mentions "a succession of young women," and there seems to have been a more serious affair with a contralto from the Metropolitan Opera. For the remaining years of his life, from 1918, when he first met her, another woman known only as Myrtle was his mistress, accompanying him to the theater and joining him for cruises to Europe. Myrtle seems to have become the congenial companion that ill health and consequent withdrawal from society, as well as her personality, meant that Rana could not be.[20]

Beginning in the early postwar years, Rana's increasing weight threatened her with serious heart problems. Later it became common for her to stay at home and for Pauline Schwab to accompany her son to social or public occasions in Loretto or Williamsburg. Even so, as in other spheres of his life, sentiment provided a fitful warmth to a relationship from which deep commitment and love had withdrawn—or never been present. Examples may be found in a diary that Schwab wrote in his own hand, apparently only when they were at Immergrun for the summer and beginning at the end of May 1920, before construction of this comfortable retreat had been fully completed. From the start the tone of his entries makes it difficult to recognize it as the work of one of the nation's leading industrialists: "May 29th. Saturday—We arrived to-day from New York. Our hearts are so full of joy and happiness in our lovely mountain home that Rana felt a daily diary of our personal doings and those of our Dear Friends while here, would be an interesting record for future years. Hence this little daily record. May it contain only records of happiness and contentment, and especially records of restored health to my Dear 'Old Lady.' This is the ardent wish of its first recorder—Lad." Almost five months later he

Charles M. Schwab in the gardens at Immergrun in the early 1920s.
Courtesy of the Hagley Museum and Library, Wilmington, DE.

closed the diary for that season on a note of deep contentment: "This has been a summer of happiness and rest. I have spent practically the whole of the summer here as this diary will show. Rana has been well all year until the past week. I never thought I would learn to love the quiet restfulness of Immergrun as I have this year." Yet even in its shangri-la atmosphere it was impossible to be wholly cut off from the wider world. Two nights before he closed the record, a "crazy man" from Altoona who claimed to be looking for Schwab was caught by two of the staff and after a struggle taken off to the county "home."[21]

Next spring, during a time of sharp depression when national employment was lower than at any time since 1914 and unemployment reached 3.6 million, he recorded their arrival at Immergrun in terms again more appropriate for a literary romantic:

Saturday April 30th 1921. Left New York this morning for Immergrun. We decided this year to make our yearly Wedding Day journey to the house we love so much where we could spend the day alone in comfort and happy thankfulness for the many blessings we have had in 38 years of married life. We have had a strenuous week in New York. The most important event being the reception and presentation by the New York Chamber of Commerce. Rana was present and it was most pleasing and creditable but we were both worn and tired when we boarded the *Loretto* this morning for our annual journey. It was a rainy day and when we reached Cresson at 8pm it was pouring rain, but soon from out the darkness the welcome light of Immergrun greeted us, and when we stepped into the hall our hearts were overflowing with happiness and thankfulness for all our blessings and good fortune. The house was a perfect bower of flowers and the warm blazing fire made us quickly forget the inclement weather. Dinner was waiting and we soon retired to quiet, peaceful and happy rest. No one knows we are here except our household.[22]

The Late 1920s and the Great Depression

In February 1927 Schwab celebrated his sixty-fifth birthday. Again it amazed him to contemplate how long he had been in the steel business and how much he had achieved. Now he was as old as Andrew Carnegie had been during the last six months of the Carnegie Steel Company. For almost a quarter century since then he had worked to build another great company. Yet, even at this age, unlike his mentor, model, and friend, he was unready to retire completely from business and devote himself to leisure, cultivation of wider interests, or more public responsibilities. Instead, for the remainder of his life he acted the part of a business elder statesman or guru. Generally it was a rather sad period, the drift both of his own life and of the times seeming to conspire against him. It began promisingly enough.

In the 1920s Schwab was one of the world's outstanding steel makers, and he used this eminent position to advocate the restructuring of industry in the leading producing nations. As early as 1923, speaking to the British Chamber of Commerce in New York, he urged an extension of cooperative action from the national to the international dimension. His proposals included an agreement between American, British, and French industrial concerns to end destructive competition in foreign markets and an implied assumption that Germany would join in when its industry had recovered its competitiveness. Such an association could make the distribution of orders more economical and efficient. The International Steel Cartel of the later 1920s proved such advice had fallen on receptive ears.[23]

In spring 1928 Schwab was awarded the Bessemer Gold Medal by the Iron and Steel Institute in London. Presenting it, the president reminded members that the medal was "the highest honour we have to bestow" and "the hall-mark of outstanding technical ability and efficiency so far as the iron and steel industry is concerned." The occasion prompted much Schwab-type humor and a good deal of sentiment, and the recipient took the opportunity to give his assessment of the essence of the long-term American achievement in iron and steel and some good, if rather impracticable, advice to his hosts. He said he often wondered how people in Britain managed to design plant with such small outputs as compared with those in America, yet he did not feel his own country deserved the credit it was so often given: "Taking a mill that ran 365 days a year on one size of rod or sheets, if it were not possible to get good costs under those conditions for all that was produced they would be pretty bad engineers." For Britain he recommended protection from continental dumping, followed by concentration in fewer, bigger plants and the securing of similar economies of scale: "If I were a dictator of the iron and steel industry in Great Britain, I would form all your companies into three or four great companies, and put them forward with all the economies of management that would come from that, and then I would say, use your influence and great position in the world to do for your government what they ought to do for you." Bethlehem Steel that year produced 76 percent as much steel as all the works in Britain.[24]

Four years later he was the honored guest at another London presentation, this time to receive the Melchett Medal of the relatively recently established Institute of Fuel. It was intended as recognition for original research or professional administration or construction work of an outstanding character involving the scientific properties or use of fuel; Schwab was chosen for his general distinction, not because he fit the specifications. In his speech of acceptance he turned again to the British steel industry. It had at last been given tariff protection, on the condition that the industry would draw up a program to put its plant in much better shape. Schwab suggested the number of works should be reduced by four-fifths and that those plants that survived should be kept continuously at work.[25] In fact, those who listened were no better placed to forget and cancel out the distinctive industrial history of their own country than was someone from a different tradition able to fully understand the nature or causes of its problems.

At home Schwab succeeded to positions that made him the unrivaled voice of much of the nation's basic manufacturing industry. In 1927 he became president of the American Society of Mechanical Engineers. Much more significant, both symbolically and in terms of influence, was his election, after Gary's death in August, as president of the American Iron and Steel Institute.[26] He occupied this position for seven years. Given his own temperament, it was understandable that in the early years of his presidency he lent his talents and considerable oratorical reputation to attempts to persuade the nation that prosperity could be a permanent state and later, that despite increasingly obvious signs to the contrary, recovery of prosperity lay just around the corner. In 1926 the United States produced 49.1 million metric tons of crude steel. Output dipped sharply in 1927 before reaching new peaks at 52.4 million in 1928 and 57.3 million in 1929. This recovery and the more general glow of material well-being in the 1920s provided the happy context for the last high points of his career.

From some points of view, the general business situation in the 1920s did indeed seem to promise an early realization of the millennium—materially conceived. Successive presidential administrations avowed what now seems a simplistic devotion to business. At an AISI reception in May 1921, in the middle of a sharp depression, President Harding set the tone in a statement that in retrospect seems the dreariest of banalities but at the time conveyed a brassy confidence: "Business is the biggest thing on earth and I am for business." A few evenings later this generous sentiment brought a predictably appreciative, though not an eloquent, response from Gary: "Now, sitting and standing here, we say that so long as our President is possessed with that idea we think he is the biggest thing on earth, and we are for him and his administration." President Coolidge was equally positive, and in 1928 as Herbert Hoover accepted the Republican Party's nomination, he set himself a worthy target: "[W]e shall soon, with the help of God, be in sight of the day when poverty will be banished from this nation."[27] Early in 1929, as Coolidge concluded his presidency, he observed that the economy was "absolutely sound." Confidence from the politicians was matched by that of leading industrialists. Early in 1929, stating his conviction that national wealth was bound to grow, John Raskob, vice president of General Motors, added, "I am firm in my belief that anyone not only can be rich, but ought to be rich."[28]

The favorable statements from leading figures of the day seemed con-

firmed by the records of business. In February 1929 a report on recent
economic changes in the United States was completed. The chairman of
the group that produced it was Herbert Hoover, by now president, and
Raskob had been a member. Their inquiry focused on the remarkable
growth in the nation's economy since 1921. Though they were outlining an
economic situation, the authors recognized social and cultural gains had
also resulted. From sober statement they moved to celebration:

> The committee, like other observers, was early impressed by the de-
> gree of economic activity in these seven years. It was struck by the
> outpouring of energy which piled up skyscrapers in scores of cities;
> knit the 48 States together with 20,000 miles of airways; moved each
> year over railroads and waterways more than a billion and a half
> tons of freight; thronged the highways with 25,000,000 motor cars;
> carried electricity to 17,000,000 homes; sent each year 3,750,000 chil-
> dren to high school and more than 1,000,000 young men and women
> to college; and fed, clothed, housed and amused the 120,000,000 per-
> sons who occupy our twentieth of the habitable area of the earth.

But, though it found so many reasons for national self-congratulation, it
sounded a cautionary note: "Underlying recent developments is an attitude of mind which seems to be characteristically American. Our nation
is accustomed to rapid movement, to quick shifts in status; it is receptive
to new ideas, ingenious in devices, adaptable. Our economy is in large
measure the embodiment of those who have made it. Our situation is
fortunate, our momentum is remarkable. Yet the organic balance of our
economic structure can be maintained only by hard, persistent, intelli-
gent effort; by consideration and sympathy; by mutual confidence, and by
a disposition in the several human parts to work in harmony together."[29]
This seemed to imply that men of Schwab's background and value system
could continue to flourish. Even so Schwab began his leadership at the
AISI by recommending caution.

In mid-autumn 1927 at his inauguration Schwab spoke to AISI members—and through them to the public at large—about the large outlays
steel companies had made in recent years, but he recognized that in some
respects their industry was lagging compared with other leading sectors
of the economy. Returns on the $8.9 billion in capital they had invested
were inadequate; indeed in a striking statement he pointed out that "on
average we are not earning as much on our investment as we would if we
had put our money in gilt-edged bonds." His own company had cut pro-

duction costs by $7.27 per ton between 1923 and 1927, but prices for finished products had fallen by more than that. As a result, despite high activity, profits were not keeping pace. Bethlehem paid a 5 percent dividend in each of the four years up to 1923 but managed only 2.5 percent in 1924 and over the next two distributed only on preferred shares.[30] Perhaps he was giving signs of his age in the form of a wish to play for safety. Relative newcomers were pressing hard on established, bigger firms, and in these circumstances he even came to see some merit in the values of his predecessor: "As Judge Gary so often expressed it, live and let live. These works are here and we have our customers and we have our trade and we have our position, and therefore we must try to respect our relative positions and see if we cannot do something toward the betterment of our returns, profits and businesses."[31] It would have been difficult to imagine the young Charlie Schwab of summer 1900, busy on ambitious plans for Conneaut, or a few years later the champion of the Grey mill, happy to opt for the status quo.

On a number of occasions he made remarks about the human dimensions of business that seemed sensible, humane, and wholly acceptable but became trite when it was seen from whose lips they came. The phrasing and vocabulary suggested strongly that he had not written the speeches himself, though whether or not they were written by the public relations man, Ivy Lee, as Hessen implies, is unknown. An interesting example was his response, on 28 December 1927, to the presentation of the E. H. Harriman Memorial Medal at the American Museum of Safety: "Amazing progress has been made in bringing about efficient and economical production. The modern scientist has enabled us to manipulate machines through his penetration for us into the secrets of chemistry and physics. But the transcendent machine is the human being, the man with feelings, with sensibilities, with hopes and fears and responsibilities. It is the human being of whom we are thinking more than ever today, and the businessman is a poor manager whose primary thought is not to bring about a fuller life and finer existence for the human beings with whom he comes into contact." A moralist would find it difficult to quarrel with such aims, but at the same time he was making clear he remained wedded to the most conventional of economic policies as the route to these admirable ends. Meeting the editor Clarence Barron in New York he told him that he liked Hoover but doubted he could win a presidential election. Schwab had another possible candidate in mind: "I think that Mellon may be the next President. I don't think he is too old. [By the time of the election Mellon was well into his seventy-fourth year.] The people have been educated to see how he has reduced expenses, handled the national finances and what a success he has made."[32]

At the end of 1928, Hoover having been elected, Schwab assured the press that the nation's apparent general good fortune was indeed securely based, though the strength of his case seemed to owe more to the warmth with which he conveyed it than to logical proofs:

> Perhaps the most significant thing on the American horizon today is this: Our prosperity is not mere dollar prosperity. Because of that fact it is all the more likely to endure. The wealth which is the foundation of our prosperity is not merely the wealth of gold and silver and raw materials. The United States is wealthy in the older, or original sense of that word—in the sense you get when you hyphenate the word, as wealth, meaning well-being. In other words, America's best assurance for continued prosperity is general well-being, which exists on a scale never before rivalled by any people in history.[33]

Schwab was now striving to bolster the business success already achieved, but occasionally he revealed fears that the good times were not, after all, part of the essential order of things: "We have reached in this country an amazing degree of general prosperity. American business on the whole no longer faces an uphill climb. The problem today is an entirely new one. It is what to do to make prosperity permanent." Inevitably the commercial press warmed to a man who generally communicated positive sentiments. As one journalist rather excessively put it in spring 1929, "For moral guidance much of the world for many centuries has taken heed of the Ten Commandments. For business guidance it may well accept the philosophy of industrial success as recently propounded by Mr. Charles M. Schwab."[34]

Through much of 1929 industrial values continued to rise. U.S. Steel shares, which were 138.125 on 3 March 1928, reached 261.75 eighteen months later. On 5 July Willis King, who had joined Jones and Laughlin ten years before the young Schwab traveled from Loretto to Braddock, responded to an invitation from *Iron Age* with his own upbeat assessment of business: "The country is prosperity-minded, and only a great shock can disturb its optimism. Conditions seem to me as ideal as we can ever hope for, and the year 1929 will, I believe, hold the record in tonnage and profits."[35] The year justified King's optimism about production and profits, but his evaluation of continuing economic health would soon seem to have come from the edge of a precipice. After the high points of September the

stock market faltered; by 4 October U.S. Steel shares were down to 204.
A week earlier Schwab had been in Pittsburgh to address the chamber of
commerce. In his speech he said, "Prophecy is a dangerous thing, but I
feel that Pittsburgh is going to be the greatest center for iron and steel for
all time." At this time the American Iron and Steel Institute presented him
with a clock for his desk to commemorate the fifty years he had spent in
steel since transferring from the Braddock grocery to the surveying team
in the Edgar Thomson yards. As one financial journal put it, he could be
regarded as "the classic example of what an American boy can do with his
life."[36] A few days later he was in Dearborn for another anniversary, the
great celebration Henry Ford had arranged to remember Edison's inven-
tion of the incandescent lamp on 21 October 1879. Soon after he returned
home, steel stocks were crumbling. On Thursday morning, 24 October,
U.S. Steel opened at 205.5; it closed that day at 193.5. Next day, addressing
the AISI, Schwab began with an all too obvious attempt to shore up a col-
lapsing structure: "In my long association with the steel industry I have
never known it to enjoy a greater stability or more promising outlook than
it does today." (At the AISI banquet at this time he was reported to have
begun a speech more realistically, saying, "[A]fter what has happened in
Wall Street, it would probably be quite correct for me to start my remarks
to you with the words: 'Friends and former millionaires.'")[37]

The worst day of this uncertain period was Tuesday, 29 October, on
which selling took place on a huge scale. By 13 November U.S. Steel shares
were down to 150. The AISI president continued to talk up the economy.
On 10 December, with dark days matching the dark times, he maintained
the battle line: "Never before has American business been as firmly entrenched for prosperity as it is today."[38] On Friday evening, 13 December,
he was host at his Riverside Drive home to the twenty-eighth annual re-
union and dinner of the Carnegie Veterans Association. Giving an address that, strangely, focused on the general decay of the religious faith
some of them had held in their youth, William Dickson ended by looking
ahead. His somber tone, although it referred especially to their individual
circumstances, also fit the wider mood of that midwinter season. It could
well have been a Stoic exhortation from the twilight years of imperial
Rome: "As the years are passing ever more swiftly, let us, then, without
waiting for those gray days to come, have the satisfaction of giving utter-
ance to our mutual affection."[39]

In spite of the gloom and uncertainties of fall 1929 it was some time
before the crisis on Wall Street was reflected by the main indicators from
Schwab's industry. The production of crude steel in 1929 was almost 5

million net tons or 9.5 percent more than in 1928, the previous record, and nearly a quarter greater than in the year of largest wartime production. At the end of the year Bethlehem had on hand its biggest order book since 1920–$86 million as compared with an average of less than $61 million over the last eight years. Operations in 1929 averaged 91.8 percent of capacity, and though in the last quarter that figure slipped sharply to 76.8 percent, there was a rally to 80.8 percent in the first quarter of 1930. On 18 February 1930 Schwab spent the day as usual at his office at 25 Broadway before celebrating his sixty-eighth birthday with a "quiet family dinner party" at Riverside. He announced that he intended to retire from all business activities except those connected with Bethlehem Steel.[40] That year both he and Grace appeared in the list drawn up by James W. Gerard, a former American ambassador to Germany, of the sixty-four men "who ruled America." Now things were rapidly sliding into an undeniable crisis. The steel output for 1930 was sharply down; it shrank even more dramatically in 1931, and by the following year, at 15.1 million net tons, it was lower than in any year since 1901 (see table 14 in appendix B).

As the run-down continued, Schwab undertook two last, major services for Bethlehem Steel. They were linked and led to a further decline in his power to influence "his" company's future course. From the acquisition of Lackawanna and Cambria in the early 1920s Bethlehem Steel had been the predominant steel producer east of the Alleghenies, indeed far more in command there than U.S. Steel had at any time been in the national steel markets as a whole. Schwab later stated that U.S. Steel had agreed to stay out of the eastern areas if Bethlehem kept out of areas west of the Allegheny Mountains. Disagreement over the rights to the Grey beam mill (which, after Gary's death, Bethlehem took to expensive litigation) and a more aggressive policy generally from U.S. Steel were factors that encouraged Schwab and Grace to reconsider their company strategy. In fall 1929 Bethlehem very closely followed its bigger rival in acquiring steel capacity on the Pacific coast, and a strong argument for securing a place in the industrial areas west of the Appalachians was that the districts with the largest and most rapidly growing steel consumption were in that region. Bethlehem was concentrated in heavy steels, whereas the biggest increase in demand was for lighter, flat-rolled steels. Together the changes in composition and location of demand persuaded those who controlled Bethlehem to look to combination with an important and well-situated steel maker in these lines. As its name suggests, the Youngstown Sheet and Tube Company (YS&T) concentrated on these very products. In 1901, when he was president of U.S. Steel, Schwab was offered help in

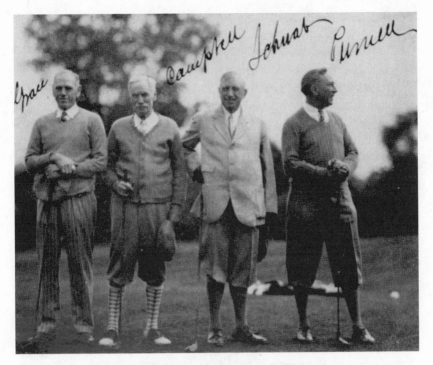

Charles M. Schwab and partners at the Youngstown
Country Golf Club, c. 1929 or 1930.
Reprinted from the *Youngstown Sheet and Tube Bulletin*.

arranging to buy the then newly formed YS&T. The executive committee declined the offer. Since then YS&T had grown into a major company
with integrated plants both in the Valleys district and in the Chicago area.
For the present discussion, the details of the negotiations for Bethlehem
to absorb YS&T are not material. The main negotiator for Bethlehem was
Grace, but Schwab's role was still important. There are pictures of the
two men meeting, apparently rather self-consciously, on the Youngstown
Country Club golf course with James A. Campbell and Frank Purnell of
YS&T.[41]

Early in March 1930 it was announced that along with Grace and
Cyrus Eaton, who represented a group of YS&T stockholders opposed
to the link, Schwab would speak in Youngstown. With Grace he issued
a statement assuring doubters that, if the amalgamation went ahead, the
local company would survive as a separate entity with its own headquarters and executive officers. At this point complications began to crowd in.
There was for instance a rumor that, through his old Carnegie Steel asso-

ciate Julian Kennedy, Schwab had tried to buy a small group of shares at an enhanced price in order to increase the number of votes in favor of the merger.[42] There was soon agreement both from the two boards and from shareholders to go ahead with the merger, but a minority group from YS&T took their opposition to the court of common pleas. In December the amalgamation was declared illegal. In the course of the inquiries that led to this decision, Schwab's position was weakened when the dissenting Youngstown group argued that Bethlehem paid excessive bonuses to its chief officers.

The battle to defend YS&T exposed the Bethlehem bonus system to public scrutiny. It became clear that through his control of the allocation of bonuses Schwab had exercised a power of which most shareholders were unaware. The system had long existed, and Cotter neatly defined it as "nothing more or less than the setting of a cash premium on personal efficiency and endeavor."[43] The system put those eligible for bonuses under tremendous pressure, for it ensured that "each man is constantly keyed up to the highest pitch of efficiency of which he is capable." In 1929 the company distributed bonuses totaling $3.42 million to fourteen or fifteen of its officers. Grace was by far the largest beneficiary. When he testified that his annual salary was $12,000, those in the courtroom laughed; that year he was also paid a bonus of $1,623,753. Schwab received $150,000 a year as chairman, but no bonus. During 1931 the planned merger with YS&T was called off, but disclosure of the bonus payments caused a revolt among Bethlehem shareholders. Their own returns were suffering from the dwindling activity, the 1931 common stock dividend being only $6.4 million compared with $19.2 million the year before. A small group formed a "Protective Committee for the Stockholders of the Bethlehem Steel Corporation" to try to ensure that ordinary investors no longer suffered from deductions to support such large distributions. On 2 March 1931 Schwab sent a long letter to the stockholders. In it he listed the bonuses paid to individuals over the years; he also explained that the system had started as soon as he became sole owner of Bethlehem in August 1901 and that he had controlled decisions about its operation. In summer 1931 Bethlehem Steel came to an agreement with the Protective Committee under which Schwab lost this power.

Month after month as the depression continued and deepened Schwab kept up the pretense that all was or soon would be well. In May 1930 he tried to inspire confidence in seven hundred steel men at the Hotel Commodore during the twenty-seventh annual meeting of the AISI. He thought 1930 would be a year of normal progress: "I have never known a time when steel management had equipped itself so well to gauge accurately the factors that it should take into account in charting its progressive course. Accordingly, after weighing all factors, I am sure I voice the opinions of steel men generally when I say that looking ahead, the prospects for the future of steel are assuring." In October at the opening of the James Ward Packer Electrical Engineering Laboratory at Lehigh University, he took the opportunity to reach out for a technological fix for their difficulties: "Science will cure unemployment. New industries will arise from our laboratories. That is the basis of American progress."[44] Next May he still managed a brave face at the AISI meeting, his presidential address acknowledging there had been some price cutting, but he tried to encourage his members with a maritime metaphor: "We want to keep pulling for the shore. We must not lose headway by resting on our oars, but we can be cheered by the knowledge that 'the tide is coming in.'" Prolonged applause acknowledged his statement, yet his rallying cry seemed rather flat: "Let us go along feeling optimistic, trying our best to be optimistic, practicing Christian Science in our business and believing that we are going to do better, and have happiness in the doing of it." Speaking next, James Farrell was more critical of the conduct of many in their industry.[45] Things were in fact getting worse, and as Frederick Lewis Allen put it, as months of depression went on one after another, Schwab's "easy optimism came to seem like the standard product of an age gone by." In 1931 Bethlehem orders in hand fell by $11 million or more than a quarter; net income that year was a diminutive $100,000. By autumn and winter even Schwab was losing his veneer of confidence. He now urged, "The Federal budget must be halved in order to protect our national credit."[46] As 1932 began Bethlehem was drifting into major losses, but the problem was general—in the first quarter of the year the five leading steel companies failed by $25 million, or some $12.50 per gross ton, to earn the interest, depreciation, or other charges on their output. U.S. Steel stock reached a low of 21.25. Schwab had now moved from optimism to casting about for an explanation of their plight: "That is where we have been brought by reckless, suicidal competition," he said in his AISI presidential address that spring.[47] A few weeks before, on his seventieth birthday, he emphasized once again that he was withdrawing from active involvement in business.

New Deal and Old Thinking

On 24 February 1932, a few days after his seventieth birthday, Schwab wrote to Grace to thank the managerial staff at Bethlehem for the large compendium of their congratulations he had been sent. His gracious response to "all of the Bethlehem boys" was in words that showed he now thought of himself as having withdrawn from business conflicts: "This book from the men in the mill, the production fellows, the accounting men, the lawyers, the management fellows, from the mines, the shipping, the railroads, and every part of our business, was a heart-warming and beautiful tribute. Words cannot begin to express the happiness which this has given me. I love to sit in my study in the evening, turn over the pages of this book and see your faces as I read your kindly words." Not all views of him were as benign as theirs. A few months earlier the *New Republic* had described him as "a born actor": "[W]ith his baritone voice, his ready flow of language, his golden-toothed smile and, above all, his marvelous gift of bursting into tears without a moment's notice, he knows how to fascinate enemies, Senators, government prosecutors, justices and rebellious stockholders."[48]

More than thirty years before Carnegie had written in *The Gospel of Wealth,* "The saddest of all spectacles is that of an elderly man occupying his last years in grasping for more dollars."[49] In 1930, Schwab's fortune of about $300 million was, in nominal terms, roughly equal to what Carnegie had received from the sale of his company to U.S. Steel in 1901. When Carnegie died in 1919 almost all his wealth was gone; by the time of Schwab's death he too would have no money left. The difference between them was that Carnegie gave his money to what he and generally others regarded as worthy causes; Schwab lost his because of bad investments, the general depreciation of commercial values, and simply by living beyond his means.

Given his age and the times, Charlie Schwab was now increasingly out of step with contemporary economic, social, and political conditions. In fall 1931 his former colleague and assistant, William Dickson, sent him a clipping about the thoughts of the former Ford Motor Company mogul and now progressive Republican, Sen. James Couzens, on the administration of big corporations. Dickson asked Schwab what he thought of Couzens's remarks. Schwab reacted defensively: "I am just back from the Mountains and overwhelmed with affairs, but some day soon let us have a luncheon. I would like to talk further with you." There is no record that the matter was taken up again. When the American Iron and Steel Institute met in spring 1932, Bethlehem steel output was at only 20 to 21 percent of capacity. Schwab declared to his members that he still favored the traditional harsh medicine prescribed by conventional economic wisdom for hard times. His opinion was shared by most other leaders in steel, such as Tom Girdler and Ernest Weir. That year in the course of a Senate inquiry into the depression, the chairman of U.S. Steel, Myron Taylor, was honest enough to say, "I have no remedy in mind."[50] In October in London Schwab sounded another clarion call for holding on in the assurance that good times would come again, but his optimism had a hollow ring, more than ever seeming like whistling in the dark: "There was a great danger in times like these of getting into a blue funk. They had in the world today the great resources which always had existed. They had to a greater extent than ever the knowledge of how to utilize those resources. Their difficulties today had not been with the lack of essential wealth, but in the dislocation of economic machinery. They had emerged from difficulties before and would do so again, advancing to ever higher standards of well-being." Back in the United States he praised Hoover's Reconstruction Finance Corporation but continued to advocate tax cuts at the federal, state, and municipal level.[51] Soon America would have a leader with new ideas, for in the presidential election that fall Herbert Hoover received 59 electoral votes and Franklin D. Roosevelt, 472.

The new administration could not take over the reins of government until the president's inauguration on 4 March 1933. During the uncertain winter weeks of the interregnum it felt to an impressionable observer that an uncharacteristic drabness had possessed New York: "It seemed as if the very color of the city had changed. From an elegant bright gray by day and sparkling gold by night, the afternoons had grown haggard, the nights mournful."[52] About this time, in a striking departure from his long-maintained, outwardly confident style, Schwab at last admitted, "I'm afraid, every man is afraid." Publicly, the president of AISI, now with an annual salary from Bethlehem Steel of about $250,000, was open-minded enough to welcome the new administration. That May, in the middle of the whirlwind of the first hundred days in which the main elements of the New Deal were put in place, in his sixth annual presidential address to the Iron and Steel Institute he made reference to Roosevelt's program for price stability and expressed the hope it might fulfill the old ambition of leading firms in the industry to do away with price cutting. But the new National Recovery Administration (NRA) code for steel was less acceptable, and Schwab went to the White House for consultations. At first he argued that his obligation to Bethlehem shareholders stood in the way of accepting the code. Then in mid-August Roosevelt signed the Code of Fair Competition for Steel, and the board of directors of the American Iron and Steel Institute was given the responsibility of administering it. A year later Schwab formally welcomed the "Steel Code" and even managed to summon up some enthusiasm for the new regime: "For the first time in my half-century in the steel industry, I have seen a year when the business of the industry could be conducted on a common sense basis." The 1934 annual meeting of the AISI marked the end of another strand in Schwab's career; after presiding over the proceedings "with usual geniality" and citing his age and the state of his health as his reasons, he stepped down. Acknowledging his services, the directors of AISI spoke of his opinions and judgments as those of a master; in turn he bade them the most affectionate of farewells: "I want you all to know how deeply I appreciate your ever kindly and friendly attitude and help to me as President and Chairman of the Institute, and my love, esteem and admiration for all the members of the Institute will always remain a bright spot of my life."[53] Henceforth the business world was one in which his long experience seemed less an asset than a legacy of a bygone age. Even at Bethlehem, his own creation, he seemed more and more an anachronism. Its great projects and new growth points were the hot strip mills and ancillary plant installed at Sparrows Point and Lackawanna.

Old business friends and those who meant even more to him were rapidly passing from the scene. William Abbott, under whom he had served at Carnegie, Phipps and Company at Homestead in the late 1880s, died in 1930. Julian Kennedy, a rival for promotion nearly half a century before, passed on in 1932. In May 1934 he was deeply upset by the death of William Corey, who was just sixty-eight; three months earlier Schwab had celebrated his seventy-second birthday. At the end of 1936 Schwab and Farrell were honorary pall bearers at the funeral of an old business rival, the eighty-five-year-old Willis King of Jones and Laughlin. Far more upsetting than any of these was the death of his mother Pauline in March 1936 in her ninety-fourth year.

When Grace took over as president of the AISI he joined the chorus of outspoken disapproval of government policies to revive the economy: "I believe the chief barrier to recovery is political—the economic uncertainties underlying too many experiments and the proposals to regiment American business and labor. . . . It is about time we had a little old-fashioned economy, that we encouraged efficiency and thrift, and stopped holding out false illusions based on the theory that the resources of the states are unlimited." In the year in which he made those comments unemployment averaged 10.6 million or 20.1 percent of the civilian labor force. In his second presidential address Grace referred to what he saw as the most serious problem facing the nation: "the menacing attempt to exercise a political control of our economic and personal lives." He asked

George M. Verity, Charles M. Schwab, and Eugene G. Grace *(left to right)*, 1934.
Courtesy of the National Canal Museum, Easton, PA.

his fellow industrialists, "Shall freedom of initiative and freedom of enterprise survive, or shall social and economic existence be dictated and controlled by Government? This is the momentous issue confronting us."[54]

Schwab's public references to Grace were always in terms of unqualified in praise. In 1920, identifying integrity as a primary requirement for
a man of business, he had singled out his president as exemplifying this
virtue. Twelve years later he told the press, "I consider Mr. Grace the
ablest executive for the business that I ever knew. Grace and I have always made a good team. Grace is the keen, calculating business executive.
I am a dreamer, a sentimental man in business. No business can be truly
successful unless it has sentiment in it." As his presidency of AISI ended,
he presented the organization's highest honor, the Gary Medal, to Grace.
The occasion gave both men a chance to reveal more of their relationship.
Schwab was typically effusive and generous:

> For me to be able to present this award to a man with whom I have
> been associated, who has been my closest business colleague and
> friend for over 30 years, and who I know, perhaps better than any-
> one else, possesses those sterling qualities which have made him the
> outstanding figure which he is in our industrial life, is indeed grati-
> fying. It is one of the happiest moments in my life. . . . Thoroughness
> and study, knowledge of how to deal with men, practical experience
> in the mills, executive training both abroad and at home, wartime
> service, the policy of forging ahead without trampling on his col-
> leagues—such are the qualities which have brought him to the fore-

front in our industry, equipped with this experience and a character of the highest quality.

In an interesting variant of words he had once used about Carnegie, he now referred to Grace as "the dearest friend I have in the world." Then he added a patriotic flourish: "[H]e has always gone forward with optimism and Americanism as the dominating spirit within his soul." Responding, Grace was equally generous but concise and "businesslike" in his remarks: "It is hardly necessary for me to tell this group that whatever I have accomplished is due solely to the opportunity, support and guidance given me throughout this entire period by my dearest and closest friend and associate, Mr. Schwab. Never was there a more generous or unselfish man." Away from the warm euphoria—and the stage management—of such a presentation, perhaps the best indication of the real nature of the relationship between Schwab and Grace came in brief remarks from them some years later. A year or so after his speech at the Gary Medal presentation Schwab commented on Grace to the reporter Sidney Whipple. He was again loud in his praise but ended with a few significant words: "He is a man of quick decisions and unswerving loyalty. . . . Whatever he does he does well. He has the greatest power of concentration I have ever seen in any man. Ours has been one of the happiest of associations, although there is no levity in him." Ten years later, Grace set himself the aim of giving a "human picture of the man himself." In the course of it he said, "It was typical of his friendliness that thousands of men referred to him as 'Charlie' or 'CM.' But I had such great respect for him, I always called him Mr. Schwab."[55]

There is no evidence that Schwab really grasped the deep suffering of millions of his fellow citizens during one of the most traumatic phases of the nation's history. A good illustration of the great gulf that separated him from them was provided by his response to the squatter camps of the times. As early as winter 1930–1931 there began to appear settlements of the dispossessed that, sardonically, were often given the name "Hoovervilles." Arthur M. Schlesinger summarized their origin and condition: "With no money left for rent, unemployed men and their entire families began to build shacks where they could find unoccupied land. Along the railroad embankment, beside the garbage incinerator, in the city dumps, there appeared towns of tar paper and tin, old packing boxes and old car bodies." By 1934 one of the largest of these "villages" within New York City was located on Riverside Drive at Seventy-fourth Street. Edward Robb Ellis evocatively—and provocatively—described its character and setting:

Thin-faced men, many of them veterans, had used discarded boards, sheets of corrugated tin, strips of tar paper and wire to put together a cluster of shanties for themselves and their families. They cooked scraps of food over open tins within sight of passengers on the double-decked buses that rolled up and down the Drive. . . . A stone's throw away from these miserable huts, there loomed one of the most magnificent mansions in America, the home of Charles M Schwab. . . . Merely by lifting their eyes, the residents of Hoover Village could see the iron picket fence enclosing the spacious grassy lawns and the granite chateau with twin minarets 100 feet high. . . . Deep underground was a vault that could hold 20 tons of beef—enough to feed a family of five for 80 years. This pleasure palace also contained a $50,000 organ, a marble swimming pool, a gymnasium, a billiard room with 10 tables, bowling alleys, a mahogany wine closet, three elevators and a private chapel with a marble altar weighing 10 tons.

But what was most remarkable was not the huge difference in command over material provision that divided Schwab from these near neighbors so much as the strange combination of his apparently genial attitude to unemployed working men with a deep-seated inability to comprehend their real plight. In spring 1934, returning from Europe, he expressed surprise on learning that the squatters had been ordered to break camp and move on. He spoke to a reporter in a tone as unrealistically benign as Ellis's was bitter: "We visited back and forth. They had been up to my house and very kindly assisted us around the grounds in getting rid of the heavy snows of last winter. Mrs. Schwab frequently drove down to visit them in their homes. And I also called on them many times. When we had a surplus of produce from our farm at Loretto, Pennsylvania, we were happy to share it with them. They had looked forward to staying there, I know, until business improved. We shall miss them. They were not bad neighbors at all." Sometime in 1935 or 1936 in conversations with the journalist Sidney Whipple he revealed the core of his political economy. It was simple enough: "There is one unalterable law—the law of supply and demand. If we had let Nature take her course, the world would have been able to work out its own destination."[56] What this course of inaction might have meant for the well-being of his erstwhile squatter neighbors he did not spell out.

After withdrawing from active involvement in Bethlehem Steel and standing down from AISI Schwab had more time to pursue other interests. He played bridge, long one of his favorite pastimes, and in 1933 he donated a trophy to be competed for in international competition—with the request that an invitation for Germany to take part should be withdrawn if Jews were not allowed to participate. In spring 1936 he showed reporters his vast collection of first editions on the first floor of Riverside and told them, "I read a great deal now, and in addition to this, I have another library upstairs."[57] He continued to travel. Early in 1931 Rana, in a departure from the norm, traveled with him to Cuba to visit President Gerardo Machado, who had ruled tyrannically since 1924 in an administration John Gunther later described as "one of the most vicious governments that ever existed in the Western Hemisphere."[58] Schwab was feted everywhere in the world as an elder statesman in steel. When he received the Melchett Medal, he had been invited to dinner in the Pinafore Room of the Savoy Hotel by a party that was led by Sir Charles Wright of Guest, Keen & Baldwins Iron and Steel (GKB) and included many of the heads of the most important British companies. Most valued of all, his foreign visits gave him opportunities to meet old friends. At least one of these friends was widely regarded as scarcely if any more respectable than Machado.

Whenever Schwab returned from Europe the press would ask for his impressions, and some of his responses were interesting, especially those concerning armaments, a very lively issue during and after the 1934–1935 congressional hearings into the munitions industry (the Nye Committee). In early 1935 while allegedly visiting the Riviera for health reasons, he met up with Basil Zaharoff, the widely detested arms salesman who had formerly been with Vickers. Zaharoff now owned the Casino in Monte Carlo, the very establishment in which Schwab had compromised his position as head of U.S. Steel. When Schwab arrived home he was invited to comment on Bernard Baruch's suggestion that wartime earnings should bear a heavy tax. Schwab agreed that profit should be modest but pointed out that if it was taken away altogether, the makers of munitions would withdraw from the trade. Asked about Zaharoff, he characterized him as a brilliant man of business and then provided a stunning understatement: "He is what I would call an international merchant. . . . I told him recently that his one mistake was in not taking the press into his confidence. That caused all this 'mystery' business." A year later, on his seventy-fourth birthday, war and armaments were again brought up. He described as "ridiculous" the idea that armament firms fomented war. He was asked if munitions, as distinguished from munitions makers, did not make for war: "Ah, that is a very different thing," Schwab said. "If the whole world decided armaments should not be made, there is nobody who would be faster and quicker at the top of the list than I. I think war is [he searched for a word] indescribable." Then, with fantasy rather than hyperbole getting the better of him, he spoke of Zaharoff as "one of the finest, most estimable, most beloved of men." That spring, returning from a six-week rest in the spa town of Bad Nauheim, he reported Germany to be in fine condition and that Hitler was "really popular, because they credit him with bringing order out of chaos."[59] A few weeks before that, German forces had reoccupied the Rhineland, and Europe was on the slippery slope to World War II. In November 1936 Basil Zaharoff died suddenly.

In the mid-1930s the setbacks experienced by labor unions after Frick's handling of the Homestead strike and the labor management policies Schwab had followed afterward were at last reversed. In August 1931, attending the funeral of his brother-in-law Alva Dinkey, he remarked to William Dickson, "Billy, when I review our past history, I am very much ashamed of the way we treated our labor. In my opinion, the working men have higher standards than the average of our class." A few months later he said, "Fifty years ago our working men were treated as machines; now they are treated as human beings." Both statements may have been true, but they did not change the formal arrangements between management and workers. There had been improvements, including the introduction of company unions, but industry-wide unionization not only did not exist, but most of the industry was adamant that it never would. But in July 1935 Congress passed the National Labor Relations Act, which marked a major though general step toward the end of the company union system. A much more vital blow within the steel industry was struck in March 1937 when, unexpectedly, U.S. Steel agreed with the Steel Workers Organizing Committee (SWOC) of the Congress of Industrial Organizations (CIO) to accept full union representation. That summer U.S. Steel avoided the labor disputes that affected many other steel companies, including Bethlehem Steel; in one instance the water supply at Johnstown was dynamited. Even more reminiscent of earlier unhappy events at Bethlehem Steel, Grace arranged for company police to be supplied with revolvers, rifles, shotguns, and even machine guns. Tear gas was made available, and undercover agents were hired to spy on anyone attempting to organize a union. Schwab was away at the time, spending four weeks taking the "cure," but upon arriving home he said he was very disturbed about the strike—and hurried off to Loretto to get more information. A year before, visiting the new Lackawanna strip mill, he had revealed how important to him it was to be well thought of: "It hurts me—it hurts me very much—to be branded as nothing but a greedy, selfish, self-seeking, mercenary, merciless fellow, callous toward workmen and toward every-body else."[60]

Through this decade there were family occasions to be enjoyed, in-cluding his and Rana's wedding anniversary celebrations and regular vis-its to Loretto. An interesting insight into his life there came from an inde-pendent source in July 1935 when the Historical Society of Western Penn-sylvania, in its fourth successive historical tour into the countryside and into the past, visited the Altoona district. At Loretto they passed by Im-mergrun and visited Saint Michael's Church, where Schwab joined them, chatting for a time to old friends and being introduced to other members of the party. During a luncheon in the Penn-Alto Hotel in Altoona he was the principal speaker. "Chatting" rather than speaking formally, he urged the audience to preserve sentiment in human relations and referred to the roles of time, chance, and place in molding human life and their impor-tance when, as then, all seemed chaos. He confessed that though he re-tained hope, he was out of step with the spirit of the times: "I am worried because I cannot plan for the future, but I have been optimistic all my life and I am not going to change. I believe in the spirit of the people of this country, and I believe that we are going to see things restored to the usual course. All that we have at present is the result of individual initiative, exercised not for personal gain but because of the urge to progress. The future, my friends, will be individualistic rather than cooperative." The recorder of the occasion added that no one present would ever forget "the running fire of anecdotes with which the speaker enlivened his discourse and illustrated his points."[61]

Now and again he displayed some of the old sentimentality. An ex-treme example was when, in May 1937, he again took up the diary of his and Rana's visits to Loretto. His last entry had been made in October 1921; the new one was an expression of feelings that linked him with millions of the aging looking back nostalgically on life:

> I have just found through Minnie [Rana's sister] my old diary of May 1920. Today, through the goodness of God, we celebrate our 54th wedding anniversary, and it seems fitting I should write something in this old book of our day's doings and celebration. . . . Dear old Immergrun never looked so lovely nor any home sweeter. Today we had a busy day, meeting all the members of our families. . . . We then visited Sister Mary [his sister] at the convent and Rana took her a beautiful poem engraved on silver and written by Rana herself to be placed on the old clock which she had presented to the convent. The

Charles and Rana Schwab on their fiftieth wedding anniversary, 1933.
Courtesy of the National Canal Museum, Easton, PA.

Mother Superior and Mary were delighted. We then had a drive and now are settled for the day. After 54 years of married life together one naturally thinks of the past—what busy and yet happy years they were. After all these years together I love my old wife with deeper affection than ever before. To me she is the greatest and best woman in the world and now that life naturally is nearly ended for both of us we have no real regrets. Many vicissitudes, many troubles, but much contentment and happiness, many honors have come to us in these years, but the lasting impression is that of a happy life together. This is a true and sincere expression. CM Schwab.[62]

In 1934 Schwab had told reporters, "I am lightening my load. I am not giving much time to business anymore, and I am only spending several hours a day at my office at 25 Broadway. I am finding quiet and relaxation at my various clubs and in playing cards"—though he had just retired as president of the whist club at 9 East Sixty-second Street, which he had headed for some twenty years. But he added, "As for retiring from Bethlehem Steel, that I will never do. It is my greatest monument, and I am proud of it."[63] Eventually it began to appear anomalous to some that he should receive a large salary as Bethlehem's chairman for life. Apart from appearances at the annual meetings, he seemed to drift away from the company he had created. Whatever his kind words, his leading protégé took little regular account of him. Grace's engagement diaries made no mention of him at all in 1934, and on the day on which Schwab lunched at Bethlehem in May 1935 Grace seems to have been in New York. Next year Grace's diary again did not refer to Schwab even once.

During the proceedings at the 1932 annual general meeting, Bethlehem stockholders expressed unhappiness about Schwab's $250,000 annual salary. In response Grace pointed out that no such payment could fully reward their chairman for all he had done. Three years later two stockholders were bold enough to suggest that Schwab had outlived his usefulness to the company, but an overwhelming majority of stockholders supported him and Grace became so outraged that he threatened the two dissidents with physical violence. The problem returned in 1938 when depression made a sharp return. The general meeting provided an opportunity for a group of stockholders to try to secure a ruling that, if the quarterly common stock dividend was passed, their chairman should either serve without a salary or should at least take a 10 percent cut. After sitting silently for three hours listening to the arguments, Schwab spoke and indicated how deeply he had been hurt: "I have devoted my life to the Bethlehem Steel Corporation. This company owes me a debt which it can never repay." The enthusiastic applause that greeted this statement came from all but four stockholders.[64]

Schwab's health was now failing. In spring 1932, he sailed on a three-week recuperative trip abroad. During autumn 1933 he was confined to Doctors Hospital for two weeks, listed as a rest cure patient. Next year on several occasions after his return from Europe he was in the same hospital, usually suffering from what was described as fatigue. In late spring 1937 he "took the cure" in Europe and after a nineteen-day heat wave that summer was once more in the hospital for several days. By 1938 he suffered from neuritis. There even seemed to be some indication of mental decline, though it may have been "diplomatic" rather than real. In summer 1938 he gave evidence in a court case involving the puzzling loss of any record of $215,730 spent in the publication of an index of articles from the American Society of Mechanical Engineers, of which he had been president in the late 1920s. The judge was reported as saying, "Mr. Schwab, who was president, showed an almost inconceivable ignorance of everything connected with the affairs of the society, and his answers to page after page of inquiries, as to details or generalities, were reduced to almost invariable repetition of 'I don't know' or 'I don't remember' or 'I did not know.'"[65]

By the second half of the 1930s the range of his activities was narrowing. Already peripheral in the business world, Schwab now saw his wealth and social life begin to shrink. At the end of 1936, indicating that he and Rana now found their Riverside home too big, Schwab suggested New York City should pay four million dollars for the property and make it a residence for Mayor LaGuardia. Failing to convince the potential buyer they had identified, they had to hold on to it. By 1938 Schwab had given up his luxury yacht *Alicia,* and though he still retained his private railroad car, he and Rana rarely visited Immergrun. They seldom entertained at Riverside, so that the "epicurean and table-talk marvels of days gone by have virtually ceased."[66] By the following midwinter the last phase of a long and distinguished life had unmistakably begun.

End of a Working Life

Rana Schwab had been in ill health and a virtual invalid for about three years when on 2 May 1938 she and Charlie celebrated their fifty-fifth wedding anniversary. In words that revealed much about their marriage, they were reported as saying, "It seems like a few short years since we started our happy companionship." On Christmas Day in 1938 Rana suffered a severe heart attack. She was confined to bed and early on the morning of Thursday, 12 January, died in her sleep. She was seventy-nine. At 3 p.m. on Saturday, 14 January, a minister of the Dutch Reformed Church conducted her funeral at Riverside, and she was buried in Woodlawn Cemetery. Schwab, soon to be seventy-seven, was now without his "balance wheel."

In spite of the loss, in the second week of February he set out for his usual winter cruise to the Mediterranean, this time on the Italian liner *Rex.* He explained he was going solely for the rest and would stay on the ship. In early March he closed Riverside, moving first to a hotel and then into a "small" apartment at 290 Park Avenue. At about the same time he shut and put up for sale his home in Bethlehem. By April the furnishings from Immergrun were sold, and in a few weeks the house itself was on the market. Yet, though having lost his homes and now alone in the profoundest sense of lacking the closest of family ties, he could still be warmed by the admiration of an unusually wide range of business friends. There can be little doubt that their sentiments for him were genuine for by this time neither preferment nor material gain could be expected in return. In short, though he was an old man, Charlie Schwab was, as always, able to charm. This ability was vividly illustrated in late April 1939.

A final important dinner was given in his honor in New York, this time at the Roosevelt Hotel. In the course of the evening he was praised as the nation's number one salesman. Modestly, he denied he deserved such an honor. Tom Girdler, the head of Republic Steel and forthright opponent of the New Deal, who may well have felt discomfort at the very name of the building in which they were meeting, declared, "I wish to God he was younger and had the inclination so that we could make him President of the United States to lead us out of this depression." There were laudatory telegrams from various quarters. The president of the Boston Chamber of Commerce, communicating the admiration of his organization, wrote, "Heartiest congratulations upon richly deserved honors, accorded you tonight. Your optimism and driving force have been an inspiration to the development of American industry throughout the thrilling years of the twentieth century. A thousand good wishes." Generous remarks came from former business rivals. James Farrell, who was born three days before Schwab, had arrived in Pittsburgh only a little later, and first knew him in Braddock when they were both young men working for different iron and steel firms, recalled not only Schwab's business abilities but also his personal qualities as he had experienced them during his own presidency of U.S. Steel and at the American Iron and Steel Institute: "Having had many business dealings with you, I can say without equivocation that never did I come away from any of these without having a greater respect for your instinctive business and commercial ability and a higher regard for you as a man." The much younger Benjamin Fairless, then president of United States Steel, was more direct: "Dear Charlie . . . I have yet to meet your equal as a salesman. I speak feelingly but honestly." Overseas friends sent greetings. Telegrams came from Lord Dudley, president of the Iron and Steel Institute, and from Robert Hilton, president of the British Iron and Steel Federation. Another was from Sir William Firth, the leading maverick among the heads of British steel companies, who said, "You have more than earned any medal that may be presented to you. You have also earned [the] admiration, respect and affection of your competitors throughout the world. I wish you long life and much happiness."[67] In fact this long, distinguished, and colorful life was rapidly drawing to its close.

During the summer Schwab traveled once more to Europe. At the beginning of August, on a flight from Paris to London, his plane was caught in a storm and he became violently sick. He arrived at the Savoy Hotel in central London, and it was there on 9 August that he suffered a heart attack. After two weeks of rest, he was reckoned fit to travel home. On his return journey he was accompanied by Dr. Edward Gordon, the British doctor who had been treating him. They arrived in New York on the SS *Washington* on Thursday, 31 August. The man who had crossed the Atlantic so frequently and had come back with so much business was now carried from the liner on a stretcher. He was driven by ambulance to the Park Avenue apartment that had been his home since spring. Next day he arranged for a telephone reply to Grace, who had expressed a wish to visit him. The tone of his message indicated weariness but above all showed a remarkable, cheerful resilience: "My dear boy, I am safely home in my own bed after a most difficult and trying experience. I thank you for your kind message and of course at the earliest opportunity I shall be very glad to see you. Sir Charles Wright [of the British firm GKB], Quincy Bent [vice president of Bethlehem Steel] and everybody have been most attentive to me in my difficulty. I am so happy that everything seems to be going well with you. CMS."[68]

Samuel Brown, his own doctor, who had been in Czechoslovakia when Schwab became ill, came home from Europe. After examining his patient, he ordered two more weeks of bed rest but was said to have expressed a belief that after that he might be up again, although it was reported afterward that Schwab's friends had known he would not recover. Over the next few days, as Schwab lay in his bed, the European nations he had visited so often and known so well drifted into the horrors of a second great war. It is not known whether he managed to read the newspapers or, if so, how he reacted to the prospect of new and indeed unprecedented levels of demand for his firm's products. As things turned out, relatively little time was left for reflection. Dr. Brown had made clear that the recovery he hoped for would depend on his patient not having another heart attack. A second attack came, and, with his brother Edward at his bedside, Charlie Schwab died at his home at 9:30 on the evening of Monday, 18 September 1939.

It was at once widely acknowledged that a great American had passed from the scene, a man whose life had spanned all the economic, social, and political transformations that separated the Civil War from World War II. Throughout a majority of those years, and in a most vital sector of its business activity, he had been a key player. On the day after his death, Eugene Grace issued a statement to all employees about "Bethlehem's founder and our friend." His remarks were far from perfunctory; on this occasion they had the ring of genuine emotion. They set their subject within a personal, company, and national setting. Further interest lies in what they emphasized and what they omitted:

In paying tribute to Charles M. Schwab, I speak of one of my deepest friendships. Everyone will mourn his loss. In the many years of association with him we have had a chance to know thoroughly the generosity and warmth of his character, his honesty, his friendliness and his gift for inspiring others. Mr. Schwab was a pioneer in realizing the importance of the human element in industry, believing in encouragement and opportunity for every employee. He proved by experience that praise brings out the best in men, and he discarded the slave-driving tradition once prevalent in industry in favor of a policy of commendation and reward for work well done. Mr. Schwab was always a solid and enthusiastic believer in the future of America. His early predictions on the growth of the steel industry were thought fantastic and yet he lived to see most of them come true. He stood for American principles, for the American way of life, and he continuously affirmed that if America retains her tradition of enterprise, the progress of the country will be assured. Mr. Schwab was a man of great faith. He was a tower of strength to the age in which he lived and an inspiration for future generations. As a mark of respect to his more than half a century as the country's outstanding figure in the steel industry, as a great American, and for his 35 years of outstanding service to Bethlehem, flags will be flown at half-mast in all plants and properties until after his burial and a period of three minutes' silence will be observed throughout the organization, during which there will be a cessation of all possible operations, at 10.00 a.m.–Eastern Daylight Saving Time–Thursday, September 21st, the time at which his funeral services will be held.[69]

On the day of the funeral a congregation of fifteen hundred gathered in Saint Patrick's Cathedral, New York, for a solemn High Mass of requiem. At least another thousand stood outside in Fifth Avenue or the neighboring streets. Grace was an honorary pall bearer. Among those present were J. D. Rockefeller Jr. and James Farrell. The interment took place at the Gate of Heaven Cemetery in Westchester County, but the following spring Schwab's remains were moved to Cresson to be reburied near his parents. By this time his effects were being sold. The furniture and furnishings on which he had spent so lavishly were auctioned over three days in March and realized only $17,760; a few weeks earlier his silver sold for $24,000.[70] Three years later a tax appraisal of his estate appeared. His New York home had cost $8 million to build and furnish, and the house and estate at Immergrun had been valued at $3.5 million. Before the financial crash of 1929 his wealth was perhaps $300 million. Riverside Drive had been disposed of before his death to the Chase Manhattan Bank. On 3 October 1942 his thousand-acre Loretto estate, which had once employed one hundred gardeners and had cost about $100,000 a year to maintain, was sold by auction for $57,000. Most of Immergrun went to Saint Francis College for $32,500. Even so, what was revealed by the tax appraisal was startling enough; at the time of his death his assets amounted to $1.39 million but his obligations were $1.73 million.[71] Long before the insolvency of this former multimillionaire's estate was revealed, many evaluations of the man and of his part in America's development had already appeared.

One of the most generous—and also one of the most discerning—comments had been written almost twenty years before his death, in the form of the "recollections" of Willis King. His remarks on Schwab's business qualities have already been quoted, but King ended by focusing on the man: "Schwab is the best after dinner speaker I have ever heard. . . . His speeches to young men at schools and colleges are wonderfully impressive, full of good advice given in such an attractive and impelling way as to arouse enthusiasm and ambition. A 'fellow of infinite wit,' generous to a fault, and lovable to a degree not given to many, I count our long friendship one of the most pleasing incidents in my business life." In the early aftermath of Schwab's death, Horace E. Lewis, also of Jones and Laughlin and like Schwab a man who had worked his way up from the mills to top management, spoke of his understanding, kindliness, and vision. James Farrell recognized that America had lost an inspiring industrial leader and mentioned not only his "force of personality" but also his humble beginnings: "I like to think of Charles Schwab as I knew him at Braddock, where we were working in separate plants, and frequently walked home together after the day's toil." The New York correspondent for the *Times* of London described Schwab as a "self-made man" who had attained a position in the industry "second only to that of his master and friend Andrew Carnegie."[72] Contemporary assessments of his place in the economy's growth were generally positive, and there were records of Schwab's own thoughts regarding his place in economic history. It is important to recognize, however, that both he and most of the outside critics were biased observers. To some extent this bias was because of the nature of the times and partly because of a wholly understandable wish to think and record the best of those who have recently passed away. His former colleagues and associates thought of him as a very human elder statesman of the business world; he had always wanted to present himself as an industrial romantic who could scarcely understand his fame and wealth.

He had once claimed to be puzzled by his own success but had been unable to keep his sense of humor out of his assessment: "Here am I, a not over good business man, a second-rate engineer. I can make poor mechanical drawings. I play the piano after a fashion. In fact, I am one of those proverbial Jacks of all trades who are usually failures. Why I am not, I can't tell you." On another occasion he had remarked, surely disingenuously, "I have always looked at myself as a builder rather than a financier. That I have money is accidental." In 1928 he seemed to attribute success to good fortune: "Luck, opportunity, chance—call it what you will—there is certainly something that gives some men more than an even break." To Sidney Whipple a few years later he revealed his opinion of his own mental processes: "I do not sit and figure things out. . . . I simply get the 'flash.' It is instinctive, and I am not conscious of thought."[73] In these respects Schwab seems to have been doing less than justice to his powers of reasoning; certainly some of the detailed cost assessments he made at Homestead in the mid-1890s suggested that at least then he relied on something more substantial than "flash." On his seventieth birthday he had presented himself as a dreamer but explicitly recognized that his vision was confined to the world of industry, a far cry from the soaring aspirations and even the achievements of Andrew Carnegie. He set his position at Bethlehem Steel within a broader framework, though some might regard it as woefully lacking in depth: "That company is my own child, the soul of my life. It is my monument, that I hope will stand as something worthy to be connected with. . . . I am a dreamer. I am a sentimental man in business or in anything else. No business will be happy and successful unless it has sentiment in it." In this interview he revealed the secret of his success, his ability to attract and to motivate men with more technical expertise than he had, an invaluable quality he shared with Carnegie: "Men do their best work under the stimulus of appreciation. I've been smart in one respect. That was in picking men like Grace and encouraging them."[74] At the end, it was his own human qualities that outsiders praised most.

Iron Age recognized that a magnetic smile, contagious optimism, tact, and friendliness had made up his great talent of organizing men to work together. When it was noted that he was "Charlie" to his workers, it was all too easy to take a further step and romanticize his techniques of human resource management. The New York correspondent of the London *Times* put a favorable gloss on this aspect of his working life: "One of the secrets of his success was that he understood the handling of men, not by concessions to their extreme agitators, but by his brusque and cheerful manner, and above all by his personal example when hard work was to be done." From the opposite perspective the *Labor Advocate* made a legitimate point but was equally narrow and therefore unbalanced when it simply labeled him "a bitter foe of organized labor."[75]

Schwab had for more than a generation been a picturesque figure among American industrialists, a man of "pungent and witty speeches, often impromptu and always full of individuality." On such occasions, notwithstanding his seniority and experience, he conveyed to his listeners "an almost boyish sportiveness." There were numerous jokes, some of them crude, but many others memorable.[76] Many men were easily bowled over by his personality. Foreigners were as readily bewitched as his compatriots. In consequence they may have exaggerated his business expertise, glossing over any deficiencies by making primary reference to his human qualities. An example of this practice may be found in his relations with the Iron and Steel Institute in London. In May 1928 when he was given the Bessemer Gold Medal, the president, Benjamin Talbot, remarked that it was unusual to find combined in one person the three vital qualities of scientific knowledge, technical ability, and administrative capacity. They did not really question whether Schwab was in fact an exception to this rule; instead Talbot said that "in Mr Schwab we have an outstanding example of such a combination linked with force of character, as the result of which he has, by his own ability and energy, forged his way to the leading position in the great iron and steel industry of the United States of America."[77] Eleven years later in a eulogistic memoir, the *Engineer* revisited this medal ceremony. Unlike Talbot, the anonymous obituary writer acknowledged that by modern standards Schwab could not be claimed to be a leading technical expert but that he possessed a far more important quality: "that indefinable something that gives its owners power through sympathy." "Charlie" to his workpeople and to thousands of steel workers and engineers, "he emanated as it were human kindness and sympathy, and even those who but knew him for the passing moment, or were merely in his presence, were attracted to him. We recall to this day the astonishing demonstration which had followed the presentation of the Bessemer Medal." At the presentation dinner Schwab had stood to make some characteristic remarks, "a typical American post-prandial speech in which good fellowship, good advice and good stories were mingled. Not a person in the room but was moved by it; not a person, we venture to say, who did not feel that 'Charlie' was his own intimate friend. We all rose to our feet and cheered him, and afterwards he was surrounded by scores of men, many complete strangers, who wished to touch him, to shake him by the hand, to be able to say afterwards, 'I knew Charlie Schawb.'" The unknown British writer of this account recognized that the subject of his praise had "blended sentiment with shrewd business in a way that seems almost incomprehensible to a people like ours who are rather ashamed of sentiment and seek to hide it even when they feel it." Finally, the writer found in sentiment sufficient excuse for any apparent commercial harsh- ness: "'Charlie' was beloved by his workpeople. As a business man he could be hard and shrewd, but underlying it was a human sympathy and understanding which drew his fellows to him."[78]

Later assessments of Schwab have not always been so kind. It is true that Hessen ends his biography, the fullest, most scholarly survey of the man, on a positive note, though some of his imagery seems a good deal less impressive now than when he wrote it in the early 1970s: "[T]he real monuments to Schwab's life, and the living testament to his memory, are the steel mills and shipyards, the blast furnaces and bellowing smoke stacks which mark the skyline of America. Perhaps the greatest symbols of Schwab's life can be seen from the center of Park Avenue in New York City, as one looks up at skyscrapers built with the Bethlehem beam. There Schwab might well invoke the words of Horace: 'If you want to see my monuments, look around you.'"[79]

Over the years a myth similar to that about Carnegie grew up around Schwab until it became difficult to break through the traditional crust to find the real man. There was much to support this myth, but even the comments of those who had known him tended to gloss over faults and to use rosy colors rather than realistic ones. This tendency was perhaps un- derstandable when in 1950 E. R. Weidlein, who had been well acquainted with him, gave the Charles M. Schwab Memorial Lecture to the American Iron and Steel Institute. Weidlein claimed, "He was a man who discerned his place in the world, and never doubted that it was a good world, or that God made it." A few years later, one of his secretaries praised him as "a fine Catholic gentleman. He was kind and good natured, and I can't re- member him ever saying one word in anger." A steel man who had known him—who indeed during the depression had echoed the conventional eco- nomic wisdom of his seniors in condemning interventionist government— looked back from the perspective of the 1960s and, now using a rather dif- ferent basis for his assessment, was less sure than Hessen and penetrated a good deal further than those who had given him sweeping praise. Admitting that Schwab had been "Mr. Steel" to the American people, as well as "by all odds the nation's most gifted after-dinner speaker," Clarence Randall of Inland Steel came to a harsh summing up:

> Each man must be judged by the standards of his own generation. The contemporaries of Charles Schwab rated him a huge success, but he would not be accepted today. He would not measure up as a leader of industry because he was entirely self-centered. . . . deep down inside he was insensitive to the world about him. . . . He lacked a vitalizing sense of social responsibility, either for himself or for big business as a whole. . . . Money was his god. Not money that could be used to create a heritage for underprivileged Americans, after the manner of Andrew Carnegie, but money that would serve his own purposes, and add to his personal satisfactions. And the sad sequel is that this way of life brought to him its own retribution, for in the end he lost most of his money.

When young, Randall had greatly admired him, but now "I find a tragic note in the thought that one who possessed such extraordinary gifts should have had so little impact upon the total welfare of his country."[80] Though by no means treating him harshly in his study of Andrew Carnegie, John F. Wall shortly afterward summed up Schwab in two penetrating sentences of a brief biographical article: "Schwab always enjoyed the good life to the fullest. As generous to his friends as he was to himself, he traded in futures and lived for the present," and "Schwab deserved his title of Star Salesman and no product was he more successful in selling than himself."[81]

At Carnegie Steel as well as at Bethlehem Schwab had without question proved himself to be an exceptional steel man. To some extent he shared Carnegie's characteristics, but the way he used his wealth and the harsher national economic context of his years of retirement showed how narrow his vision was when compared with that of his old mentor. Carnegie had given millions to libraries, set up various institutions, and donated for such special purposes as the Hero Fund. He had educated himself and mixed with men of distinction in fields distant from his own, though certainly not always avoiding the temptations of social climbing. In his later years he campaigned for peace and for a prototype League of Nations. In short, whatever the circumstances of its acquisition, his wealth once made was used with discrimination and for the wider good of humanity. By contrast, before the remnants of his own fortune disappeared during the hard years of the 1930s, when Schwab had given money away it was often in sentimental projects, some of which revived memories of boyhood, such as paving the road between Loretto and Cresson and building convents in both places, churches in Braddock, and a school in Homestead. An endowment of $2 million was given to Saint Francis College, which he had attended after grade school. Of wider vision there was little or no evidence. In his home he had been noted for his fondness for "rich" things—"books, paintings, deep and costly carpets and walls paneled in dark woods," but even there nostalgia and sentiment rather than discriminating taste seem to have ruled. The *New York Times* noted, "[O]nce, being interviewed in the library of his Riverside Drive home, the walls of which were virtually covered with fine editions of the world's most famous books, he turned the conversation to his boyhood and recalled how he tended the horses in the stable and drove the mail coach. Impulsively he pulled out a copy of *Black Beauty*. 'Here,' he said, 'is one of the finest books that was ever written.'"[82]

In short, in marked contrast with Carnegie—or even with Frick, of whom Schwab once admiringly remarked that before he was done "he knew art"—he cannot be said to have achieved anything enduring except in business. Yet within that world of steel, over a remarkable period of almost sixty years, he had shown outstanding qualities as plant manager, superintendent, company and corporation president, and industry elder statesman. At the Emergency Fleet Corporation he had applied these talents to a completely different field of work, again with exceptional success. These achievements were all in manufacturing, and to this field his aspirations for the future were confined. In a way he had summed it all up ten years before he died: "[W]hen I look about me and see the multitude of friends that I have after 49 years of business association with men, when I see the great lines of smoking stacks and blazing furnaces that have come into being because of my interests and activity in life; and when I see a work that I set out to do successfully accomplished and meeting the approval of my fellow men, then a real thrill comes into my heart and I feel that I have done something worth-while."[83] In many ways he was limited. Yet more than sixty years after his death, although much may be found to criticize, his uncomplicated, infectious enjoyment of exceptional material success makes it impossible to be unimpressed by Charlie Schwab.

APPENDIX A

GUESTS AT THE 1900 DINNER IN HONOR OF
CHARLES M. SCHWAB

This is a partial list of those present at the University Club, New York, on Wednesday, 12 December 1900, at a dinner honoring Schwab. The listing is from a telegram that Albert Case sent on 13 December 1900 to J. McSwigan in Pittsburgh. There were inaccuracies in Case's list, however. For instance, Carnegie (see below) was only present for a short time, and Henry Phipps (see below) did not attend.

E. D. Adams (?), capitalist and American representative of the Deutsche Bank

James W. Alexander (1839–1915), president, Equitable Life Assurance Company

George F. Baker (1840–1931), president, First National Bank, New York, and New York Clearing House

Charles C. Beaman (1840–1900), lawyer, Evarts, Choate and Beaman, and president, University Club

August Belmont (1853–1924), August Belmont and Company (banking)

Hon. Cornelius N. Bliss (1833–1911), Bliss, Fabyan and Company, and former secretary of the interior

James A. Burden (1833–1906), president, Burden Iron Company, Troy, NY

James G. Cannon (1858–1916), vice president, Fourth National Bank, New York

Andrew Carnegie (1835–1919) (see introductory paragraph)

Albert C. Case (1851–1918), credit manager and junior partner, Carnegie Steel

John Claflin (1850–1938), merchant, H. B. Claflin and Company

George Coppell (?), Maitland, Coppell and Company (banking)

Eugene Delano (1866–1920), banker, Brown Brothers and Company, New York

Gen. Louis Fitzgerald (1838–1908), president, Mercantile Trust Company

James B. Forgan (1852–1924), president, First National Bank, Chicago

R. N. Galloway (?), president, Merchants National Bank

Elbridge T. Gerry (1837–1927), lawyer

Edward H. Harriman (1848–1909), chairman, Union Pacific Railroad Company

George G. Haven (?–1908), director, National Bank of Commerce and numerous railroads

A(?). L. Hopkins (?), capitalist

Adrian Iselin (?–1925), A. Iselin and Company (banking)

Brayton Ives (1840–1914), banker and president of Metropolitan Trust Company

Morris K. Jessup (1830–1908), president, New York Chamber of Commerce

A. D. Juilliard (1836–1919), capitalist, A. D. Juilliard and Company

John Kennedy (1830–1909), banker and director of railroad companies

Edward King (1833–1908), banker and president, Union Trust Company

Charles Lanier (1837–1926), banker, Winslow, Lanier and Company, and railroad executive

John A. McCall (1849–1906), president, New York Life Insurance Company

Darius O. Mills (1825–1910), banker, financier, and owner of New York hotels

J. Pierpont Morgan (1837–1913), J. P. Morgan and Company

George A. Morrison (1832–1916), president, American Cotton Oil Association

Levi P. Morton (1824–1920), banker and former vice president of the United States

Henry D. Nicoll, physician

Frederick P. Olcott (1841–1909), president, Central Trust Company

Alexander E. Orr (1831–1914), merchant, former president of New York Chamber of Commerce

Henry Phipps (1839–1930) (see introductory paragraph; perhaps the actual guest was Lawrence Phipps, nephew of Henry)

Right Reverend Henry C. Potter (1834–1908), Episcopal bishop of New York

Judge James H. Reed (1853–1927), lawyer and president, Pittsburgh, Bessemer and Lake Erie Railroad

Henry H. Rogers (1840–1909), president, Standard Oil Company

Jacob Schiff (1847–1920), banker, Kuhn, Loeb and Company

J. Edward Simmons (1841–1910), president, Fourth National Bank, New York

Charles Stewart Smith (1832–1909), former president, New York Chamber of Commerce

John A. Stewart (1822–1926), president, United States Trust Company

Frederick D. Tappen (1829–1902), president, Gallatin National Bank, and vice president, Metropolitan Trust Company

George G. Williams (1826–1903), president, Chemical National Bank

R. T. Wilson (?), R. T. Wilson and Company (banking)

Right Reverend George Worthington (1840–1908), Episcopal bishop of Nebraska

APPENDIX B

STATISTICAL DATA

TABLE 1 **Pig iron and steel production capacity at main Carnegie Steel works in specific months, 1895, 1896 (tons)**

	Pig iron (October 1896)	Crude steel (May 1895)
Homestead	none	60,000
Edgar Thomson	80,000	45,000
Duquesne	60,000	40,000
Lucy Furnaces	25,000	

Sources: C. M. Schwab to D. Evans, 27 May 1895; C. M. Schwab to J. G. Pangborn, 20 October 1896, both in United States Steel Corporation archives, Pittsburgh, PA.

TABLE 2 **Labor costs of product in various Homestead departments, 1888 to 1897 (dollars per ton)**

	1888	1889	1890	1891	1892 (First half)	1893	1894 (May/ June)	1896	1897
Converting mill	2.01	1.87	2.18	1.96	1.96	1.13	0.84	0.81	0.65
Open hearth I	3.97	3.61	3.53	3.60	3.30	2.41	1.70	1.67	1.09
Open hearth II			3.89	2.99	2.55	2.24	1.54	1.38	0.94
32-inch mill	1.72	1.31	1.78	1.68	1.70	1.13	0.75	–	–
Plate mill		5.06	6.28	5.50	5.01	4.89	2.63	–	–
23-inch mill	8.01	7.76	8.69	8.24	8.27	7.73	4.24	–	–
33-inch finishing	10.80	9.16	10.11	8.80	7.93	7.59	3.84	–	–

Sources: C. M. Schwab to H. C. Frick, 3 July 1894; W. E. Corey to C. M. Schwab, 27 January 1898, both in Henry Clay Frick Papers, University of Pittsburgh.

TABLE 3 **The United States iron and steel industry and the Carnegie Steel Company, 1895 and 1897–1900**

	1895	1897–1900 (annual average)
U.S. crude steel production (thousand gross tons)	6,115	9,229
U.S. rolled iron and steel output (thousand gross tons)	6,190	8,824
Carnegie Steel share of national crude steel output (percent)	23.9	25.7
Carnegie Steel net profits (thousand dollars)	5,000	17,375

Sources: P. Temin, *Iron and Steel in Nineteenth-Century America: An Economic Inquiry* (Cambridge, MA: MIT Press, 1964), and Carnegie Steel papers, United States Steel Corporation archives, Pittsburgh, PA.

TABLE 4 **Carnegie Steel and selected steel companies' production of crude steel and their earnings, 1900**

	Crude steel output (thousand tons)	Utilization of capacity (percent)	Estimated earnings (millions of dollars)	Earnings per ton (dollars)
Federal Steel	1,225	48.0	10.0	8.16
National Steel	1,400	66.6	8.0	5.71
American Steel Hoop	–		13.0	
American Steel & Wire	490		6.0	12.24
National Tube	250		4.0	16.00
American Tin Plate	–		5.0	
American Sheet Steel	150		2.0	13.33
Total above	3,515		48.0	13.65
Carnegie Steel	2,970	76.1	40.0*	13.47

*This figure, which was not in Schwab's table, has been added by the author. See the discussion in chapter 2 (especially note 80) about the reliability of the profit figures reported by Carnegie Steel.

Source: Based on C. M. Schwab to A. Carnegie, 24 January 1901, Andrew Carnegie Papers, Library of Congress.

TABLE 5 **United States and U.S. Steel Corporation production of pig iron, steel, and rolled products, 1901–1904**

	Total production in United States (thousand gross tons)			U.S. Steel Corporation share of United States total (%)		
	Pig iron	Steel	Rolled products	Pig iron	Steel	Rolled products
1901	15,878	13,474	12,349	43.2	65.7	50.1
1902	17,821	14,947	13,944	44.8	65.2	51.3
1903	18,009	14,535	13,208	40.4	63.1	51.2
1904	16,497	13,860	12,013	44.7	60.7	47.8

Source: H. R. Seager and C. A. Gulick, *Trust and Corporation Problems* (New York: Harper and Brothers, 1929), 258.

TABLE 6 **Production and income of the United States Steel Corporation,**
1901–1904

	Crude steel					
	Production (thousand gross tons)	Percentage of capacity utilized	Percentage of total U.S. output	Steel products shipped (thousand gross tons)	Net income (million dollars)	Net income per ton of crude steel ($)
1901 (9 months)	8,933		66.3		61.4	6.87
1902	10,920	97.2	65.7	7,958	90.3	9.26
1903	10,275	81.8	63.5	7,258	55.4	6.04
1904	9,422	72.8	61.0	6,540	30.3	3.60

Sources: Based on D. A. Fisher, *Steel Serves the Nation* (New York: United States Steel Corporation, 1951), 224–25; A. Cotter, *United States Steel* (New York: Doubleday, Page, 1921). It will be noted that according to these sources the share of national output was slightly higher than in the figures reported by H. R. Seager and C. A. Gulick in *Trust and Corporation Problems* (New York: Harper and Brothers, 1929); the trend was very similar.

TABLE 7 **Bethlehem Steel Corporation works at inception, December 1904**

	Capital stock (million dollars)	Plant and activities
Bethlehem Steel, Bethlehem, PA	15.0	Bethlehem steel works and Juragua iron mines
Harlan and Hollingsworth, Wilmington, DE	1.0	shipyard, car building plant
Union Iron Works, San Francisco, CA	2.0	shipyard and machine shops for mining equipment, etc.
Samuel L. Moore, Elizabethport, NJ	0.3	iron foundries, machine shops, marine repairs
Carteret Improvement Society, Staten Island, NY	0.3	facilities for car building, foundries, etc.
Eastern Shipbuilding Corp., Groton, CT	0.3	shipbuilding plant
Crescent Shipyard Corp., Elizabethport, NJ	0.3	shipbuilding—linked with S. L. Moore
Bath Iron Works, Bath, ME	0.5	shipbuilding facilities
Hyde Windlass, Bath, ME	0.1	steam windlasses and auxiliary engines

Source: Bethlehem Steel, annual report for 1905, Hagley Museum and Library, Wilmington, DE.

TABLE 8 Steel production, employment, orders, manufacturing profits, and net income of Bethlehem Steel, 1912–1918

	Steel production (net tons)	Number of employees (monthly avg.)	Orders on hand at end of year (thousand $)	Net manufacturing profit (thousand $)	Net income (thousand $)
1912	732,777	11,965	29,282	4,847	2,064
1913	834,462	15,052	24,865	8,530	5,123
1914	670,220	15,586	46,513	9,378	5,590
1915	819,986	22,064	175,433	23,783	17,763
1916*	1,846,979	47,013	193,374	60,092	43,594
1917	2,564,815	64,772	453,309	51,002	27,321
1918	2,608,590	93,964	328,946	53,418	15,930

*1916 figures include major acquisitions.

Sources: Bethlehem Steel, annual reports for 1912–1928, and, for orders on hand, reports of Bethlehem Steel annual meetings, Hagley Museum and Library, Wilmington, DE.

TABLE 9 Bethlehem Steel Corporation share of U.S. matériel produced during the Great War

Product	Bethlehem Steel	Bethlehem Steel share of U.S. output
Finished guns for Army or Allies	3,570	60%
Gun forgings (largely for France)	Enough for 11,000 finished guns	65%
Finished naval mounts	599	–
Armor plate	34,705 net tons	–
Shell steel	897,178 tons	–
Ammunition	–	40%

Sources: Bethlehem Steel, annual report for 1918, Bethlehem, PA, and J. K. Mumford, "The Story of Bethlehem Steel, 1914–1918" (unpublished manuscript, Bethlehem Steel, 1943).

TABLE 10 Gross tonnage of merchant vessels launched in 1910, 1913, and 1919–1924 (thousand tons)

	1910	1913	1919	1920	1921	1922	1923	1924
United Kingdom and Ireland	1,143	1,932	1,620	2,056	1,538	1,031	646	1,440
United States (seagoing)	178	228	3,580	2,349	1,004	97	96	90
World*	1,804	3,285	6,648	5,735	4,346	2,445	1,567	2,199

*Great Lakes tonnages are excluded.

Source: Lloyd's Register Book quoted in *Encyclopedia Britannica* (1929), *s.v.,* "Shipbuilding: World Statistics."

TABLE 11 **Gross tonnage of merchant vessels owned in various countries on June 30, 1910, 1914, and 1925 (thousand tons)**

	1910	1914	1925
United States (seagoing)	2,762	2,970	12,949
United Kingdom	17,516	19,257	19,441
France	1,882	2,319	3,512
Germany	4,333	5,459	3,074
Japan	1,147	1,708	3,920
World*	39,655	46,737	62,276

*Excludes U.S. Great Lakes tonnages.

Source: Encyclopedia Britannica (1926), s.v. "Shipbuilding," by W. S. Abell.

TABLE 12 **Distribution of rolled steel to selected fields of consumption, 1923, 1926, and 1929 (thousand gross tons)**

	Railroads	Building and construction	Automobiles	Total consumption
1923	8,700	5,000	3,550	32,300
1926	8,200	6,800	5,000	34,850
1929	6,900	6,700	7,300	40,600

Source: Iron Age, January 1931.

TABLE 13 **United States operating rates for rolling mill capacity by product group, 1929 (percentage of capacity used)**

Sheet and light plate	89.2
Structural shapes	86.7
Plate	78.1
Rails	70.5
Tubular products	65.7

Source: Edwin P. Nourse, America's Capacity to Produce (Washington, DC: Brookings Institution, 1934), 264.

TABLE 14 **Bethlehem Steel Corporation, 1929–1934**

	Crude steel output (million tons)	Operating rate (% capacity)	Share of U.S. output (%)	Orders on hand at year end (thousand $)	Net income (loss) (million $)
1929	8.22	91.8	11.8	86,061	42.2
1930	5.95	61.7	13.3	68,426	23.8
1931	3.72	38.6	13.0	41,515	0.1
1932	1.81	16.9	11.9	30,569	(19.4)
1933	2.94	28.0	11.4	67,685	(8.7)
1934	3.65	34.9	12.5	56,818	0.6

Sources: Bethlehem Steel, annual reports (Hagley Museum and Library, Wilmington, DE), and AISI Yearbooks for the years indicated.

NOTES

Abbreviations

AISA	*American Iron and Steel Association*
AISI	*American Iron and Steel Institute*
BAISA	*Bulletin of the American Iron and Steel Association*
EMJ	*Engineering and Mining Journal*
IA	*Iron Age*
ICTR	*Iron and Coal Trades Review* (UK)
ITR	*Iron Trade Review*
JISI	*Journal of the Iron and Steel Institute* (UK)
NYT	*New York Times*
TAIME	*Transactions of the American Institute of Mining Engineers*
TINA	*Transactions of the Institute of Naval Architects and Marine Engineers*

Sources of Letters

(In a few cases it proved impossible to identify the source of the letter quoted.)

FP	Frick Papers
HML	Hagley Museum and Library
AC/LC	Andrew Carnegie Papers, Library of Congress
NCM	National Canal Museum
PL/PSU	Pattee Library, Pennsylvania State University
USS	United States Steel Corporation (U.S. Steel)

Preface

1. C. M. Schwab, *Some Reflections on Big Business,* 553.
2. *NYT,* 1 September 1939.

Chapter 1: Early Years to Homestead

1. C. M. Schwab quoted in Hendrick, *Life of Andrew Carnegie*, 264.

2. For other examples of inaccuracies obscuring a true account of the early years of C. M. Schwab, see the *Braddock News* article from 1892, reprinted in *BAISA*, October 1892.

3. C. M. Schwab quoted in Hendrick, *Life of Andrew Carnegie*, 264; C. M. Schwab, "Address at the Memorial Service for Andrew Carnegie," 6.

4. C. Baer, introductory notes to "Inventory of Bethlehem Steel Papers," 1982, HML; Associated Press survey of C. M. Schwab's life, September 1939.

5. Hendrick, *Life of Andrew Carnegie*, 263–65.

6. Grace, "C. M. Schwab," 6; Hessen, *Steel Titan*, 15, 16; Wall, *Andrew Carnegie*, 531.

7. *BAISA*, 10 September 1901, 131; Farrell quoted in *IA*, 3 October 1929, 915.

8. Hessen, "C. M. Schwab," 379.

9. *TAIME* 18 (1889–90): 623; C. M. Schwab, "The Huge Enterprises Built Up by Andrew Carnegie," 514; Holley statement in Wall, *Andrew Carnegie*, 320; *BAISA*, 15 February 1879.

10. Statistics from *AISA* (1878), 78.

11. *JISI* 1 (1881): 134; *BAISA*, 10 April 1901.

12. C. M. Schwab quoted in *The Royal Blue Book*, 92, and in S. B. Whipple, "Notes from Interviews in Preparation for a Biography of Charles M. Schwab" (c. 1936), 29, 33, Box 17, Bethlehem Steel Corporation Papers, HML (cited hereafter as Whipple, "Notes from Interviews"); *BAISA*, 10 April 1901.

13. Whipple, "Notes from Interviews"; C. M. Schwab in *AISI Yearbook* (1936), 268.

14. There is a discrepancy in the records about Carnegie's gift. Hessen, quoting Whipple, refers to ten twenty-dollar gold pieces (Hessen, *Steel Titan*, 28); Grace indicates that it was ten twenty-dollar bills (Grace, "C. M. Schwab," 7). Given the character of Carnegie, the former seems more likely.

15. The purchase was announced in the various Pittsburgh newspapers on 16 October 1883.

16. *IA*, 15 April 1886; *BAISA*, 6 April 1887.

17. *Braddock News* quoted in *BAISA*, October 1892; Whipple, "Notes from Interviews," 21.

18. See, e.g., Whipple, "Notes from Interviews," 15, and other instances.

19. Whipple, "Notes from Interviews," 34, 35.

20. Statistics on Carnegie Steel Company from USS archives.

21. Whipple, "Notes from Interviews," 21.

22. A. Carnegie to W. Abbott, 28 December 1888, AC/LC.

23. A. Carnegie to W. Abbott, 7 August 1889; A. Carnegie to Carnegie Brothers, 23 October 1888, both in AC/LC.

24. H. C. Frick to H. Phipps, 6 January 1890; A. Carnegie to H. C. Frick, letter received on 22 January 1890, both in FP.

25. C. M. Schwab to H. C. Frick, 1 September 1890; H. C. Frick to C. M. Schwab, 2 September 1890, both in FP.

26. C. M. Schwab to H. C. Frick, 27 September 1890; H. C. Frick to C. M. Schwab, 29 September 1890, both in FP.

27. H. C. Frick to C. M. Schwab, 28 September 1891, FP.

28. C. M. Schwab to H. C. Frick, 20 October 1890, FP.

29. C. M. Schwab to H. C. Frick, 2 October 1890, FP.

30. C. M. Schwab to H. C. Frick, two letters dated 1 January 1891; H. C. Frick to C. M. Schwab, 1 January 1891, all in FP.

31. C. M. Schwab to H. C. Frick, a third letter dated 1 January 1891, FP.

32. C. M. Schwab to H. C. Frick, 22 October 1891, FP.

33. H. C. Frick to C. M. Schwab, 17 January 1891, 22 April 1891, 26 June 1891, all in FP.

34. Lauder letter to Leishman enclosed in H. C. Frick to C. M. Schwab, 21 August 1891; H. C. Frick to J. Morse, 14 September 1891; H. C. Frick to C. M. Schwab, 14 October 1891, all in FP.

35. A. Carnegie to H. C. Frick, 7 January 1892, FP.

36. Carnegie, *Autobiography of Andrew Carnegie*, 254.

37. For the present writer's account of the strike, see Warren, *Triumphant Capitalism*, 75–97.

38. *BAISA*, 30 November 1892.

39. A. Carnegie to H. C. Frick, 4 May 1892, 10 June 1892, both in FP. See also A. Carnegie, testimony to Industrial Relations Commission, 1915, quoted in *NYT*, 12 August 1919, 9.

40. A. Carnegie wire to Frick quoted in Carnegie, *Autobiography of Andrew Carnegie*, 232; quotation and summation in Wall, *Andrew Carnegie*, 565, 561, 575; H. C. Frick cable to A. Carnegie, 18 November 1892, quoted in Harvey, *Henry Clay Frick*, 172.

41. S. A. Ford to H. C. Frick, 18 October 1892, FP.

42. C. M. Schwab, testimony of 6 July 1894 to U.S. Congress, Special Subcommittee of the Committee on Naval Affairs Investigation of Armor Plate Contracts, 1894, quoted in Hessen, *Steel Titan*, 39.

43. C. M. Schwab to H. C. Frick, 16 October 1892, FP.

44. *BAISA*, 26 October 1892.

45. H. C. Frick to T. Morrison, 18 October 1892; H. C. Frick to Curry, Dillon et al., 18 November 1892, both in FP; Harvey, *Henry Clay Frick*, 177. See also Hessen, *Steel Titan*, 38; Dickson, *History of the Carnegie Veterans Association*.

46. Marsching, "Charles M. Schwab," 25.

47. C. M. Schwab to H. C. Frick, 19 October 1892, FP.

48. H. C. Frick to C. M. Schwab, 19 October 1892, 22 October 1892, both in FP.

49. *Pittsburgh Commercial Gazette*, 19 October 1892, quoted in *BAISA*, 26 October 1892.

50. A. Carnegie to H. C. Frick, 9 November 1892, FP.

51. C. M. Schwab to H. C. Frick, 26 October 1892, FP.

52. Burgoyne, *The Homestead Strike of 1892*, 221, 229, 230; Hessen, *Steel Titan*, 39, 40; Yellen, *American Labor Struggles*, 78, 97; Foner, *History of the Labor Movement in the United States*, 217; *National Labor Tribune*, 12 January 1893; H. C. Frick to various partners, 18 November 1892, FP.

53. C. M. Schwab quoted in Whipple, "Notes from Interviews," 70, 71.

54. H. C. Frick to C. M. Schwab, 21 November 1892, FP.

55. A. Carnegie to H. C. Frick, 17 November 1892, FP.

56. "The Story of Charles M Schwab," *Bethlehem Review*, 18 February 1932.

Chapter 2: Manager and Executive

1. H. C. Frick to C. M. Schwab, 21 November 1892, FP.

2. C. M. Schwab to H. C. Frick, 19 October 1892, FP.

3. H. C. Frick to C. M. Schwab, 6 December 1892; C. M. Schwab to H. C. Frick, 8 December 1892, both in FP; G. Lauder to A. Carnegie, 2 August 1893, AC/LC.

4. For background see Warren, *Triumphant Capitalism*, 153–57.

5. *Pittsburgh Dispatch*, 12 March 1893; C. M. Schwab to H. C. Frick, 3 July 1894, recalling 1 May 1894. See also C. M. Schwab to H. C. Frick, 27 March 1894; H. C. Frick to C. M. Schwab, 27 March 1894; C. M. Schwab to H. C. Frick, 4 April 1894, all in FP.

6. C. M. Schwab to H. C. Frick, 12 April 1894, FP.

7. *Pittsburgh Commercial Gazette*, 7 July 1894, quoted in *BAISA*, 18 July 1894; C. M. Schwab, testimony, 11 May 1901, U.S. Industrial Commission, Report 13, 448; Hessen, *Steel Titan*, 45–58, appendix B.

8. Tarbell, *The Nationalizing of Business*, chap. 13; Faulkner, *American Economic History*, 519, 520; Closson, "The Unemployed in American Cities," 181, 258; C. M. Schwab to H. C. Frick, 17 May 1893, FP.

9. *Pittsburgh Dispatch*, 11 December 1893.

10. C. M. Schwab to H. C. Frick, 24 May 1894, FP.

11. C. M. Schwab to H. C. Frick, 3 July 1894, FP.

12. C. M. Schwab to H. C. Frick, 14 November 1894, USS; C. M. Schwab to H. C. Frick, 16 November 1894, FP.

13. C. M. Schwab to H. C. Frick, 21 December 1894; C. M. Schwab to J. Leishman, 14 June 1895, 29 January 1896, 6 April 1896, all in USS.

14. C. M. Schwab to D. Evans, 27 May 1895, USS; C. M. Schwab to H. C. Frick, 17 November 1894, FP.

15. C. M. Schwab to J. Leishman, 22 December 1896, USS.

16. C. M. Schwab to H. C. Frick, 1 September 1893, FP.

17. C. M. Schwab to H. C. Frick, 28 November 1894; C. M. Schwab to H. C. Frick, 11 December 1894, both in FP.

18. C. M. Schwab to H. C. Frick, 18 October 1894; C. M. Schwab to H. C. Frick, 17 November 1894. See also C. M. Schwab to H. C. Frick, 27 November 1894, all in FP.

19. C. M. Schwab to H. C. Frick, 21 December 1894, USS; H. C. Frick quoted in *Pittsburgh Commercial Gazette*, 22 December 1894, reprinted in *BAISA*, 2 January 1895.

20. C. M. Schwab, "Advantages of Location for Open-hearth Plants as Compared with Bessemer," memorandum, 6 July 1895; C. M. Schwab to A. Carnegie, 5 May 1896, both in AC/LC.

21. C. M. Schwab to P. T. Berg, 21 November 1894, USS.

22. A. Johnston in Bethlehem Papers, Box 1770, HML.

23. C. M. Schwab to H. C. Frick, 24 July 1894, FP; C. M. Schwab to J. Leishman, 8 December 1896, USS.

24. C. M. Schwab to H. C. Frick, 6 February 1893, 16 February 1893, both in FP.

25. C. M. Schwab to H. C. Frick, 3 July 1894, FP.

26. C. M. Schwab to J. Leishman, 12 August 1896, USS.

27. H. C. Frick to A. Carnegie, 7 August 1893, FP.

28. H. C. Frick to C. M. Schwab, 4 April 1894; H. C. Frick to A. Carnegie, 10 April 1894, both in FP.

29. H. C. Frick to A. Carnegie, 7 June 1894, AC/LC.

30. H. C. Frick to A. Carnegie, 7 September 1895, FP.

31. C. M. Schwab quoted in *New York Herald Tribune,* 19 February 1933.

32. *Pittsburgh Leader,* 2 May 1893; Carnegie Steel board, minutes, 11 September 1900, AC/LC; personal visit on 1 October 1987, for which I am grateful to the current owner, Dr. Dixon.

33. *Pittsburgh Leader,* 2 May 1893; Mrs. H. M. McCully to author, 1975; *BAISA,* 10 December 1903; *Souvenir of Loretto Centenary 1799–1899,* 367; C. M. Schwab to J. Leishman, 12 July 1895, USS.

34. H. C. Frick to C. M. Schwab, 21 November 1892; C. M. Schwab to H. C. Frick, 17 May 1893, both in FP.

35. *Pittsburgh Chronicle Telegraph,* 1 February 1893. This labor situation is discussed at some length in Warren, *Triumphant Capitalism,* 103–107.

36. C. M. Schwab to H. C. Frick, 17 May 1893, FP.

37. Ibid.

38. C. M. Schwab to H. C. Frick, 25 June 1894, 21 June 1893, 10 December 1894, all in FP.

39. C. M. Schwab to H. C. Frick, 7 January 1894, USS; C. M. Schwab to H. C. Frick, 7 September 1893, 20 September 1893, both in FP.

40. T. S. Newton to C. M. Schwab, 27 June 1893; C. M. Schwab to A. Carnegie, 21 May 1896, both in AC/LC.

41. Brody, *Steelworkers in America,* 17, 28.

42. C. M. Schwab to H. C. Frick, 19, 20, 24 July 1894, FP; C. M. Schwab to J. G. Leishman, 15 January 1896, USS.

43. C. M. Schwab to A. F. Malloy, 16 July 1895, 1 August 1895, 24 February 1896, USS.

44. A. Carnegie speech quoted in *ITR,* 10 November 1898. See also *BAISA,* 20 November 1898.

45. Garland's interviewee quoted in Alderson, *Andrew Carnegie;* Dreiser, *The Carnegie Works at Pittsburgh,* 16–17.

46. *Pittsburgh Leader,* 16 July 1893; *Philadelphia Press,* 28 June 1893.

47. Schwab quoted in *IA,* 21 September 1939, 32B.

48. A. Carnegie to H. C. Frick, 7 February 1897, 2 February 1897, respectively, FP.

49. Carnegie Steel Company notice, 12 February 1897, quoted in *BAISA,* 20 February 1897.

50. C. M. Schwab to H. C. Frick, 9 April 1897, FP; A. Carnegie to C. M. Schwab, 18 October 1897, AC/LC.

51. C. M. Schwab to H. C. Frick, 22 November 1897, FP.

52. Miller, *Men in Business;* Schwab quoted in P. L. Payne, "The Emergence of the Large-Scale Company in Great Britain, 1870–1914," 537; *BAISA,* 25 November 1903; Eggert, "Alva Dinkey."

53. Joseph Schwab to C. M. Schwab, included as an attachment to Carnegie Steel company minutes, 26 March 1900, AC/LC.

54. C. M. Schwab to H. C. Frick, 3 December 1897, 9 December 1897, FP; minutes of Carnegie Steel operating departments, 27 May 1899, 9 June 1899, 2 August 1898, AC/LC .

55. *IA,* 9 June 1898, 30; Warren, *Triumphant Capitalism,* 181–85.

56. J. Gayley, testimony, in U.S. Congress, *Hearings before the Committee on Investigation of the United States Steel Corporation (Stanley Committee),* I, 424 (hereafter cited as U.S. Congress, *Hearings before the Stanley Committee*); A. Carnegie to U.S. Tariff Commission, 1908, *Hearings,* Document 1505, 1262, 1263; C. M. Schwab to U.S. Tariff Commission, 1908, *Hearings,* Document 1505, 1629. Regarding Schwab's claims about the cost of producing rails, see Montagu, *Trusts of Today,* 11; *IA,* 14 April 1904, 18; *BAISA,* 25 October 1903, 1 January 1909.

57. H. C. Frick to A. Carnegie, 10 September 1897; quotations from C. M. Schwab to H. C. Frick, 24 September 1897, 29 September 1897, all in FP.

58. C. M. Schwab to H. C. Frick, 29 September 1897; H. C. Frick to W. Scranton, 16 December 1897; C. M. Schwab to H. C. Frick, 5 January 1898, all in FP; record of agreement of 15 November 1897, 46, AC/LC.

59. C. M. Schwab to H. C. Frick, 26 September 1898, FP.

60. C. M. Schwab, testimony, in U.S. Congress, *Hearings before the Stanley Committee,* 1285; Whipple, "Notes from Interviews," 52, 53, 104.

61. Minutes of Carnegie Steel operating departments, 21 August 1897, AC/LC; C. M. Schwab to H. C. Frick, 6 November 1897, FP; minutes of Carnegie Board of Managers, 6 July 1897, AC/LC.

62. C. M. Schwab to H. C. Frick, 29 September 1897, 26 September 1898, 6 November 1897, FP.

63. A. Carnegie to Board of Managers of Carnegie Steel Co., 18 September 1897; C. M. Schwab to A. Carnegie, 5 October 1897; A. Carnegie to C. M. Schwab, 16 October 1897, all in AC/LC.

64. A. Carnegie to C. M. Schwab, 18 October 1897; C. M. Schwab to A. Carnegie, 23 August 1898, both in AC/LC.

65. C. M. Schwab to H. C. Frick, 24 September 1897; H. C. Frick to C. M. Schwab, 25 November 1897, both in FP.

66. A. Carnegie to H. C. Frick, 31 November 1897; H. C. Frick to A. Carnegie, 4 December 1897, both in AC/LC.

67. A. Carnegie to G. Lauder, 28 November 1897, AC/LC.

68. H. C. Frick to A. Carnegie, 22 November 1897; H. C. Frick to C. M. Schwab, 12 January 1898, 18 February 1898, all in FP.

69. A. Carnegie quoted in Harvey, *Henry Clay Frick,* 90; A. Carnegie statement to *Pittsburgh Commercial Gazette,* quoted in *BAISA,* 8 February 1893.

70. A. Carnegie to H. C. Frick, 5 February 1898, FP.

71. C. M. Schwab to H. C. Frick, 6 January 1898, FP; Warren, *Triumphant Capitalism,* 225–29.

72. H. C. Frick to C. M. Schwab, 7 August 1898; H. C. Frick to C. M. Schwab, 24 January 1899; C. M. Schwab to H. C. Frick, 27 January 1899, all in FP.

73. U.S. Bureau of the Census, *Historical Statistics of the United States,* 572.

74. H. C. Frick to C. M. Schwab, 10 May 1899, FP.

75. C. M. Schwab to H. C. Frick, 26 September 1899, FP. The whole crisis is covered in Warren, *Triumphant Capitalism,* 240–68.

76. A. Carnegie to G. Lauder, 25 November 1899, AC/LC.

77. A. Carnegie to President and Managers of Carnegie Steel Co., 26 November 1899, quoted in Whipple, "Notes from Interviews," 62.

78. C. M. Schwab, handwritten note to A. Carnegie, 27 November 1899, AC/LC.

79. C. M. Schwab to H. C. Frick, 3 December 1899, FP.

80. Early drafts of this section had a simpler, more optimistic title, "Annus Mirabilis." Since then inquiries pursued by Charles R. Morris have thrown serious doubt on the reliability of the 1900 profit figures on which that choice of heading depended. I wish to stress that the credit for uncovering this discrepancy is wholly his.

81. *Pittsburgh Dispatch,* 28 January 1900; *BAISA,* 1 June 1900, 25 March 1903; *NYT,* 2 May 1903; Weisberg, DeCourcy, and McQueen, eds., *Collecting in the Gilded Age,* 95.

82. *Pittsburgh Post,* 7 January 1900.

83. A. Carnegie to C. M. Schwab, received 22 February 1900, USS; J. W. Gates to A. Carnegie, 28 March 1900, NCM; A. Carnegie to C. M. Schwab, n.d. (c. spring 1900), AC/LC.

84. *Pittsburgh Times,* 20 January 1900; Wilgus, *The United States Steel Corporation in Its Industrial and Legal Aspects,* 61, 62.

85. C. M. Schwab, "The Huge Enterprises Built Up by Andrew Carnegie," 505, 511, 512.

86. Peacock report and Bope description quoted in C. R. Morris to author, 12 August 2004.

87. Wall, *Andrew Carnegie,* 779; A. Carnegie, cable to Board of Directors, 7 July 1900; A. Carnegie to C. M. Schwab, 2 February 1900, both in AC/LC; *ITR,* 29 November 1900, 18; 13 December 1900, 10; *Pittsburgh Dispatch,* 17 March 1901.

88. *BAISA,* 15 May 1900; A. Johnston, report of 20 August 1900, HML.

89. A. Carnegie to Board of Managers, 11 July 1900, AC/LC; Bridge, *The History of the Carnegie Steel Company,* 358; C. M. Schwab to A. Carnegie, 28 July 1900, AC/LC; Warren, *Triumphant Capitalism,* 273–75.

90. A. Carnegie to C. M. Schwab, 12 and 22 January 1900, AC/LC; *EMJ,* 28 July 1900, 15.

91. A. Carnegie to C. M. Schwab, 4 June 1900, 6 July 1900, AC/LC.

92. A. Carnegie to C. M. Schwab, 17 April 1900, 18 May 1900, AC/LC.

93. H. Phipps to C. M. Schwab, 31 August 1900, AC/LC.

94. *BAISA,* 15 May 1900, 85; *IA,* 6 September 1900, 20; A. Carnegie to A. W. Mellon, 28 August 1900; A. W. Mellon to H. C. Frick, 7 September 1900, both in FP; H. Phipps to C. M. Schwab, 31 August 1900, AC/LC.

95. A. W. Mellon to H. C. Frick, 4 May 1900, FP.

96. Bridge, *The Inside History of the Carnegie Steel Company,* 358; A. Carnegie to Carnegie Steel Company, 21 February 1899; A. Carnegie to C. M. Schwab, 4 June 1900, 7 August 1900, all in AC/LC; C. M. Schwab quoted in *Engineering* (UK), 15 February 1901, 210.

97. C. R. Morris to author, 12 August 2004; Carnegie, *Autobiography of Andrew Carnegie,* 255; Bridge, *The Inside History of the Carnegie Steel Company,* 295; A. Carnegie's note on the valuation of Carnegie Company, January 1901, is in USS.

98. C. M. Schwab, penciled note made December 1900 (seen by author in the Bethlehem Steel Corporation library, 1979).

99. Tarbell, *The Life of Elbert H. Gary,* 110; C. M. Schwab comment to Whipple, "Notes for Interviews."

Chapter 3: U.S. Steel

1. Carnegie Steel Company minutes, 6 November 1900, AC/LC; Allen, *Lords of Creation,* 1.
2. C. M. Schwab testimony quoted in *BAISA,* 1 September 1911.
3. A. Carnegie to G. Lauder, 8 December 1900, AC/LC.
4. Hessen, *Steel Titan,* 114, 115; Whipple, "Notes from Interviews"; A. Case, telegram to Carnegie Steel, 13 December 1900; H. Phipps to C. M. Schwab, 14 December 1900, both in USS; Wall, *Andrew Carnegie,* 784.
5. Carnegie associate quoted in Tarbell, *The Life of Elbert H. Gary,* 111.
6. Schwab comment from Whipple, "Notes from Interviews," 86; A. Case telegram, 13 December 1900, USS.
7. J. H. Reed quoted in Hendrick, *The Life of Andrew Carnegie,* 488; *BAISA,* 1 September 1911; C. M. Schwab, testimony, 11 May 1901, U.S. Industrial Commission, Report 13, 1901, esp. 450–52. Apparently no transcript of Schwab's speech survives; perhaps there never was one. As he recalled and others recorded in various places, these points made up the substance of what he said. Almost exactly a year later he spoke to the Bankers' Club of Chicago about economies in the steel industry. This address, which seems to have been more vague and less exciting than that of December 1900, was reported in the trade press; see *IA,* 26 December 1901, 26, 27; *BAISA,* 10 January 1902. See also Jones, *The Trust Problem in the United States,* 205n.
8. Wall, *Andrew Carnegie,* 784; Hessen, *Steel Titan,* 116; Allen, *Lords of Creation,* 20.
9. Grace, "C. M. Schwab," 5; Whipple, "Notes from Interviews," 86.
10. Tarbell, *The Life of Elbert H. Gary,* 112; Grace, "C. M. Schwab," 14; Hessen, *Steel Titan,* 116.
11. Newspaper report quoted in Urofsky, *Big Steel and the Wilson Administration,* xxiv; Jones, *The Trust Problem in the United States,* 197.
12. Casson, *The Romance of Steel,* 189; J. W. Gates quoted in *ITR,* 10 August 1911, 233–34.
13. J. W. Gates, testimony, 27 May 1911, in U.S. Congress, *Hearings before the Stanley Committee,* 31.
14. A. Carnegie to G. Lauder, 1 January 1901, AC/LC.
15. C. M. Schwab quoted in Whipple, "Notes from Interviews," 86–87.
16. A. Carnegie to C. M. Schwab, n.d. (c. December 1900), 7 January 1901, and "Friday" (apparently 25 January 1901), AC/LC; Wall, *Andrew Carnegie,* 787.
17. Hessen, *Steel Titan,* 118; C. M. Schwab to Stanley Committee, quoted in *BAISA,* 1 September 1911; Hughes, *The Vital Few,* 264, 265.
18. Casson, *The Romance of Steel,* 189.
19. R. Bacon, testimony, 14 June 1913, U.S. Congress, *Hearings before the Stanley Committee,* 216, AC/LC; *National Cyclopaedia of American Biography* (1930), vol. C, *s.v.* "Julian Kennedy"; Tarbell, *The Life of Elbert H. Gary,* 115, 117, 121, 122; Whipple, "Notes from Interviews," 87, 88.
20. C. M. Schwab, testimony, 4 August 1911, U.S. Congress, *Hearings before the Stanley Committee*; Whipple, "Notes from Interviews," 91; Carnegie, *Autobiography of Andrew Carnegie,* 255–56.
21. A. Carnegie to G. Lauder, 24 January 1901, AC/LC.

22. C. M. Schwab to A. Carnegie, 24 January 1901; A. Carnegie, memo headed "Schwab/Morgan," undated (c. late January 1901), both in AC/LC.

23. Directors of Carnegie Steel Co. to A. Carnegie, 4 February 1901, AC/LC.

24. A. Carnegie to G. Lauder, 5 February 1901; H. Phipps to C. M. Schwab, 25 February 1901; A. Carnegie to H. Phipps, 10 March 1901; A. Carnegie to G. Lauder, 12 March 1901, all in AC/LC.

25. *Pittsburgh Dispatch*, 11 February 1901; *Pittsburgh Post*, 13 February 1901; *Pittsburgh Leader*, 13 February 1901; Grace, "C. M. Schwab," 17.

26. *NYT*, 4 September 1901, 1; *BAISA*, 10 October 1901, 25 October 1903. Carnegie's comment about millionaires' libraries is from Carnegie, *The Empire of Business*, 136. The Schwab papers at NCM include six large volumes of plans, photographs, and impressions of Riverside and its interiors; see also Holbrook, *The Age of the Moguls*, 278; *NYT*, 15 July 1902, 14; Mrs. H. M. McCully to author, 7 October 1975; *NYT*, 11 May 1947; Cotter, *The Story of Bethlehem Steel*, 21. I am informed by Lance Metz that the bronze figure known as *The Puddler* is now in the sculpture garden of the Allentown Art Museum in Allentown, Pennsylvania.

27. U.S. Industrial Commission, Report 13, 1901, 452 (emphasis added).

28. *BAISA*, 10 April 1901, 52; Burnley, *Millionaires and Kings of Enterprise*, 52; *NYT*, 19 September 1939.

29. *BAISA*, May 1901; R. S. Baker, "What the United States Steel Corporation Really Is and How It Works," *McClure's Magazine* 18, no. 1 (November 1901), quoted in *BAISA*, 25 November 1901.

30. *National Cyclopaedia of American Biography* (1917), vol. XIV, s.v. "C. M. Schwab."

31. Tarbell, *The Life of Elbert H. Gary*, 95; Barron, *They Told Barron*, 86.

32. C. M. Schwab quoted in Barron, *They Told Barron*, 86.

33. *BAISA*, 10 May 1903.

34. C. M. Schwab quoted in U.S. Industrial Commission, Report 13, 1901, 452, 455.

35. C. M. Schwab quoted in *ICTR* (UK), 30 April 1926, 738.

36. C. M. Schwab to A. Carnegie, 20 May 1901, AC/LC.

37. Tarbell, *The Life of Elbert H. Gary*, vii; C. M. Schwab quoted in Whipple, "Notes from Interviews," 92, 113; Garraty, *Right-Hand Man*, 99.

38. C. M. Schwab testimony quoted in *IA*, 22 May 1913, 1263.

39. C. M. Schwab testimony quoted in Tarbell, *The Life of Elbert H. Gary*, 186.

40. U.S. Steel Executive Committee minutes, 9 April 1901; C. M. Scwhab quoted in U.S. Steel Executive Committee minutes, 10 April 1901, both in USS.

41. C. M. Schwab testimony quoted in Tarbell, *The Life of Elbert H. Gary*, 155; Frick quoted in Casson, *The Romance of Steel*, 293.

42. U.S. Steel Executive Committee minutes, 9 April 1901, 10 April 1901, 11 April 1901, USS.

43. Ibid., 1 July 1901.

44. Ibid., 2 July 1901; Schwab to Perkins quoted in Garraty, *Right-Hand Man*, 96, 97.

45. U.S. Steel Executive Committee minutes, 11 July 1901, USS.

46. *BAISA*, 2 January 1902.

47. A. Carnegie to G. Lauder, 19 January 1902, AC/LC; Whipple, "Notes from Interviews," 112.

48. H. U. Faulkner, "Elbert H. Gary," in *Dictionary of American Biography* (1927–58).

49. C. M. Schwab quoted in Garraty, *Right-Hand Man*, 2:99; C. M. Schwab quoted in *BAISA*, 10 May 1904; C. M. Schwab and J. P. Morgan quoted in Grace, "C. M. Schwab," 21.

50. *BAISA*, 25 February 1902.

51. U.S. Steel Executive Committee minutes, 1 April 1902, 29 April 1902, USS.

52. *BAISA*, 25 August 1902, 10 September 1902.

53. C. M. Schwab to A. Carnegie, 2 October 1902, AC/LC; H. C. Frick to J. Strain, 8 October 1902, FP.

54. C. M. Schwab quoted in Hessen, *Steel Titan*, 140; *NYT*, 26 December 1902; *BAISA*, 10 January 1903; Warren, *Triumphant Capitalism*, 303.

55. *BAISA*, 25 March 1903; C. M. Schwab statement, 4 August 1903, USS; *BAISA*, 10 May 1903.

56. *BAISA*, 25 May 1903; C. M. Schwab statement quoted in *BAISA*, 25 August 1903; C. M. Schwab testimony quoted in O'Connor, *Steel–Dictator*, 71.

57. Copy of message from G. W. Perkins to C. M. Schwab, n.d., USS.

58. U.S. Steel announcement and other quotations from *BAISA*, 25 August 1903.

59. U.S. Steel Finance Committee minutes, 15 September 1903, 6 October 1903, USS.

60. *BAISA*, 10 October 1904.

61. Quotation from *IA*, 21 October 1909, 1219.

62. *EMJ*, 6 November 1909, 940; C. M. Schwab testimony to Stanley Committee quoted in *IA*, 22 May 1913, 263; Schwab dinner speech quoted in *IA*, 21 October 1909, 1219.

63. Schwab quoted in Whipple, "Notes from Interviews," 92, 94, 107, 112, 113, 121.

64. Schwab quoted in *Pittsburgh Press*, 20 November 1904.

65. Lesley, *The Iron Manufacturers Guide to the Furnaces, Forges, and Rolling Mills of the United States*, 433.

66. A. Carnegie, "Steel Manufacture in the United States in the Nineteenth Century."

67. A. Charles (Camden, NJ), writing in *The Shipbuilder* (UK), spring 1908, 237, 238.

68. A. Carnegie quoted in *BAISA*, 15 March 1898.

69. *BAISA*, 25 September 1902. See also Metz, "The Arsenal of America," 269.

70. James Smith quoted in *Engineering* (UK), 20 November 1903, 705; Holbrook, *The Age of the Moguls*, 185.

71. Hessen, *Steel Titan*, 147; *BAISA*, 25 June 1903.

72. Seager and Gulick, *Trust and Corporation Problems*, 196n.1. Chapter XII of their book provides a general account of the U.S. Shipbuilding Company.

73. *BAISA*, 10 October 1904, 10 November 1904.

74. *BAISA*, 10 August 1904, 10 October 1904, 10 November 1904; quote about Max Pam from Seager and Gulick, *Trust and Corporation Problems*, 204.

75. Faulkner, *The Quest for Social Justice, 1898–1914*, 37; "artistic swindle" quote from Yates, ed., *Bethlehem of Pennsylvania*, 202.

Chapter 4: Bethlehem Steel

1. *BAISA,* 1 November 1893.

2. C. M. Schwab to H. C. Frick, 20 December 1894, USS; H. C. Frick to C. M. Schwab, 6 October 1894, FP.

3. H. C. Frick to A. Carnegie, 7 June 1894, FP; C. M. Schwab report, "Advantages of location for open hearth plant as compared with Bessemer," 6 June 1895, AC/LC.

4. C. M. Schwab to H. C. Frick, 26 September 1897, FP.

5. Quotation from *BAISA,* 10 September 1901.

6. E. N. Hartley, "C. M. Schwab," in *Dictionary of American Biography* (1927–58); Hovey, *The Life Story of J. Pierpont Morgan,* 268, 269.

7. "Memorandum of matters to be taken up with Mr. Schwab," Archibald Johnston Collection, HML; Cotter, *The Story of Bethlehem Steel,* 6; Mumford, "The Story of Bethlehem Steel, 1914–1918," 5.

8. C. M. Schwab to E. M. McIlvain, 7 March 1902, HML.

9. C. M. Schwab to E. M. McIlvain, 17 October 1903, 14 April 1904, 27 May 1904, HML.

10. C. M. Schwab quoted in *BAISA,* 25 August 1904.

11. C. M. Schwab to E. M. McIlvain, 27 May 1904, HML; *JISI* 2 (1904): 344–45.

12. Note regarding Schwab's recollections in W. B. Dickson collection of C. M. Schwab materials, PL/PSU.

13. *IA,* 2 February 1905, 401; *BAISA,* 15 February 1905; Grace, "C. M. Schwab," 23, 24.

14. Grace, "C. M. Schwab," 24, 27; C. M. Schwab to E. M. McIlvain, 21 January 1906, HML; *IA,* 5 July 1906, 13.

15. Grace, "C. M. Schwab," 50; Whipple, "Notes from Interviews," 154; C. M. Schwab (c. 1913 or 1914), quoted in "Forging America," *Allentown (PA) Morning Call,* December 2003, 29.

16. A. Johnston to E. Grace, 19 July 1906, HML; *BAISA,* 1 March 1905.

17. A. Carnegie to J. G. Leishman, 6 April 1896; C. M. Schwab to A. Carnegie, 6 July 1898, both in AC/LC.

18. C. M. Schwab to E. M. McIlvain, 27 May 1904, HML.

19. *IA,* 3 May 1906, 1479.

20. Grey mill file, NCM.

21. H. Grey to C. M. Schwab, 17 July 1906, NCM.

22. H. Grey to C. M. Schwab, 27 October 1908; C. M. Schwab to H. Grey, 21 November 1908; E. G. Grace to H. Grey, 12 June 1909, all in NCM; Grace, "C. M. Schwab," 25.

23. C. M. Schwab quoted in *IA,* 9 January 1908, 168.

24. C. M. Schwab to A. Johnston, 21 November 1908, HML; Schwab and Stotesbury exchange quoted in Grace, "C. M. Schwab," 25.

25. Carnegie and Schwab to U.S. Tariff Commission, 1908–1909, 1787, 1669, 1627.

26. Warren, *Triumphant Capitalism,* 323; Bethlehem Steel, annual report for 1909, HML.

27. Bethlehem Steel, annual reports for 1909, 1913, HML; Bethlehem consolidated operating data, *Bethlehem Review,* March 1955, 6; *EMJ,* 25 January 1913, 246.

28. *EMJ*, 16 February 1907, 355.

29. *IA*, 2 February 1905, 4011.

30. C. M. Schwab to D. B. Whitaker, 20 January 1908, HML; *EMJ*, 7 January 1911, 74.

31. A. Johnston, memo of New York meeting about Sanford ore, 13 July 1907, HML.

32. *EMJ*, 9 October 1909, 758; 25 December 1909, 1270; 2 July 1910, 40; H. C. Turnbull to C. M. Schwab, 27 November 1909, HML.

33. C. M. Schwab quoted in Whipple, "Notes from Interviews," 134.

34. Newspaper clippings from August 1911, in Dunbar Furnace Company Papers, HML.

35. Whipple, "Notes from Interviews," 36; *EMJ*, 10 January 1914, 82; 14 August 1915, 293.

36. *IA*, 9 April 1914, 931; Whipple, "Notes from Interviews," 150; *EMJ*, 29 July 1916, 243.

37. Bethlehem Steel, annual reports for 1919, 1922, HML; Mitchell, *International Historical Statistics*, 416.

38. C. M. Schwab to J. Fritz, quoted in Whipple, "Notes from Interviews"; *IA*, 24 November 1910, 198. I am grateful to Lance Metz for information about the Linderman mansion.

39. Cotter, *The Story of Bethlehem Steel*.

40. A. Johnston memo to C. M. Schwab, n.d., HML; *IA*, 24 February 1916, 497; "Schwab's Bonus Men," *Collier's*, 13 May 1916, 7; R. Hessen, "E. G. Grace," in *Dictionary of American Biography* (1927–58); *IA*, 4 August 1960.

41. Whipple, "Notes from Interviews," 132; C. M. Schwab quoted in *ITR*, 28 December 1905, 1; C. M. Schwab testimony quoted in *IA*, 15 February 1912, 419.

42. Quotation from *IA*, 18 April 1912, 1003.

43. Quotations from *BAISA*, 1 December 1910; Yates, ed., *Bethlehem of Pennsylvania*, 213.

44. Quotations from *IA*, 18 April 1912, 1003; 18 January 1912, 184.

45. Baer, introductory notes to "Inventory of Bethlehem Steel Papers," HML. In detail the increases may have been slightly different.

46. A. Johnston to C. M. Schwab, November 1901; E. M. McIlvain to C. M. Schwab, 13 May 1902, 17 October 1903, all in HML.

47. J. F. Meigs to C. M. Schwab, 14 May 1904, HML.

48. C. M. Schwab to A. E. Borie, 17 May 1904, HML.

49. Bethlehem Steel, annual report and annual meeting statistics; C. M. Schwab to A. Johnston, 2 December 1907, all in HML.

50. C. M. Schwab to P. Morton, 27 June 1904, HML.

51. M. Quay quoted in Gabriel, *The Course of American Democratic Thought*, 153; H. C. Frick to C. M. Schwab, 29 January 1914, FP; *NYT*, 11 August 1923, 16 December 1923.

52. C. M. Schwab to McIlvain, 23 February 1905, HML.

53. C. M. Schwab to E. M. McIlvain, 29 May 1905, HML.

54. A. Johnston to B. Penrose, 5 March 1906; B. Penrose to A. Johnston, 23 March 1906, both in HML; *BAISA*, 20 July 1906, 1 August 1906; Bethlehem Steel, "Memo Political," 8 October 1906, HML; Misa, *A Nation of Steel*, 314n.29.

55. *BAISA,* 25 July 1904; McIlvain to C. M. Schwab, 17 November 1904; Harvey Fisk and Sons to C. M. Schwab, 17 April 1907, 24 April 1907, all in HML; La Follette quoted in Pringle, *The Life and Times of William Howard Taft,* 1:681; M. Hunsiker to H. C. Frick 28 August 1905, FP; J. M. Falkner to S. Rendel, 21 February 1908, Armstrong-Whitworth records, Newcastle upon Tyne, UK.

56. C. M. Schwab to E. G. Grace, 26 September 1913, HML.

57. *BAISA,* 15 May 1905; *IA,* 25 May 1905, 1681; *Detroit News,* 22 May 1918.

58. *New York Commercial,* 30 September 1907.

59. C. R. Flint to C. M. Schwab, 14 November 1905, HML.

60. A. Johnston to C. M. Schwab, 8 May 1908; C. M. Schwab to A. Johnston, 12 May 1908, both in HML.

61. A. Johnston to C. R. Flint, 26 November 1908, HML.

62. *EMJ,* 4 November 1911; *Times* (London), 18 November 1911, 21; the log of the *Loretto,* September to November 1912, HML.

63. A. Johnston inquiries of 11 January 1909, 17 February 1909, 24 February 1909, 27 February 1909, HML.

64. Bethlehem Steel, annual report for 1906, HML; *EMJ,* 20 June 1908, 1252; Jane, *Fighting Ships,* 157.

65. *EMJ,* 29 October 1910, 885.

66. C. M. Schwab, memorandum of conversation with F. T. Bowles, 22 January 1907, HML.

67. Excerpt from C. M. Schwab address to the Commercial Club, 24 January 1910, HML.

68. Bethlehem Steel, annual report for 1909, HML; Society of Naval Architects and Marine Engineers, *Historical Transactions* (1893–1943, 1945), 203, 204.

69. P. D. Cravath to C. M. Schwab, n.d. (c. 1 May 1910); C. M. Schwab to P. D. Cravath, 9 May 1910; log of the *Loretto,* all in HML.

70. A. Johnston to J. E. Mathews, 10 April 1913; C. M. Schwab to F. T. Bowles, 26 April 1913, both in HML.

71. A. Johnston to J. E. Mathews, 5 May 1913, HML.

72. Baer, introductory notes to "Inventory of Bethlehem Steel Papers," HML; Cotter, *The Story of Bethlehem Steel,* 45.

73. Bethlehem Steel, annual report for 1913; C. J. Harrah to C. M. Schwab, 28 April 1913; C. M. Schwab to C. J. Harrah, n.d., all in HML; obituary of F. T. Bowles in *TINA* (1927), 293.

74. Morgan, *FDR: A Biography,* 190, 191.

75. *Detroit Journal,* (n.d.) 1912.

76. "A Fair Offset" in *BAISA,* 15 January 1905; G. F. Sullivan (Ehler's son-in-law) to author, 12 July 1974.

Chapter 5: World War I

1. C. M. Schwab quoted in *EMJ,* 5 April 1913; *IA,* 9 April 1914, 932; *EMJ,* 25 April 1914, 875; *NYT,* 6 August 1914; Urofsky, *Big Steel and the Wilson Administration,* 90, 91.

2. J. A. Schwab to C. M. Schwab, 15 April 1914; Father McGettingen to C. M. Schwab, 13 June 1914; C. M. Schwab to Rana Schwab, 27 July 1914, all in HML.

3. *NYT,* 2 and 10 October 1914; W. H. Page to E. M. House, 11 October 1914, quoted in Hendrick, *The Life and Letters of Walter H. Page,* 1:341; Churchill, *The World Crisis, 1911–1918,* 232; *NYT,* 22 October 1914.

4. J. R. Jellicoe to W. S. Churchill, 31 October 1914, in Gilbert, *Churchill,* Companion Volume III, 241 (emphasis added); Fisher letter to Lambert quoted in Marder, *Fear God and Dread Nought,* 3:66. (Elswick was the main plant of the Armstrong-Whitworth Company.)

5. C. M. Schwab, 11 April 1917, quoted in *IA,* 19 April 1917, 991; C. M. Schwab to Churchill, 14 May 1915; A. Johnston notes on 1914 visits to Great Britain, both in HML; Urofsky, *Big Steel and the Wilson Administration,* 90, 91.

6. Whitaker, *Whitaker's Almanack* (1913), 105.

7. Churchill, *The World Crisis, 1911–1918,* 232; A. Johnston notes on 1914 visits to Great Britain, HML.

8. Hessen, *Steel Titan,* 212, 213; Schwab comment reported in *EMJ,* 21 November 1914, 930; *NYT,* 26 November 1914.

9. Leishman quote recollected by C. M. Schwab in Whipple, "Notes from Interviews," 191–93.

10. C. M. Schwab to Churchill, Fisher, and Jellicoe, 14 May 1915, all in HML; *NYT,* 24 and 26 March 1915; J. Fisher to C. M. Schwab, 27 May 1915, HML; *Times* (London), 9 September 1919; J. R. Jellicoe to C. M. Schwab, 5 June 1915; C. M. Schwab to J. R. Jellicoe, 7 July 1915, both in HML. (Jellicoe was Schwab's guest during his visit to New York early in 1920.)

11. W. S. Churchill to C. M. Schwab, 17 July 1915, HML.

12. Urofsky, *Big Steel and the Wilson Administration,* 90, 91; A. Johnston notes, HML.

13. H. C. Frick to C. M. Schwab, 27 March 1915, FP; Bethlehem Steel, annual reports and report of annual general meeting, HML.

14. S. Rea to C. M. Schwab, (n.d.) March 1913; C. M. Schwab to S. Rea, 20 March 1913, both in HML.

15. *IA,* 6 January 1917, 37; *EMJ,* 16 October 1915, 654; 6 November 1915, 772; *IA,* 24 February 1916, 12 October 1916, 829; W. H. Donner, Report on the Sparrows Point works of the Maryland Steel Company, 15 January 1906, FP; C. M. Schwab quoted in *Fortune,* April 1941, 142.

16. *IA,* 1 November 1917, 1036.

17. Bethlehem Steel, annual reports for 1915, 1916, 1917; "Bethlehem Steel Company appeals to the People Against the Project to spend $11 million of the Peoples' Money for A Government Armor Plant," all in HML; *NYT,* 22 December 1916; Baer, introductory notes to "Inventory of Bethlehem Steel Papers," HML. See also Roosevelt, *The Roosevelt Letters,* 2:267.

18. Yates, ed., *Bethlehem of Pennsylvania,* 213; *NYT,* 13 May 1917, 23 December 1918. See also Mumford, "The Story of Bethlehem Steel, 1914–1918."

19. *Shipbuilder* (January 1917): 7.

20. Society of Naval Architects and Marine Engineers, *Historical Transactions* (1945); *Shipbuilder and Marine Engine Builder* (March 1933): 127.

21. Western Pennsylvania Biographical Association, *Western Pennsylvanians* (1923), 383; *Encyclopedia Britannica* (1922), s.v. "Shipping," by W. L. Marvin.

22. *NYT,* 23 April 1918; A. Carnegie to C. M. Schwab, 17 April 1918; C. M. Schwab to A. Carnegie, 21 April 1918, both in AC/LC; *IA,* 23 April 1925, 1191; J. A. Schwab to C. M. Schwab, 18 April 1918, NCM.

23. President's Conference on Unemployment, *Report of the Committee on Recent Economic Changes in the United States* (1929), 80; *TINA* (1918), 243–54; Grace, "C. M. Schwab," 35; *Encyclopedia Britannica* (1922), *s.v.* "Pennsylvania"; Piez quoted in *San Francisco Examiner,* 4 July 1918.

24. *EMJ,* 4 May 1918, 84; 27 April 1918, 809; *Times* (London), *The History of the War,* 260; *Encyclopedia Britannica* (1922), *s.v.* "Pennsylvania."

25. *NYT,* 3 May 1917.

26. C. M. Schwab's and subsequent quotes from *Times* (London), *The History of the War,* 263.

27. Piez quoted in *IA,* 11 February 1926.

28. C. M. Schwab to Engineers' Club of Philadelphia, November 1923, quoted in *IA,* 29 November 1923, 1447; *EMJ,* 1 June 1918, 1010.

29. Quotations from *IA,* 4 July 1918, 11; and *Chicago Journal,* 28 June 1918.

30. *NYT,* 25 and 26 July 1918; Western Pennsylvania Biographical Association, *Western Pennsylvanians* (1923), 383; *Times* (London), *The History of the War,* 278; C. M. Schwab quoted in *Tacoma Ledger,* 18 July 1918.

31. C. M. Schwab to A. Carnegie, 5 September 1918, AC/LC; *NYT,* 26 September 1918.

32. *IA,* 6 June 1918, 1461, 1462.

33. All quotations from *TINA* (1918), 290–95.

34. *IA,* 15 May 1919, 1292; 5 June 1919, 1505.

35. C. M. Schwab to J. Poynton, summer 1919, AC/LC. For details of the contacts with Carnegie in the summer of 1919 I am indebted to Lance Metz.

36. A. Carnegie to C. M. Schwab, 28 November 1896; C. M. Schwab to A. Carnegie, 22 December 1908, both in AC/LC; *NYT,* 12 August 1919; Whipple, "Notes from Interviews," 84, 85; C. M. Schwab to J. Poynton, summer 1919, AC/LC; C. M. Schwab speech quoted in *NYT,* 21 March 1920.

37. C. M. Schwab quotations from Whipple, "Notes from Interviews," 6, 85, 238, 248; Weisberg, DeCourcy, and McQueen, eds., *Collecting in the Gilded Age,* 102; Frick visitor book, FP.

38. Whipple, "Notes from Interviews," 126.

39. Quotations from *Cardiff Echo* (UK), 19 June 1918.

40. C. M. Schwab, *Emergency Fleet News,* quoted in *IA,* 31 October 1918, 1113.

41. Wright, *Economic History of the United States,* 752–53. For a more favorable international comparison see *New York Journal of Commerce,* 23 May 1918. The headline appeared in the *New York Evening Post,* 15 June 1918. Note that the figures quoted in the text differ from those of Lloyd's Register Book as shown in table 10, appendix B.

42. On the Traylor wooden yards see Rodriguez, "Samuel Traylor," 95–114; *Encyclopedia Britannica* (1922), *s.v.* "Shipping."

43. *Concise Dictionary of American History* (1963), 1026; Jennings, *A History of Economic Progress in the United States,* 673.

44. Bound account of the dinner of November 1921, HML.

45. *Manchester Guardian Commercial* (UK), Reconstruction Supplement, 31 May 1923, 254.

46. *NYT,* 21 January 1921.

47. *Times* (London), 27 January 1921, 9; *NYT,* 3 March 1921.

48. *NYT,* 18 April 1925; *IA,* 23 April 1925, 1189, 1190.

49. G. N. Scott to C. M. Schwab, 19 April 1919; C. M. Schwab to G. N. Scott, 21 April 1919, both in NCM.

50. C. M. Schwab, *Succeeding with What You Have,* 10, 14, 42.

51. Jeans, *American Industrial Conditions and Competition,* 11, 59, 61, 62.

52. Tarbell, *The Life of Elbert H. Gary,* 153; Ingham, *Making Iron and Steel,* 152; quotations from U.S. Steel minutes, 1 October 1901, 12 November 1901, USS.

53. C. M. Schwab quoted in *BAISA,* 10 May 1907.

54. *EMJ,* 12 August 1911, 301.

55. F. A. Whelan, "'I Can Stand It,'" 63, 76; G. G. Thorpe to A. Johnston, 23 Aug 1909, HML.

56. U.S. Commissioner of Labor, *Report of the Commissioner of Labor on the Strike at the Bethlehem Steel Works,* 15, 20, 25, 26, 129; Schwab statement quoted in Vadasz, "The History of an Industrial Community," 194.

57. Bethlehem Strikers to Governor of Pennsylvania, 4 March 1910, PL/PSU.

58. Statement and circular of the Committee of Striking Workmen at Bethlehem, 7 April 1910, in U.S. Commissioner of Labor, *Report of the Commissioner of Labor on the Strike at the Bethlehem Steel Works,* Vadasz, "The History of an Industrial Community," chap. 7.

59. Hessen, *Steel Titan,* 202; Whelan, "'I Can Stand It,'" 63–80; C. M. Schwab's shouted statement quoted by R. Bartram in *Allentown Morning Call,* 31 March 1999; Adams, *Age of Industrial Violence, 1910–15,* 189–94.

60. C. M. Schwab quoted in Urofsky, *Big Steel and the Wilson Administration,* 278, 284.

61. C. M. Schwab quoted in *IA,* 20 May 1920, 1484.

62. C. M. Schwab, "Today's Problems," 5, 6.

63. *Times* (London), 23 February 1923, 11.

64. Barron, *They Told Barron,* 82, 83 (emphasis added).

65. Schwab quoted in *IA,* 29 November 1923, 1447.

66. *Johnstown (PA) Tribune,* 12 June 1902.

67. *BAISA,* 10 October 1901; unattributed clippings about the new church; C. M. Schwab and R Schwab to Father Kittell, 10 October 1899, all in HML; Mrs. H. M. McCully to author, April 1973.

68. Hessen, *Steel Titan,* 252. I owe details of the commemoration of Rana Schwab to Lance Metz.

Chapter 6: The Process of Retiring

1. Cotter, *United States Steel,* 100, 101; W. L. King, "Recollections and Conclusions from a Long Business Life."

2. Roosevelt, *The Roosevelt Letters,* 1:355; C. M. Schwab comments from *Cincinnati Enquirer* quoted in Noyes, *The War Period of American Finance, 1908–1925,* 286; C. M. Schwab quoted in *AISI Yearbook* (1921), 259.

3. C. M. Schwab quoted in *Times* (London), 30 April 1921, 10.

4. C. M. Schwab speeches quoted in *IA*, 16 December 1920, 1644; 26 October 1922, 1066; *Bethlehem Review*, 18 February 1932, 1–11.

5. *Manchester Guardian Commercial* (UK), Reconstruction Supplement, 31 May 1923, 854.

6. J. W. White to C. M. Schwab, 6 May 1908, HML.

7. Grace, "C. M. Schwab," 53; *IA*, 5 April 1923; Bethlehem Steel, annual report for 1922, HML.

8. C. M. Schwab speeches quoted in *IA*, 29 November 1923, 1447; 5 November 1925, 1263; *NYT*, 14 May 1927.

9. C. M. Schwab address to Iron and Steel Institute quoted in *JISI* 1 (1928): 703; C. M. Schwab's 1919 comment reported by *New York American* quoted in *IA*, 5 November 1925, 1263 (compare with E. G. Grace speech quoted in *IA*, 8 January 1925, 125); Schwab's Kamchatka remark quoted in Hessen, *Steel Titan*, 254; *New York World*, 19 August 1923; see also remarks in *Times* (London), 23 February 1923, 4.

10. *NYT*, 9 April 1924.

11. C. M. Schwab quoted in *IA*, 7 January 1926, 73; *JISI* 1 (1928): 206; *AISI Year-book* (1928), 40.

12. *EMJ*, 15 December 1906, 1143; 26 January 1907, 207; 13 April 1907, 731; 11 July 1908, 101; *Pittsburgh Press*, 16 March 1958; *NYT*, 26 January 1923.

13. *BAISA*, 25 July 1904; Hessen, *Steel Titan*, 142; *NYT*, 22 April 1923, 25 July 1924. For details on Chicago Pneumatic tools I am grateful to Lance Metz.

14. *ICTR* (UK), 4 May 1928, 631, 632; quotation from Allen, *Lords of Creation*, 39.

15. Hellman, *Lanes of Memory*, 69.

16. C. M. Schwab to Clarence Barron, 30 March 1921, quoted in Barron, *They Told Barron*, 36.

17. American Guide Series, *Pennsylvania*, 393; Swetnam and Smith, *Historic Western Pennsylvania*; Hessen, *Steel Titan*, 250; "statues" description and C. M. Schwab address quoted in *Pittsburgh Post-Gazette*, 19 March 1939.

18. Bethlehem Steel records (Harlan and Hollingsworth), HML; *Altoona (PA) Mirror*, 5 April 1975.

19. Hessen, *Steel Titan*, 251; Donehoo, *Pennsylvania*, 1710; *Pittsburgh Post-Gazette*, 31 March 1936.

20. C. M. Schwab to Rana Schwab, 27 July 1914, HML; Hessen, *Steel Titan*, 292, 293.

21. C. M. Schwab diary, 29 May 1920, 13 and 15 October 1920, HML.

22. Ibid., 30 April 1921.

23. *Times* (London), 19 March 1923; Hexner, *The International Steel Cartel*.

24. C. M. Schwab quoted in *JISI* 1 (1928): 206, 207.

25. *Engineering* (UK), 28 October 1932, 513; *Times* (London), 20 October 1932, 16.

26. See tributes to E. H. Gary in *ITR*, 18 August 1927, vii, viii.

27. Harding quoted in *AISI Yearbook* (1921), 239; Gary quoted in Schlesinger, *The Crisis of the Old Order*, in Oates, *Portrait of America*, 2:201, 202; Hoover quoted in Spencer, *The Sinews of American Capitalism*, 264. See also Giesbrecht, *The Evolution of Economic Society*, 245.

28. Quotations from Spencer, *The Sinews of American Capitalism*, 265.

29. President's Conference on Unemployment, *Report of the Committee on Recent Economic Changes in the United States* (1929), x, xxii.

30. C. M. Schwab quoted in *ICTR* (UK), 15 June 1928, 902, 907; Skinner, *The Stock Exchange Yearbook for 1931.*

31. C. M. Schwab quoted in *IA,* 3 November 1927, 1230.

32. C. M. Schwab speech quoted in *IA,* 5 January 1928, 71; Barron, *They Told Barron,* 177–78.

33. C. M. Schwab quoted in *ICTR* (UK), 21 December 1928, 905.

34. *The Sales Timer,* February 1929; *EMJ,* 25 May 1929; C. M. Schwab, "Ten Commandments of Success," quoted in *IA,* 30 May 1929, 1485.

35. W. L. King quoted in *IA,* 11 July 1929, 95.

36. C. M. Schwab, address of 26 September 1929, quoted in *IA,* 3 October 1929, 914; *New York Daily Investment News,* 15 October 1929.

37. C. M. Schwab quoted in *Wall Street Journal,* 28 October 1929.

38. Allen, *Only Yesterday,* 456, 457; C. M. Schwab quoted in Schlesinger, *The Crisis of the Old Order,* as cited in Oates, *Portrait of America,* 2:268.

39. Dickson, *History of the Carnegie Veterans Association.*

40. *NYT,* 19 February 1930, 14.

41. U.S. Steel Executive Committee minutes, 25 June 1901, USS; *Youngstown Sheet and Tube Bulletin,* December 1967, 9.

42. *NYT,* 20 March 1930, 44; 1 April 1930, 49; 6 May 1930, 42.

43. Cotter, *The Story of Bethlehem Steel,* 18, 19.

44. C. M. Schwab speeches quoted in *NYT,* 10 May 1930; *IA,* 15 May 1930, 1463; 23 October 1930, 1156.

45. C. M. Schwab speech quoted in *AISI Yearbook* (1931), 38, 39, 46; *IA,* 29 October 1931, 1121.

46. Allen, *Lords of Creation,* 39; *AISI Yearbook* (1931), 340; C. M. Schwab quoted in *AISI Yearbook* (1932), 30.

47. Schwab speech quoted in *AISI Yearbook* (1932), 32.

48. C. M. Schwab to E. Grace, 24 February 1932, PL/PSU; *New Republic* 67 (15 July 1931): 220, quoted in Vadasz, "The History of an Industrial Community," 163.

49. Carnegie quoted in Wilgus, *The United States Steel Corporation in Its Industrial and Legal Aspects,* 19.

50. W. B. Dickson to C. M. Schwab, 3 October 1930; C. M. Schwab to W. B. Dickson, 6 October 1932, both in PL/PSU; *AISI Yearbook* (1932), 30, 32, 40.

51. C. M. Schwab quoted in *Times* (London), 20 October 1932, 16; *New York Herald Tribune,* 9 November 1932.

52. H. Clurman quoted in Morison, Commager, and Leuchtenburg, *The Growth of the American Republic,* 2:483.

53. Ellis, *A Nation in Torment,* 349; C. M. Schwab quoted in *AISI Yearbook* (1934), 22; *IA,* 31 May 1934.

54. E. G. Grace quoted in *IA,* 30 May 1935, 15; E. G. Grace at AISI, on 28 May 1936, *AISI Yearbook* (1936).

55. *NYT,* 21 March 1920; *IA,* 25 February 1932, 512; *AISI Yearbook* (1934), 134–36; report of AISI meeting in *IA,* 31 May 1934; Whipple, "Notes from Interviews," 237; Grace, "C. M. Schwab," 3.

56. Schlesinger, *The Crisis of the Old Order,* quoted in Oates, *Portrait of America,* 2:274; Ellis, *A Nation in Torment,* 152–53; Whipple, "Notes from Interviews," 220–21.

57. C. M. Schwab quoted in *NYT,* 29 May 1936.

58. Gunther, *Inside Latin America*, 362; *NYT*, 29 March 1935.

59. C. M. Schwab quoted in *NYT*, 19 February 1936, 29 May 1936.

60. Notes about C. M. Schwab in W. B. Dickson Collection, PL/PSU; T. Girdler quoted in *IA*, 31 May 1934; Perkins, *The Roosevelt I Knew*, 352, 353; *New York Herald Tribune*, 18 June 1937. See also "Forging America," *Allentown (PA) Morning Call*, December 2003, 67, 68.

61. *Western Pennsylvania Historical Society Magazine*, September 1935, 170, 172, 173.

62. C. M. Schwab diary, May 1937, HML.

63. C. M. Schwab quotes from 1934 reported in *NYT*, 19 September 1939.

64. *IA*, 14 April 1932, 10; C. M. Schwab's quote reported in *NYT*, 19 September 1939.

65. *NYT*, 19 September 1939; *New York Herald Tribune*, 18 June 1937; judge quoted in *Pittsburgh Press*, 12 June 1938.

66. *NYT*, 19 December 1936; *Boston Post*, 19 February 1938.

67. Girdler quoted in *NYT*, 28 April 1939; *IA*, 4 May 1939; telegrams of April 1939, HML.

68. C. M. Schwab to E. G. Grace, record of telephone message, 1 September 1939, HML.

69. E. G. Grace, statement to employees of Bethlehem Steel noting the death of C. M. Schwab, 19 September 1939, HML.

70. *NYT*, 22 September 1939, 23; *IA*, 9 May 1940, 77; *NYT*, 24 February 1940.

71. *New York Herald Tribune*, 4 October 1942, 48; 17 April 1943.

72. W. L. King, "Recollections and Conclusions from a Long Business Life," 234, 235; Farrell quoted in *IA*, 28 September 1939; *Times* (London), 20 September 1939.

73. C. M. Schwab quoted in *IA*, 21 September 1939, 32B; *Times* (London), 20 September 1939; *NYT*, 19 September 1939; Whipple, "Notes from Interviews," 231.

74. C. M. Schwab quoted in *NYT*, 19 September 1939.

75. *IA*, 21 September 1939, 32B; *Times* (London), 20 September 1939; *Labor Advocate*, 28 September 1939.

76. *NYT* editorial, 20 September 1939, 26.

77. *JISI* 1 (1928): 26, 27.

78. *Engineer* (London), 29 September 1939, 330.

79. Hessen, *Steel Titan*, 304.

80. Weidlein, *The Charles M. Schwab Memorial Lecture*, 24 May 1950, 2; C. C. Kelly quoted in *Bayonne (NJ) Times*, 7 March 1961; Randall, *Adventures in Friendship*, 8, 9; E. N. Hartley, "C. M. Schwab," in *Dictionary of American Biography* (1927–58).

81. Wall, "C. M. Schwab," 973.

82. C. M. Schwab quoted in *NYT*, 19 September 1939.

83. C. M. Schwab quoted in *New York Daily Investment News*, 15 October 1929.

BIBLIOGRAPHY

Archival Collections

An important collection of papers and other materials relevant to the life and work of Charles M. Schwab was once housed in the library at the former Bethlehem Steel headquarters in Bethlehem, Pennsylvania. I conducted research in that collection (1979), but the collection has since been divided and removed to the Hagley Museum and Library in Wilmington, Delaware, and to the National Canal Museum in Easton, Pennsylvania. Some items may be found at the Pattee Library at Pennsylvania State University. Many other items of importance, including extensive correspondence, are to be found in the papers of Andrew Carnegie, collections of which are housed in the Library of Congress, in the archives of U.S. Steel in Pittsburgh and in Annandale, Pennsylvania, and in the archives of the former Bethlehem Steel Corporation at the National Canal Museum. Other important materials are in the records and papers of Henry Clay Frick now held by the Archives of Industrial Society at the University of Pittsburgh.

Books and Articles

Adams, G. *Age of Industrial Violence, 1910–15: Activities and Findings of the U.S. Commission on Industrial Relations.* New York: Columbia University Press, 1966.

Alderson, B. *Andrew Carnegie: The Man and His Work.* New York: Doubleday, Page, 1902.

Allen, F. L. *Lords of Creation: The Story of the Great Age of American Finance.* London: Hamish Hamilton, 1935.

——. *Only Yesterday: An Informal History of the Nineteen-Twenties.* Harmondsworth, England: Penguin, 1931.

American Guide Series. *Pennsylvania.* New York: Oxford University Press, 1940.

American Iron and Steel Institute (AISI) Yearbooks.

Baer, C. "Inventory of Bethlehem Steel Papers." 1982. Hagley Museum and Library.

Barron, C. W. *They Told Barron: Conversations and Revelations of an American Pepys in Wall Street.* New York: Harper, 1930.

Bethlehem Steel. *The Bethlehem Steel Company Appeals to the People against the Proposal to Spend $11 Million of the People's Money for a Government Armor Plant.* Bethlehem, PA, 1916–17.

Blood, W. H. "Hog Island: The Greatest Shipyard in the World." *Transactions of the Institute of Naval Architects and Marine Engineers,* 1918.

Bridge, J. H. *The Inside History of the Carnegie Steel Company.* 4th ed. New York: Aldine, 1903.

Brody, D. *Steelworkers in America: The Nonunion Era.* Cambridge, MA: Harvard University Press, 1960.

Burgoyne, A. G. *The Homestead Strike of 1892.* Pittsburgh, PA: Rawsthorne, 1893.

Burnley, J. *Millionaires and Kings of Enterprise.* Philadelphia, PA: Lippincott, 1901.

Carnegie, A. C. *Autobiography of Andrew Carnegie.* Boston: Houghton Mifflin, 1920.

———. *The Empire of Business.* New York: Doubleday, Page, 1902.

———. "Steel Manufacture in the United States in the Nineteenth Century." *New York Evening Post,* 12 January 1901.

Casson, H. N. *The Romance of Steel.* New York: A. S. Barnes, 1907.

Churchill, W. S. *The World Crisis, 1911–1918.* 1931. Abridged and rev. ed. London: Macmillan, 1943.

Clark, V. S. *History of Manufactures in the United States.* 3 vols. New York: McGraw-Hill, 1929.

Closson, C. "The Unemployed in American Cities." *Quarterly Journal of Economics* 8 (1893/1894).

C. M. Schwab: Man of Culture. Easton, PA: Canal Museum, n.d.

Cotter, A. *The Story of Bethlehem Steel.* New York: Moody Magazine and Book Company, 1916.

———. *United States Steel: A Corporation with a Soul.* New York: Doubleday, Page, 1921.

Craig, N. B. *The History of Pittsburgh.* Pittsburgh, PA: J. R. Weldin Company, 1917.

Dickson, W. B. *History of the Carnegie Veterans Association.* Montclair, NJ: Mountain Press, 1938.

Donehoo, G. P. *Pennsylvania: A History.* New York: Lewis Historical Publishing, 1921.

Dreiser, T. *The Carnegie Works at Pittsburgh.* Privately printed, 1899.

Eggert, G. G. "Alva Dinkey." In *Iron and Steel in the Twentieth Century,* edited by B. E. Seeley. New York: Facts on File, 1994.

Ellis, E. R. *A Nation in Torment: The Great American Depression, 1929–1939.* New York: Coward, McCann, and Geoghegan, 1970.

Faulkner, H. U. *American Economic History.* New York: Harper and Row, 1960.

———. *The Quest for Social Justice, 1898–1914.* New York: Macmillan, 1931.

Fisher, D. A. *Steel Serves the Nation.* New York: United States Steel Corporation, 1951.

Foner, P. S. *History of the Labor Movement in the United States.* Vol. 2, *From the Founding of the American Federation of Labor to the Emergence of American Imperialism.* New York: International Publishers, 1953.

"Forging America" series. *Allentown (PA) Morning Call,* December 2003.

Gabriel, R. H. *The Course of American Democratic Thought.* New York: Ronald Press, 1940.

Gage, T. "'Hands-On, All-Over': Captain Bill Jones." *Pittsburgh History* 80, no. 4 (winter 1997/98): 148–69.

Garraty, J. *Right-Hand Man: The Life of George W. Perkins.* New York: Harper, 1960.

——, ed. *Encyclopedia of American Biography.* New York: Harper and Row, 1974.

——, ed. *Historical Viewpoints: Notable Articles from* American Heritage. Vol. 2, *Since 1865.* New York: American Heritage Publishing, 1970.

Giesbrecht, M. G. *The Evolution of Economic Society.* San Francisco: W. H. Freeman, 1972.

Gilbert, M. *W. S. Churchill: The Official Biography.* Companion Volume III. London: Heinemann, 1967.

Grace, E. G. "C. M. Schwab. Bethlehem: Bethlehem Steel Corporation." Reprint of a paper presented at the first annual C. M. Schwab Memorial Lecture at the American Iron and Steel Institute, New York, 21 May 1947.

Grey, H. *The "H" Column Steel Company.* 1905. Hagley Museum and Library, Wilmington, DE.

Gunther, J. *Inside Latin America.* London: Hamish Hamilton, 1942.

Harvey, G. *Henry Clay Frick: The Man.* New York: Charles Scribner's Sons, 1928.

Hellman, G. S. *Lanes of Memory.* New York: Knopf, 1927.

Hendrick, B. J. *The Life and Letters of Walter H. Page.* Vol. 1. London: William Heinemann, 1924.

——. *The Life of Andrew Carnegie.* London: William Heinemann, 1933.

Hessen, R. "A Biography of Charles M. Schwab, Steel Industrialist." Ph.D. diss., Columbia University, 1969.

——. "C. M. Schwab." In *Iron and Steel in the Twentieth Century,* edited by B. E. Seeley. New York: Facts on File, 1994.

——. *Steel Titan: The Life of Charles M Schwab.* New York: Oxford University Press, 1975. Reprint, Pittsburgh, PA: University of Pittsburgh Press, 1990.

Hexner, E. *The International Steel Cartel.* Chapel Hill: University of North Carolina Press, 1943.

Hogan, W. T. *Economic History of the Iron and Steel Industry in the United States.* 5 vols. Lexington, MA: D. C. Heath, 1971.

Holbrook, S. H. *The Age of the Moguls.* London: Victor Gollancz, 1953.

Hovey, C. *The Life Story of J. Pierpont Morgan.* New York: Sturgis & Walton, 1911.

Hughes, J. *The Vital Few: American Economic Progress and Its Protagonists.* New York: Oxford University Press, 1973.

Ingham, J. *Making Iron and Steel: Independent Mills in Pittsburgh, 1820–1920.* Columbus: Ohio State University Press, 1991.

Jane, F. T. *Fighting Ships.* London: Sampson, Low, Marston, 1914. Reprint, Newton Abbot, England: David and Charles, 1968.

Jeans, J. S. *American Industrial Conditions and Competition.* London: British Iron Trade Association, 1902.

Jennings, W. W. *A History of Economic Progress in the United States.* New York: Crowell, 1926.

Jones, E. *The Trust Problem in the United States.* New York: Macmillan, 1922.

King, J. T. "Pittsburgh Past and Present." *Leisure Hours* 1 (October 1868).

King, W. L. "Recollections and Conclusions from a Long Business Life." 1920. Reprint, *West Pennsylvania Historical Society Magazine,* December 1940.

Lesley, J. P. *The Iron Manufacturers Guide to the Furnaces, Forges, and Rolling Mills of the United States.* New York: American Iron Association, 1859.

Marder, A. J., ed. *Fear God and Dread Nought: The Correspondence of Admiral of the Fleet Lord Fisher of Kilverstone.* 3 vols. London: Jonathan Cape, 1959.

Marsching, R. "Charles M. Schwab: A Business Biography." BA thesis, Princeton University, 1950.

Metz, L. 1992. "The Arsenal of America: A History of the Forging Operations of Bethlehem Steel." *Canal History and Technology Proceedings,* vol. 11. Easton, PA: CHTP, 1992.

Miller, W. *Men in Business: Essays in the History of Entrepreneurship.* Cambridge, MA: Harvard University Press, 1952.

Misa, T. *A Nation of Steel: The Making of Modern America, 1865–1925.* Baltimore, MD: Johns Hopkins University Press, 1995.

Mitchell, B. R. *International Historical Statistics: The Americas and Australasia.* London: Macmillan, 1983.

Montagu, G. H. *Trusts of Today.* New York: McClure, Phillips, 1904.

Morgan, T. *FDR: A Biography.* New York: Simon and Schuster, 1985.

Morison, S. E., H. S. Commager, and W. E. Leuchtenburg. *The Growth of the American Republic,* vol. 2. 6th edition. New York: Oxford University Press, 1969.

Mumford, J. K. "The Story of Bethlehem Steel, 1914–1918." Unpublished manuscript, Bethlehem Steel, 1943.

National Cyclopaedia of American Biography. 58 vols. New York: J. T. White, 1892–1964.

Noyes, A. D. *The War Period of American Finance, 1908–1925.* New York: Putnam, 1926.

Oates, S. E. *Portrait of America.* 2 vols. Boston: Houghton Mifflin, 1973.

O'Connor, H. *Steel—Dictator.* New York: John Day, 1935.

Paskoff, P. F., ed. *Iron and Steel in the Nineteenth Century.* New York: Facts on File, 1989.

Payne, P. L. "The Emergence of the Large-Scale Company in Great Britain, 1870–1914." *Economic History Review* 20 (1967): 519–42.

Perkins, F. *The Roosevelt I Knew.* New York: Viking Press, 1946.

"Pittsburgh." *Atlantic Monthly,* 21 (January 1868).

President's Conference on Unemployment. *Report of the Committee on Recent Economic Changes in the United States.* New York: McGraw-Hill, 1929.

Pringle, H. F. *The Life and Times of William Howard Taft: A Biography.* 2 vols. Hamden, CT: Archon Books, 1964.

Randall, C. *Adventures in Friendship.* Boston: Little, Brown, 1965.

Rodriguez, L. "Samuel Traylor: The Making of an Entrepreneur." *Canal History* 10 (23 March 1991): 95–114.

Roosevelt, Franklin D. *The Roosevelt Letters: Being the Personal Correspondence of Franklin D. Roosevelt.* Edited by Elliott Roosevelt. 3 vols. London: Harrap, 1950.

The Royal Blue Book. Pittsburgh, PA: International Eisteddfod, 1913.

Schlesinger, A. M. *The Crisis of the Old Order.* Boston: Houghton Mifflin, 1957.

Scholes, E. C., and T. C. Leary. "Eugene G. Grace." In *Iron and Steel in the Twentieth Century,* edited by B. E. Seeley. New York: Facts on File, 1994.

Schwab, C. M. "Address at the Memorial Service for Andrew Carnegie," 25 November 1919, Pittsburgh, PA.

——. "The Huge Enterprises Built Up by Andrew Carnegie." *The Engineering Magazine,* January 1901.

——. "Some Reflections on Big Business." In *These Eventful Years: The Twentieth Century in the Making, as Told by Many of Its Makers.* New York: Encyclopedia Britannica, 1924.

——. *Succeeding with What You Have.* New York: Century Company, 1917.

——. "Ten Commandments of Success: An Interview by B. C. Forbes with Charles M. Schwab." Chicago: La Salle Extension University, 1924.

——. "Today's Problems." New York State Chamber of Commerce, 28 April 1921.

Seager, H. R., and C. A. Gulick. *Trust and Corporation Problems.* New York: Harper and Brothers, 1929.

Seeley, B. E., ed. *Iron and Steel in the Twentieth Century.* New York: Facts on File, 1994.

Skinner, T. *The Stock Exchange Yearbook for 1931.* London: Thomas Skinner and Company, 1931.

Souvenir of Loretto Centenary 1799–1899. Cresson, PA: Swope Brothers, 1899.

Spencer, C. C. *The Sinews of American Capitalism.* London: Macmillan, 1965.

Swetnam, G., and H. Smith. *Historic Western Pennsylvania.* Pittsburgh, PA: University of Pittsburgh Press, 1976.

Tarbell, I. *The Life of Elbert H. Gary: The Story of Steel.* New York: Appleton, 1925.

——. *The Nationalizing of Business, 1878–1898.* New York: Macmillan, 1936.

Temin, P. *Iron and Steel in Nineteenth-Century America: An Economic Inquiry.* Cambridge, MA: MIT Press, 1964.

Times, The. *The History of the War.* London: The Times, 1919.

United States. Bureau of the Census. *Historical Statistics of the United States.* Washington, DC: Government Printing Office, 1960.

United States. Commission on Industrial Relations. *Hearings on Industrial Relations.* Washington, DC: Government Printing Office, 1915.

——. Commissioner of Labor. *Report of the Commissioner for Labor on the Strike at the Bethlehem Steel Works.* Washington, DC: Government Printing Office, 1910.

——. Industrial Commission. *Reports.* Washington, DC: Government Printing Office, 1899–1901.

——. Tariff Commission. *Hearings.* Washington, DC: Government Printing Office, 1908–1909.

United States Congress. House of Representatives. *Hearings before the Committee on Investigation of the United States Steel Corporation (Stanley Committee).* Washington DC: Government Printing Office, 1912.

Urofsky, M. I. *Big Steel and the Wilson Administration.* Columbus: Ohio State University Press, 1969.

Vadasz, T. P. "The History of an Industrial Community: Bethlehem, Pennsylvania, 1741–1920." Ph.D. diss., College of William and Mary, 1975.

Wall, J. F. *Andrew Carnegie.* New York: Oxford University Press, 1970.

——. "Charles M. Schwab." In *Encyclopedia of American Biography,* ed. J. Garraty. New York: Harper and Row, 1974.

Warren, K. *Triumphant Capitalism: Henry Clay Frick and the Industrial Transformation of America.* Pittsburgh, PA: University of Pittsburgh Press, 1996.

Weidlein, E. R. *The Charles M. Schwab Memorial Lecture.* New York: American Iron and Steel Institute, 1950.

Weir, E. T. "Selling Practices in the Steel Industry." In *American Iron and Steel Institute Yearbook*. New York: AISI, 1924.

Weisberg, G. P., E. M. DeCourcy, and A. McQueen, eds. *Collecting in the Gilded Age: Art Patronage in Pittsburgh, 1890–1910*. Pittsburgh, PA: Frick Art and Historical Center, 1997.

Western Pennsylvania Biographical Association. *Western Pennsylvanians*. Pittsburgh, PA: WPBA, 1923.

Whelan, F. A. 1994. "'I Can Stand It': Charles M. Schwab and the Bethlehem Steel Strike of 1910." *Canal History and Technology Proceedings*, vol. 13. Easton, PA: CHTP, 1994.

Whitaker, J. *Whitaker's Almanack*. London, 1913.

Wilgus, H. L. *The United States Steel Corporation in Its Industrial and Legal Aspects*. Chicago: Callaghan, 1901.

Wright, C. W. *Economic History of the United States*. New York: McGraw-Hill, 1949.

Yates, W. R., ed. *Bethlehem of Pennsylvania: The Golden Years*. Bethlehem, PA: Bethlehem Book Commission, 1976.

Yellen, S. *American Labor Struggles*. New York: Harcourt Brace, 1936.

INDEX